'This book offers a critical and per
ing conventional academic boundar
acknowledged leading expert on
and practically into the worlds of _____ ____ offers a range of
compelling insights into the lives of those involved in gang subcultures.
He challenges conventional views of the gang and provides a new set of
methodological tools that are designed to help him and the reader unpack
the significance of this important global phenomenon.'

Roger Matthews, *Professor of Criminology, University of Kent, UK*

'David Brotherton has spent decades of global involvement, activism and
research earning the right to write this book – and now he's written it. As
morally courageous as it is methodologically and theoretically innovative,
Youth Street Gangs illuminates what others wilfully ignore: youthful street
organizations in all their human and political complexity.'

Jeff Ferrell, *Visiting Professor of Criminology, University of Kent, UK*

'Brotherton weaves two powerful narratives through this book; the first is a
theoretical and political history of gang studies with a culminating vision for
how to locate the gang within the folds of late modernity, post-colonialism,
and global neoliberalism. The second is an eloquently written and passionate
treatise on the necessity of a critical paradigm that will help students negotiate the epistemological and methodological borders of twenty-first century
academia. It is superb!'

Tim Black, *Associate Professor of Sociology, Case Western Reserve
University, USA*

'Based on more than two decades of intensive fieldwork with street gangs,
Brotherton's new work is a call to arms for criminologists to move beyond
the pointless and pathologizing "risk factor" approach to understanding
youth gangs and to engage with our subject matter in a proper historical and
sociological fashion. I hope the field is listening, the message could hardly be
more important or compelling.'

Shadd Maruna, *Dean, School of Criminal Justice, Rutgers University
Newark, USA*

YOUTH STREET GANGS

Gangs have been heavily pathologized in the last several decades. In comparison to the pioneering Chicago School's work on gangs in the 1920s we have moved away from a humanistic appraisal of and sensitivity toward the phenomenon and have allowed the gang to become a highly plastic folk devil outside of history. This pathologization of the gang has particularly negative consequences for democracy in an age of punishment, cruelty and coercive social control.

This is the central thesis of David Brotherton's new and highly contentious book on street gangs. Drawing on a wealth of highly acclaimed original research, Brotherton explores the socially layered practices of street gangs, including community movements, cultural projects and sites of social resistance. The book also critically reviews gang theory and the geographical trajectories of street gangs from New York and Puerto Rico to Europe, the Caribbean and South America, as well as state-sponsored reactions and the enabling role of orthodox criminology.

In opposition to the dominant gang discourses, Brotherton proposes the development of a critical studies approach to gangs and concludes by making a plea for researchers to engage the gang reflexively, paying attention to the contradictory agency of the gang and what gang members actually tell us. The book is essential reading for academics and students involved in the study of juvenile delinquency, youth studies, deviance, gang studies and cultural criminology.

David C. Brotherton grew up in the East End of London, England. Dr Brotherton gained his doctorate in Sociology in 1992 and began work on street gang subcultures at UC Berkeley in the same year. In 1994, Dr Brotherton came to John Jay College of Criminal Justice at CUNY, where his research on youth resistance, marginalization and gangs led to the Street Organization Project in 1997. He has received research grants from both private and public agencies and has published widely in journals, books, newspapers and magazines. Dr Brotherton edits the Public Criminology book series at Columbia University Press and was named Critical Criminologist of the Year in 2011. He is currently Professor of Sociology at John Jay College and the Graduate Center, The City University of New York.

New Directions in Critical Criminology
Edited by Walter S. DeKeseredy,
West Virginia University, USA

This series presents new cutting-edge critical criminological, empirical, theoretical, and policy work on a broad range of social problems, including drug policy, rural crime and social control, policing and the media, ecocide, intersectionality, and the gendered nature of crime. It aims to highlight the most up-to-date author-itative essays written by new and established scholars in the field. Rather than offering a survey of the literature, each book takes a strong position on topics of major concern to those interested in seeking new ways of thinking critically about crime.

YOUTH STREET GANGS

A critical appraisal

David C. Brotherton

Routledge
Taylor & Francis Group

LONDON AND NEW YORK

First published 2015
by Routledge
2 Park Square, Milton Park, Abingdon, Oxon OX14 4RN

and by Routledge
711 Third Avenue, New York, NY 10017

Routledge is an imprint of the Taylor & Francis Group, an informa business

British Library Cataloguing in Publication Data
A catalogue record for this book is available from the British Library

Library of Congress Cataloguing in Publication data
Brotherton, David.
  Youth street gangs : a critical appraisal / David C. Brotherton.
    pages   cm. – (New directions in critical criminology ; 10)
  Includes bibliographical references and index.
  1. Gangs–United States. 2. Juvenile delinquency–United States.
  3. Problem youth–United States. I. Title.
  HV6439.U5B75 2015
  364.106′608350973–dc23
  2014038940

ISBN: 978-0-415-85627-0 (hbk)
ISBN: 978-0-415-85629-4 (pbk)
ISBN: 978-0-203-72778-2 (ebk)

Typeset in Bembo
by Out of House Publishing

For Michael and Jock

CONTENTS

FIGURES

TABLES

ACKNOWLEDGEMENTS

There are a number of people I wish to thank, whose support, insights and encouragement have allowed this work to reach a conclusion. Much appreciation is due to the many men and women of the street organizations with whom I have worked for much of the past twenty years, who gave me their time and shared with me their earnest reflections on their lives and their communities. In particular I am deeply indebted to Antonio Fernandez who continues to give his all in the struggle for peace and hope on the streets of New York and New Jersey.

My sincere thanks to my colleagues at John Jay College and the Graduate Center of the City University of New York, especially Luis Barrios, Louis Kontos, Lynn Chancer, Jayne Mooney, Barry Spunt, Susan Opotow, Bob Garot, Michael Rowan, Lucia Trimbur, Andy Karmen, Seth Baumrin, Marcia Esparza and Ric Curtis, all of whom in many different ways aided my research and provided the network of scholars essential for writing against the grain. In addition, a big shout out to my current and former graduate students Kevin Moran, Jennifer Ortiz, Albert Novelozo, Mitch Librett, Robert Weide, Yolanda Martín, Peter Marina, Ignasi Bernat, Juan Esteva, Marcos Burgos and Bronwyn Dobchuk-Lind, who together represent a new generation of scholars dedicated to changing the way we think and represent the communities in which gangs emerge and develop.

I must include a special note of gratitude to my comrades in Europe, Luca Palmas, Camilla Salazar, Carles Feixa, Amir Rostami,

Svetlana Stephenson, Noemi Cannelles, Barbara Scandroglio and Simon Hallsworth, and in South America, Mauro Cerbino, without whose support my own work would have been that much poorer and less enlightened.

Thanks also to Springer, Columbia University Press, Steve Hart, *New York Magazine*, Antonio Fernandez, Mauro Cerbino, Rita Fecher and Henry Chalfant, *New York Daily News*, Fernando Zambrano, Luca Palmas and Nik Mills for their kind permission to reproduce images and previously published material in this book. Almost last but not least much appreciation is due to Walter DeKeseredy and Tom Sutton for making this work happen through Routledge and to the invaluable help of Heidi Lee and Gail Welsh in the production and copyediting phases, and Claudia Cojocaru for great work on the indexing.

And finally unreserved thanks to my family, Elsie, Lisa, Gijs, Mia and Aidan, who have had to listen to my barbed comments on the state of the world and its misappropriation of resources for so many years. This offering is dedicated to two of the finest, most generous scholars I have had the great privilege of knowing, Jock Young and Michael Flynn, and to my grandchildren Madu and Sijmen.

INTRODUCTION

This book has been contemplated for some time as I struggled to make sense of the existing gang literature and my own experiences with gang members of every age, gender, sexuality and race/ethnicity. I had begun working with young gang members as a high school teacher in San Francisco more than twenty years ago. So many students in the school seemed to be coming only part-time, including to my own classes in social studies. I took this seriously as I grew up with youth of a similar class who also used to spend a lot of time playing truant, with many of them barely graduating (at sixteen in England) and a number entering the criminal justice system.

Consequently, I would sometimes go in search of the missing ones at night and found several of them hanging out with their homeboys and homegirls on the streets of the Mission District and other inner-city areas. I would approach them, somewhat gingerly, and ask if everything was OK as I was concerned. In this way I started to take a more concerted interest in their non-school lives and after a few months they would begin to write about their experiences in journals or talk to me after class about various personal developments. They also used to show up in class a lot more than before and it was clear that my demonstrating a genuine interest in them, their surroundings, their friends and their family, and treating them with respect, meant that we could begin to build a relationship as human beings, not just as teacher and student. From this we could make some genuine pedagogical progress. It was, of course, a Freirean approach (Freire 1970) built on trying to establish a dialogical connection between learners, regardless of our statuses in the classroom. I felt that I knew so little about them and their subcultures and yet these were so important in their lives. In order for me to relate to them as a teacher I had to understand who they were in an holistic sense and that way we could begin a journey together that might lead to a change in consciousness, or as Freire calls it, "conscientization."[1]

This early grounding in the gang worlds of San Francisco was revived as I later found myself in the same school collecting data for my dissertation on why high school students in marginalized communities "drop in" to school as well as "drop out" from it. In particular, my relationships with these students became extremely important as I pursued my postdoctoral training on alcohol and drug use among gang-involved school-age youth at the Alcohol Research Group at UC Berkeley, which involved an immersion in gang research while also working as a field researcher for the Institute of Scientific Analysis and its "Homeboy Study" under the direction of the noted ethnographer Dan Waldorf.

At first, I was fascinated by the sheer extent of the literature and that the study of gangs had such a long history in the United States, unequaled elsewhere. Nonetheless, I found myself troubled by the level of objectification of the subjects in the writing and I was unable to write simply as a neutral observer. As I had already had a different history with these groups' members whom I was now interviewing, it felt false and contrived for me to talk to them about violence, or drugs, or alcohol use when their lives were infinitely more complex and multi-dimensional. It was not long before I grew frustrated with these gang representations and the growing discord between my field experiences and many of the tropes so common in the revived gang studies. The framing of the issues, the narrow foci of the research, the lack of reflexivity and the prevalence of the stereotypes were not only in sociology but in criminology, criminal justice, public health, psychology, education and anthropology. It was not long before this unease led me to look elsewhere for guidance, seeking a different approach to what I was seeing emerge over time and what was and is being reported by so many professionals in the now gang industry. For it is an actual and virtual organization with its own international political economy based on funding from the security state and a host of non-profits and non-governmental organizations (NGOs).

Hence this book was conceived first as a way to think differently about both the form and content of "the street gang" as a contribution to the literature, given that the repetitive and almost hegemonic versions of gangs and gang members as pathological seemed to be flowing so seamlessly between the mass media, social science, the state and the array of professionals in the private sector linked to gang "interventionism." Moreover, I observed that this was not only happening in the United States but it was increasingly a global phenomenon, which underscored the degree to which US social science, and in particular its criminological and criminal justice variants, had so successfully penetrated and influenced an international discourse on a phenomenon that was always studied first and foremost within the particularities of its local habitat.

A second motivation was to take this opportunity to gather my thoughts on the non-pathological ways to interpret and study the meanings of gang life, especially given the glocalizing contexts in which we are all trying to make sense of our daily lives. I was undoubtedly encouraged and inspired to do this by my own "outsider" status in the United States as I necessarily brought a different imaginary to my gang research, coming from a background in social and political organizing in Europe and an academic training that was steeped in critical theorizing and questioning the methodologies of normative social inquiry. Consequently, the manifest function of this work is to provide a critical reading of the gang while its latent function is to prod both experienced and neophyte students of gangs into another way of thinking, knowing and observing this complex and growing social phenomenon.

A third motivation was to highlight the work of those who have provided a counter-narrative, theoretically and empirically, and in so doing I am seeking to draw links in the literature that might not be so obvious. It is in this current period that the borders of our disciplines lend themselves to such transgressions with the layered properties, meaning systems and comparative sites of the street gang presenting an appropriate subject to be criminologically reimagined.

However, I make no claims that this effort somehow amounts to an authoritative version of the critical perspective on the gang, but I would like to think that in the following pages the curious and probably somewhat frustrated reader will gain some insights into another literature on "the gang" that will lead to more curiosity and hopefully another way of interacting with a subculture that has been around since the mid- to- late 1800s (and some would argue long before).

I have attempted to lay out the text in a fairly rational order, beginning with a major problem in so many gang studies, and that is the lack of attention to any historical perspective in the presentation of data or in the approach to analysis. I argue, therefore, in Chapter 1, that not only are the gangs located in history but, of course, they *have* history and little can be understood about many of the current gang subcultures, particularly in their relationships to each other and to the surrounding community, without some knowledge of both a partic-ular and a general past. Similarly, it is important and perhaps crucial to take into consideration how previous generations have viewed the gang, which is especially the case when thinking about matters of policy and their consequences.

In Chapter 2 I discuss the various optics used to discover, research and construct the gang. Much of the current criminological and criminal justice literature privileges a Hobbesian approach to the phenomena, which is reproduced through such dominant paradigms as social control and rational choice theories. As I argue, this distinctly pathological view did not always have such currency and it is no surprise that such a perspective complements the rise of neo-liberal politics, economics and ideology in the wider society. I also point to the contributions of humanist criminology and a more recent variant that I refer to as social reproductionist.

In Chapter 3 I lay out my interpretation of the notion of resist-ance in gang studies. It should come as no surprise that little research adopts this approach and as a result the literature is long on narratives regarding individual and collective forms of conformity but short on accounts that build on the possibilities of social action and consciousness that aim for transcendence if not always transformation of the status quo.

Chapter 4 takes us into the territory of methods and lessons I have drawn and practiced over twenty-plus years of field research. I am particularly aiming this chapter at emerging students of the street gang who might be seeking permission to go outside the norms and boundaries of the usual data-gathering protocols and who feel stymied as they try to wedge their "social facts" about the gang into categories often driven by the need to serve the interests of research-granting institutions.

I follow this in Chapter 5 with a discussion of the processes and impacts of gang-related "moral panics," drawing on some of the classic literature in the field. Here I discuss not just the objectification and reification of the gang but its treatment as an object of desire and commercial exploitation, so rife under contemporary capitalism.

This leads into Chapter 6 and my reflections on the various projects I have been involved in largely during the 1990s. Much of this material is being published for the first time as I look back at my gang research experiences in San Francisco and New York City.

In the penultimate chapter (Chapter 7) I make the case for a concerted effort to develop an alternative research approach to the street gang, arguing for a critical criminology and sociology of the gang that is attuned to the massive social, economic, political and cultural changes in a globalized society. It is an extraordinary time to study this phenomenon but it requires a new set of research skills and foci going beyond the crime–violence–drugs vortex promoted, conditioned and contained by parameters set by the criminal justice industry.

Finally, I draw some conclusions, making a plea for continuing our engagement with the gang through research and policies that err on the side of empowerment and societal transformation rather than repression and the largely failed attempts to contain and control our most "deviant" subjects. In the Appendix I have included a paper that my colleague, the late Jock Young, and I wrote several years ago for an American Sociological Association conference in which we presented a dialogue between a theorist and a field researcher on the gang from a cultural criminological perspective.

Notes

1 By this Freire was talking about the development of a critical appreciation of the world through seeing, engaging and understanding society in all its political, social, cultural and economic contradictions. However, it did not just stop at an understanding, for linked to this consciousness is the obligation to act on the world in order to change; hence he called this the pedagogy of the oppressed.

1

GANGS AND THE COMMUNITY

History from below

> I shall begin with this proposition – one that is so common-place that its significance is often overlooked – that in our society, youth is present only when its presence is a problem, or is regarded as a problem. More precisely, the category "youth" gets mobilized in official documentary discourse, in concerned or outraged editorials and features, or in the supposedly disinterested tracts emanating from the social sciences at those times when young people make their presence felt by going "out of bounds," by resisting through rituals, dressing strangely, striking bizarre attitudes, breaking rules, windows, heads, issuing rhetorical challenges to the law.
>
> (Hebdige 1988:18)

Approaching the subject of gangs outside of any historical context is impossible, yet this "oversight" is precisely what characterizes most gang studies today, particularly those that come increasingly from the field of criminal justice. As Hebdige makes abundantly clear (see above) when he locates youth as a subject/object of investigation, derision and fear in history, it is only when youth are associated with "trouble" that they become worthy of society's doubtful attention – and there

FIGURE 1.1 *Bandit roost (59 Mulberry Street in New York City)*, photo taken by Jacob Riis in 1888.
Source: http://commons.wikimedia.org/wiki/File:Bandit%27s_Roost_by_Jacob_Riis. jpeg. Original source: Preus Museum, accessible at https://www.Flickr.com/photos/ preusmuseum/5389939434/in/set-72157625909173714

is no greater shorthand for this pejorative association between youth and trouble than "the gang."

In this chapter I want to discuss the various aspects of the relation-ship between the gang and history, drawing on my own research as well as that of numerous colleagues in the gang field and on a cor-pus of iconoclastic work often referred to as "history from below"[1] and its corollary in historical ethnography (see in particular the work of Comaroff and Comaroff 1992). In so doing I want to argue that renditions of the gang without history place the phenomenon at the mercy of empiricist accounts that pay scant attention to the politics of representation in an era of extreme privilege on the one hand, and pri-vation, punishment and cruelty on the other (Giroux 2012). We need to take seriously the literature that has resisted the temptation to repro-duce elite readings of deviance and deviants and instead has sought to place such claims in a historically grounded framework of indirect violence (Salmi 1993), competition over material resources and symbolic (mis)representations. Second, I argue that disregarding history's importance in the making of gangs leads to a failure to understand the multiple contours of development through which a community must emerge, particularly along the fault lines of race and class and the political economy of space. Finally, I argue that, without the historical lens, we will reproduce representations of the gang that serve the hegemony rather than a critical reading or deconstruction of the phenomenon that allows us to see how that hegemony is achieved in the first place. As Howard Zinn (2005 [1980]:11), one of the pioneers of the "people's history" approach, wrote in the introduction to his acclaimed work:

> this book will be skeptical of governments and their attempts, through politics and culture, to ensnare ordinary people in a giant web of nationhood pretending to a common interest. I will not try to overlook the cruelties that victims inflict on one another as they are jammed together in the boxcars of the system. I don't want to romanticize them. But I do remember (in rough paraphrase) a statement I once read: "The cry of the poor is not always just, but if you don't listen to it, you will never know what justice is…" If history is to be creative, to anticipate a possible future without denying the past, it should, I believe, emphasize new possibilities by disclosing those hidden episodes of the past when, even if in brief flashes, people showed their ability to resist, to join together, occasionally to win. I am supposing or perhaps only hoping, that our future may be found in the past's fugitive moments of compassion rather than its solid centuries of warfare.[2]

Not too many "saints" in the East End

I suppose coming from a highly marginalized and stereotyped community of East London (Jack London (2011 [1903]) called us the "People of the Abyss" early last century), I am loathe to accept deviance at its face value, particularly when it is said to be a societal threat. Through my own personal history of membership in both "skinhead" street corner groups and the early legions of soccer "hooligans" during the late 1960s it became clear to me that society would always cast the antics of middle-class progeny in sharply different colors and tones than those of the working-class. The "saints" would never be the ones hanging out on my block but the "roughnecks" could be seen in their small gatherings about every 100 yards. As I later learned, the presence of these "street corner societies" had little to do with the roughnecks' intrinsic properties but everything to do with those who made claims about us, telling the world who and how we were and what we stood for.

At the moment in the United States, despite massive collective and conspiratorial abuses of the financial system by banks, mortgage lenders, insurance companies, accountancy firms, ratings agencies and brokerage houses exposed by the meltdown of 2008 (Will *et al.* 2013), hardly an upper-class culprit spent a single day behind bars. Bernie Madoff was the exception, not the rule, as his ownership of the massive pyramid scheme became too big to ignore and leave unpunished in the eyes of the public. Yet his lifestyle of rampant illegal drug use, corruption and debauchery, and his working assumptions about the diverse scams of casino capitalism, went unchecked for years because such behavior was normative and shared by many of his fellow players, who happen to shape the rules by which the game is played. Do these bankers and financial titans behave like a gang, meeting secretly over time, having their own clubrooms, organizing and protecting their own territory, carrying out predatory actions against adversaries, showing loyalty to the group and so forth? Many would say they do and that they perpetrate and encourage extraordinary levels of social harm on innocent bystanders far in excess of the injuries caused by so-called "gangs."

Nonetheless, despite the obvious criminal deviance of the elites we are advised by the FBI that it is the Mara Salvatrucha street gang that is the number one organized crime group in the United States. Strange as it might seem for a street subculture to be accorded such an elevated status, when one thinks of the decades-long investigation and prosecution of the various US mafias by law enforcement agencies or the prolific organized rule-breaking of industrial and financial leaders as mentioned above, nonetheless such obviously dubious claims, made by one of the country's leading policing agencies, are rarely questioned or considered "an issue." The obvious politics behind the representation and misrepresentation are hardly ever contested.

And so it goes with most studies of gangs, whose premises are simply taken as given, with gangs usually defined and discovered by legitimated social control agencies and their broad ranks of affiliated "experts," most often drawn from the police, the criminal justice system or the correctional industry. Thus it is rare for researchers, sociologists or other social scientists to step back and reflect on the processes of epistemology (e.g. categorization and social recognition) and place such "knowledge," often coming from above, in some historical context such that it can be interrogated by a knowledge and history from below. As social scientists we should not only be asking ourselves whether our theories, categories and definitions are empirically proven but why are these the only data worthy of consideration? Why, for example, is there such a vast criminology of the gang and no criminology of genocide or war (Morrison 2006)? What properties of the group and its members are included or excluded in the analysis? How or why do certain groups get named in the first place? Who or what benefits by this process of naming, discovery and measurement? Such questions, of course, are par for the course in more critical investigative approaches or discourses such as social constructionism and labeling theory in sociology or in cultural criminology, and I shall return to some of these debates later in the book. For now I am simply raising these issues to urge us to think more critically and reflexively about the gang in history, i.e. as a social phenomenon that is said to emerge within the ebbs and flows of social, economic and political currents over time; or as a group or subculture that possesses a set of meanings that are contested and contestable in a world that, as Galeano warns, is increasingly "upside down" and dystopic.

Thus, to think about the gang in history requires us to consciously place the phenomenon we are describing in a set of intersecting, overlapping, unequal power relations where depictions and constructions of the unrighteous are frequently without merit and allowed to go unchecked, especially in the current dominant discourse of crime control, risk management and border protection. As a result the practices of a more or less rational counter-discourse have been growing, even though they might be sometimes difficult to observe when set against the tsunami of orthodox criminological and criminal justice renderings of the gang Other.

The gang in history and the gang with history

In Pearson's (1987) work on the historical emergence of the "hooligan" we see an excellent example of an historical materialist or realist approach to the construction of a deviant group, in this case the notion of the hooligan. Played out within the processes of a "moral panic," or what Pearson calls "respectable fears," Pearson interrogates the presence of the new, dangerous youth "underclass" in Britain (during the 1980s) by carefully going back into the past to uncover periods and instances when a rapidly urbanizing and industrializing England was similarly finding other dangerous "underclasses" as it struggled to cope with the lower orders increasingly transgressing their social boundaries and infiltrating the spaces of the middle and, to a lesser extent, upper classes. The results of his inquiry are prosaically told and serve to describe in some detail how ready members and representatives of the Establishment, often via their media mouthpieces, were to denigrate and condemn the behavior, modes of dress, and organizational capabilities of lower-class youth for their perceived threats to such middle-class strictures as "fair play," self-control and the "stiff upper lip."

Thus, the unruly behavior of soccer fans at games, increasingly popular as a mass spectacle at the turn of the century, the drunken comportment of working-class patrons in depraved public spaces such as "pubs," or the bawdy "music hall" influence on lower-class culture, and last but not least the sight of lower-class men and women improving their lot through pedal power, were all the topic of frequent denunciations. As Pearson (1987:66) puts it:

> undoubtedly the most extraordinary aspect of this grumbling against the tendency of the working-class to assert its noisome presence in places it clearly had no right to go, was to be found in the "bicycle craze" of the 1890s.

Pearson goes on to analyze the moral opprobrium against the feckless behavior of working-class youth in the 1920s and 1930s whilst studiously overlooking the deepening conditions of poverty and extreme exploitation during the Depression. In so doing he argues that there is a prevalence of nostalgia for an idealized, often racially pure, past, citing the example of Richard Hoggart (1957) in the 1950s, whose pioneering work on working-class culture also held to a pastoral version of the lower classes as he lamented the influence on youth of "Americanized" mass entertainment via television, film and rock and roll. Although there were, of course, oppositional narratives to these moralizing discourses from more radical and socialist commentators, Pearson reveals a general absence of self-articulated versions of daily life by the perpetrators of these transgressive behaviors, or what we now call a history from below.

Thus Pearson emphasizes that it is incumbent on social scientists to fully engage claims made about the agents of order and disorder by comparing such claims to other, past instances when social outrage was also an issue and thereby to place the present in a more revealing comparative past. Such a context is necessary to demonstrate more fully what the continuity and discontinuities are in terms of the power to represent and to concoct symbols that have lasting influence on both the private and public imaginations. As Pearson (1987:236) reminds us:

> The way to challenge the foundation of myth, to repeat, is not to deny the facts of violence and disorder. Rather, it is to insist that more facts are placed within the field of vision … When the cobwebs of historical myth are cleared away, then we can begin to see that the real and enduring problem that faces us is not moral decay, or declining parental responsibility, or undutiful working mothers, or the unparalleled debasement of popular amusements – or any other symptom of spiritual degeneration among the British people. Rather, it is a material problem. The inescapable reality of the social reproduction of an underclass of the most poor and dispossessed.

If we substitute "the hooligan" for "the gang" we have a good example of how important it is to locate deviant subjects within different periods of time and space to make sense of what Gilbert (1986) calls "cycles of outrage." In Britain this tradition of critical social historical inquiry is prevalent in many of the social sciences and particularly in criminology, but it is less so in the United States where a preference for empiricism, presentism and positivism has generally negated the virtues of an historically grounded orientation.

Nonetheless, when we look at the gang in history we often see something akin to Pearson's discoveries that compel us to take a second look at our assumptions. For example, in the discovery phase of a social group, the range of social reactions to a set of behaviors, the circumstances under which these behaviors are said to have occurred and the processes that are purported to explain the behavior's emergence. Therefore, in addition to placing the gang *in history*, doing our utmost to reveal or at least consider the dominant discourses within which it is emerging, we need to contemplate the gang *with history*.

For example, in my previous work with Luis Barrios (see Brotherton and Barrios 2004) on the New York Latin Kings and Queens, it was impossible to consider this group in the present without a grasp of its historical development, its claims to history (e.g. it named its branches after ancient indigenous peoples in the Caribbean) and, in particular, its relationship to gang subcultures not only in the New York City area but also in Chicago and later in other cities outside the United States. We found that the language of the group, its style of organization, its codes of conduct and its ideology could only be explained within this historical framework. It was only after seeing the organization within history that we could begin to understand the range of meanings members were attaching to their group experiences and the developmental processes they were describing and we were witnessing.

Yet the study is fairly exceptional in contemporary gang research, where subjects are more typically portrayed as historyless with scant attention paid to: (1) processes of individual social development; (2) the origins of the group or subculture to which the individuals are affiliated; and (3) the long-term development of the community within which the subjects reside, i.e. their setting. Consequently, gang subjects are mostly located outside of any real matrix of dynamic, intersecting structures within which human beings achieve agency and strive to make sense of their lot. In this way, the gang becomes a thing-in-itself, a deviant subspecies made real and evidenced through certain properties with characteristics that researchers suggest contribute to the social reproduction of the lower classes (Miller 1958) at best, or the destruction of community life (Yablonsky 1963) or even Western civilization (Manwaring 2005) at worst. However, any examination of history reminds us that this process is highly contradictory, with the role of gangs in such socio-political processes neither predictable nor absolute, with accommodationist, oppositional and resistance behaviors mixed with individual agency, subcultural innovation and the rituals of conformity and non-conformity playing out in structured yet fluid environments.

Gangs and the community

One way to think about the gang both in history and with history is to understand the group and its members through the experiences of the community. Joan Moore[3] in her study of intergenerational Chicano gangs in Los Angeles during the 1970s underscores the need for community context:

> The barrios are Chicano by repeated external definition both in the past and continuously in the present. It is no accident that the 350 street murals of East Los Angeles are always built around Mexican and Indian themes. Or that the high schools of the area sponsor and train folklorico dance troupes who perform at many community functions with pride and with applause. "Cultural nationalism" did not have to be invented; it is normal and expressive in the life-patterns of the community itself. The daily, weekly, and yearly rhythms of life in the barrios differ from those elsewhere in Los Angeles. They are geared to a social system that emphasizes a large and extended family and to relationships among families that (in small town fashion) go back for decades.
>
> (Moore and García 1978:52)

Thus it is difficult to see the gang outside of the making of the community from which it comes. This would seem to be an obvious point if it were not for the fact that the gang is so often conceived as a phenomenon emerging either outside of a community or else in opposition to it – neither of which is true, for some of the following reasons that I later expound upon:

- gangs are invariably tied to the race, class and gender history of the community and the changing contours of spatial and economic occupation, segregation and social reproduction;
- gangs emerge from the long-term struggles of a community against marginality and social suffering that are related to the community's quest for political empowerment, social autonomy, forms of historicity and cultural self-expression;
- gangs reflect shifts in a community's race, ethnic and class make-up as neighborhoods change in relationship to powerful global structural forces such as colonialism, imperialism and neo-liberalism as well as more local, endogenous processes such as settlement and the building of ethnic enclaves;
- the organizational, ideological and stylistic characteristics of gangs reflect the subcultural histories of a particular community and its subaltern strata;
- gangs are associated with the specific articulation of the informal economy as well as different forms of community social control;
- gangs are influenced by the varying interventions of the state over time, the constellation of "blocs" that constitute hegemonic class relations and the construction of a civil society.

Race, class and gendered histories of the community

Gangs owe their origins and practices to a particular set of class, race and gender characteristics of a community that are formed under certain socio-historical conditions. It is impossible to appreciate the diverse forms of organization, practices and styles of such groups without turning in some measure to a community's social constitution and its paths and processes of development within a capitalist political economy. For example, to understand a gang's allegiance to territorialism or its predominantly male make-up, or the development of female substrata or its race-ethnic membership, it is necessary to take into account the residential patterns of a neighborhood, the opportunity structures of a specific area and their relationship to a reserve army of labor, the classed and raced nature of schooling and the multiple socio-economic and cultural bases of identity construction particularly among globalized youth.

Moore makes this point very clear in her opposition to some of the generalizing arguments in the early gang research of Klein (1971), who situates gangs in a "stable slum" with "no attention to the adult or ethnic context" (Moore and García 1978:49). Vigil (1988) makes a similar argument in his anthropological analysis of the emergence of "cholo" and "pachuco" styles in Chicano gang subcultures, Hagedorn (2006) underlines the historical importance of urban race politics, white supremacy and hyper-ghettoization in the evolution of Chicago's black, white and Latino gangs, while the historian Schneider (1999:107) cites strong evidence of a gang–masculinity nexus in his 1960s gang study of New York City when he says:

> Young men who rejected the demands of these principal sites of adolescent socialization [i.e. school, the labor market and the family] found in street gangs the opportunity to win power, prestige, female adulation, and a masculine identity.[4]

Many gang and related youth studies highlight similar community-based histories, placing the emphasis in gang emergence on enforced spatiality (e.g. studies that situate gangs in neighborhoods characterized by racially-segregated public housing, minority-only public schooling, socio-geographical isolation ensured by freeways, policed boundaries and the intergenerational divestment of socio-economic supports (see for example the Colorado multi-site gang study of Durán (2013), the New York hip-hop history of Chang (2005), the gang female socio-linguistic account of the Latino north–south divide in California by Mendoza-Denton (2008), the political economic history of Los Angeles by Davis (1990) and Venkatesh's (2000) Chicago public housing research)). In these studies gang members are responding to their multiple marginality across generations, forming in some cases what Moore calls "quasi-institutions" rather than ad hoc groups which come and go, as may have been the case with white gangs in communities that experienced more sustained social mobility. Consequently, an account of the community's race-ethnic, class and gendered history is obligatory if gangs are to be situated. However, these histories are dynamic, filled with dialectical processes of power manifested in both oppressive and privileged class relations, conditions of expropriation and sites of resistance as well as accommodation and social reproduction. In many respects, gangs are barometers of these power relations (which are rarely separate from processes of capital accumulation) and represent their ongoing as well as changing forms. Gangs reflect at the micro level the imposition and interpenetration of extraordinary structural forces mediated and working themselves out at the most basic level of the community.

Community political struggles and historicity

Touraine's (1988) notion of historicity is critically important yet rarely brought into the analysis of US gangs. For Touraine, historicity refers to the processes by which society acts on itself to produce its own history outside of the laws of the political economy. Hence, he believed that we needed a theory of society that placed its emphasis on agency rather than determining structures "to help establish the belief that men and women are not subject to historical laws and material necessity, that they produce their own history through their cultural creations and social struggles" (1988:5). In studies of community action, resistance and subjugation it would seem obvious that such an approach would be beneficial to an understanding of the myriad processes of grassroots action, community self-organization and labor rank-and-filism that are replete in from-below histories of community development but more often than not go untold and undocumented.

It is difficult to understand the subcultural entrance of gangs without considering how and under what conditions community members exert their specific cultural legacy and identity, create new forms of sociality, discover their political voice and construct internal bodies of knowledge to withstand and make sense of the pressures of poverty, marginalization and adjustment. Of course, where the immigrant community is more middle class the processes of transition are quite different and the gang phenomenon is usually less present.

In our work with the various street organizations of New York but also in other sites such as Los Angeles, Barcelona and Quito (see Chapter 5) we have constantly seen these native and immigrant subcultures struggle to develop a knowledge of themselves and the world around them in social actions that include a range of anti-Establishment projects not normally associated with gang activity. As part of this street political process we have long observed how gangs can produce their own "organic intellectuals" charged with recording and analyzing important events drawn from their own group experiences – events that are highly valued by the group's members and are often referred to as the "knowledge."

Sometimes, of course, such "knowledge" functions as a form of myth-building as the group constructs narratives about itself which it uses to seduce prospective recruits while building a case for its own specialness (or what Katz calls street royalty). Nonetheless, this knowledge contains otherwise forgotten details of collective transgressions and resistances from the past which the dominant society prefers not to remember, recognize or validate. These can include a range of subaltern contestations to the dominant order, for example famous inmate wars against prison authorities, neighborhood struggles against police authoritarianism, inter-gang peace treaties, community campaigns for political enfranchisement, neighborhood challenges to public school bureaucracies, landlords, etc. This quest for self-knowledge is a form of counter-memory that informs and shapes social action and has to be considered in any serious inquiry into a community's history making.

Many researchers argue (see Pleyers 2012) that in the post-industrial world it is precisely this kind of historicity, in which a turn to activistic cultural forms of resistance, self-organization and agency are observed, that defines many of today's new media-savvy and horizontal social movements (e.g. the various "Occupy" movements in the United States and Europe, those collective movements associated with the Arab Spring and the ongoing protests in Brazil and Chile occasioned by extreme increases in public transportation and public education costs). Such social movements are seen as responding to the scripted market fundamentalism of neo-liberalism and in particular to a suffocating political discourse that assumes radical change to be impossible (Klein 1999), thus engendering a collective disposition of fatalism and nihilism especially in the youth.

It would seem logical to ask if such agency that is intrinsically counter-hegemonic might not be observed among certain gangs who become part of the so-called "multitude" (Hardt and Negri 2005), that disparate social class formed in opposition to the new global "empire." This is especially provocative when we consider that many radical groups in the 1960s frequently recruited from among inner-city gang populations (Dawley 1992 [1973]) and there is, of course, a long history of social banditry (Hobsbawm 1969) in pro-revolutionary narratives and popular struggles throughout much of the world. I make this point mindful of the charges of exoticism and/or heroism when describing or imagining the transformative potential of such subaltern groups.

Global structures and local dynamics

The history of a community influenced by larger global processes has to be part of the gang analysis. African-Americans moving north in the post-slavery era, Irish, Italian and East European Jewish immigrants arriving in New York and Chicago pushed and pulled by discrimination and supreme hardship inflicted by domestic elites at the turn of the century and before, Puerto Ricans entering the United States as its neo-colonial subjects after World War II, Dominicans escaping from poverty as their own democratic revolution is upended by US invasion in the 1960s, Mexicans displaced by US expansionism and then through US dependency over the course of 150 years, Central Americans fleeing from a civil war heavily financed by the United States as part of its anti-communist Cold War foreign policy during the 1980s – all these populations responding to global imperial and colonial pressures have effectively transformed much of the US landscape. Historically it is in these areas of settlement that sociology formed its ideas of social disorganization which, in turn, formed the theoretical basis for early gang studies. Missing, however, has been a larger global focus (or what some refer to as "glocal") that showed the relationship between the adaptations of youth and adults (by forming "the gang") to the broader social, political, economic and cultural processes that also were informing its subcultural emergence. The gang, therefore, never formed in supreme isolation from these global pressures but rather, either directly or indirectly, in response to them over the *longue durée* (Adamson 1998).

To correct the picture, therefore, we need to develop a more probing historical sensibility and imagination, particularly in the late modern era when globalization is a fundamental characteristic of local, national and transnational social processes. It is in this period of the "global city" (Sassen 2001), porous boundaries (Young 1999, Conquergood 1993) and "liquid modernity" (Bauman 2004) that sociologists have encouraged us to think more clearly about the role of hybridity in the formation of identities, especially around notions of race, ethnicity and class (see Gilroy's (1993) notion of the Black Atlantic for example). In the sphere of gangs this has been largely neglected, though in my own work on the Latinization of gang subcultures (see Brotherton and Barrios 2004) and in the studies of immigrant gangs in Europe by Palmas (2010) and Feixa *et al.* (2006)[5] there is increasing evidence of a new global gang literature being forged.

Subcultural histories and the gang

All gangs have substantial subcultural[6] histories as they usually move from one generation to another or develop out of other gangs over time. These histories and traditions are often important to understand and trace as they help us to see the continuities and changes in social and cultural practices over time, e.g. many New York City "gangs" have similar organizational structures with Presidents, Treasurers, Warlords or Peacemakers, etc. Many of these subcultural histories are not well known but their influences are carried over in the form of organizational norms, physical gestures, modes of communication, group-based rituals and historically based enmities and solidarities with and against other groups. Sometimes these histories are contained in the parental culture. If we understand these subcultures as "magical solutions" to marginality (P. Cohen 1972), or power-charged, innovative sub-communities (Conquergood 1993) responding to structural contradictions over which they have little control (see Brake 1985), then we should not be surprised to find a wide variety of such sub-cultures in poor neighborhoods.

For the most part, however, these subcultures remain hidden or obscured (except when constructed as highly visible targets of crime control) and it is the task of the community social scientist to unearth them as part of a broader, complex subterranean story of youth in marginalized environments. But there are other moments when these histories become celebrated by the dominant culture. This occurs when profit-seeking enterprises are able to exploit their aesthetics, styles and cultural production, as is the case with the commodification of hip-hop. In this instance we see industry marketers freely associating hybrid gang subcultures of the past with the musical, dance and graffiti scene of the present (see Chang 2005), using the gang connection to give the genre that extra legitimacy, edge and value. At this level the gang is essentially objectified, fetishized and turned into a marketing tool, effectively negating the common assumption that gangs disrupt spheres of capitalist consumption due to their anti-social behavior.

Local histories of the informal economy and social control

We have already referred to the importance of attending to the history of economic development in a community to understand the nature and emergence of gangs. It was Cloward and Ohlin who extended Merton's analysis of subcultural innovation and theorized how the mix of formal and informal economies structured the life chances of lower-class youth that led in turn to different types of gangs. However, Cloward and Ohlin's work was carried out during a high point of modernity, Keynesian economics and a period of still-developing industrialization. During the last couple of decades we have entered capitalism's post-industrial phase with the result that secure working-class jobs are increasingly scarce, with the state increasingly disinclined to regulate markets, protect employment and ensure improved standards of living for all under the ideological banner of neo-liberalism. In this era of declining industrial production in the advanced capitalist countries but increasing financial corporate control of the economy we see the extraordinary growth of the informal economic sector, in particular the illegal drugs market.

The impact on gangs of the massive increase in the drugs economy and the rise of a global narco-trafficking class aided and abetted by the money laundering activities of multinational banks has changed the activities, identities, culture and organization of numerous gangs. It is imperative to take into account the changing nature of these informal economies in relationship to the social problem of gangs and in particular to the assertion that certain gangs have become corporatized in the late modern era. Such a "finding" is very consequential for gangs in the developing world, for example Brazil, Mexico and Colombia, where narco-trafficking has become such an important means of survival for those condemned to poverty and heightened levels of relative deprivation. It is imperative to understand these local economies in relationship to the state, to its various agents who are formally committed to fight the drugs cartels but often work with them, and to the legitimate formal economy.

The state, hegemony and civil society in gang formation

In the United States it is self-evident more than twenty years into the so-called War on Drugs how important the state has become for the creation and perpetuation of gangs. Gonzales (2013) argues that cultures of control (Garland 2001) and government through fear (Simon 2007), initiated by successive elites, constitute a new form of class and racial hegemony. In other words, it is domination through the means of criminalization and in this the gang has been an important symbol against which to organize both physically and ideologically. The legal, technological and institutional apparatuses amassed by the state to defeat this supposed enemy have had an incredibly detrimental effect on the poorest and most vulnerable communities, helping to destabilize families and stigmatize generations of youth and adults forced to pass through criminal justice systems which have become the first rather than the last resort in so many types of crime. This domestic hegemony also extends to the international sphere where the US state is actively creating a new American diaspora as it deports over 400,000 legal and undocumented residents annually. Many of these deportees have come to the state's attention through anti-gang policies such as "Secure Communities", which ostensibly aim at exorcising the nation's "criminal aliens," thereby separating the good immigrants from the bad ones. Another powerful enabler of such mass social exclusion has been those policies based on the dubious criminological theory of "broken windows" – a policy made infamous by state agents who crusaded indefatigably against "quality of life crimes" which invariably were observed primarily in the poorest areas.

These state policies, largely begun in the United States, have been exported to the rest of the world and eagerly adopted there in domestic wars against the gang and other undesirables. The result is what Zilberg (2011) calls "political simultaneity" as various parts of the globe adopt the same kind of vindictive, punishing, humiliating and ultimately futile policies of crime and delinquency control that do little to address the roots of private and public insecurity and everything to reduce the problem to a simplistic struggle against pathological cultures, populations and individuals. This war against the Other, in which the gang plays such an important signifying role, produces a certain level of consensus, such that extraordinary measures of surveillance, preventive security, intelligence gathering and deterrence are tolerated. Naturally this Orwellian manipulation of civil society requires an almost constant diet of moral panics, reminding the public that the "war" is never over, our vigilance should never wane and the end of history is already here.

Conclusion

In this chapter I have sought to underscore the role of history in understanding gangs and to argue that it is impossible to make much sociological or criminological headway in gang studies without situating gangs in their historical context. Gangs are powerful indicators of the contradictions of the larger society and if we simply study them as things-in-themselves, separate from the cross-cutting tensions that mirror their development in the community, or fail to take into account their evolution over time and across space, then we are likely to produce findings and draw conclusions that simply mirror the prejudices and pathological gazes of the dominant social order.

This focus on history as a major underpinning of gang research and the epistemologies we employ is of especial importance in the current epoch of late modernity when the world is shifting at such speed with levels of reflexivity now reaching unparalleled heights. It is in this world of a mass-mediated or hyper-mediated society (Baudrillard 1994) that social actors are increasingly aware of the images of themselves (Gitlin 1980) in a mutually reinforcing process that conditions subjectivities, behavior, styles, ideologies and cultural practices. The gang is simply an example of this highly mediated, reflexive and historical process on a global scale. Consequently, the "world of gangs" (Hagedorn 2008) has to be constantly located and grounded in space, time and social setting. Such an approach flies in the face of the dominant research approach to gangs predicated on the virtues of empiricism and positivism, which simply service the dominant ideological response to poor youth through policies of naive and not so naive social containment, fear and exclusion.

Notes

1 I include here a range of influences from Eduardo Galeano, E.P. Thompson, Robin Kelley, Howard Zinn, David Montgomery, Christopher Hill, and Raphael Samuel to W.E.B. Du Bois.
2 I am, therefore, in agreement with a more general materialist approach to history and historiography summed up by Burrows and Wallace (1999:xxiv) in their encyclopedic history of New York City:

> We believe that the world we've inherited has an immense momentum; that actions taken in the past have bequeathed us the mix of constraints and possibilities within which we act today; that the stage onto which each generation walks has already been set, key characters introduced, major plots set in motion, and that while the next act has not been written, it's likely to follow, in undetermined ways, from the previous action. This is not to say that history repeats itself. Time is not a carousel on which we might, next time round, snatch the brass ring by being better prepared. Rather we see the past as flowing powerfully through the present and think that charting historical currents can enhance our ability to navigate them.

3 Vigil (1988, 2002, 2007), Hagedorn (1988, 2014) (both former students of Moore) and Venkatesh (2000) all maintain the same historico-contextual approach in their work. For example in Vigil's recent study of a housing project with high numbers of gang members a founding chapter is devoted to a history of the main gang in the area during the 1930s and 1940s.
4 Similarly Mendoza-Denton (2008) found a strong gender identity relationship to female gangs in Northern California and traced this to the

historical marginalization of the Mexican and Chicano communities in that area. The author provides a highly innovative and humanistic analysis of a Chola resistance identity to race, class and gendered pressures, invoking the term "hemispheric localism" which incorporates a distinct linguistic and embodied response to oppression and colonialism defined as "a projection onto the hemispheric political stage of processes that began locally in the history of groups of Latinos in California, and that through the processes of symbolic analogy and metonymy this meaning system becomes projected as a wider political analysis" (Mendoza-Denton 2008:87).

5 For example Palmas uses the term Latino Atlantic to describe Latino gangs in Italy.

6 By subculture I am referring to its sociological meaning, i.e. that of the formation of a socio-cultural group with its own values, norms and practices that are often at variance with the dominant culture of society. Subcultures in my interpretation usually emerge from some form of felt marginalization and asymmetrical power relationships, which are somewhat resolved through the group's cultural praxes.

2

DIVERGENT GAZES

From humanism to Hobbesian positivism and social reproduction

> If you want to understand orthodox criminology's vision of the world, the way in which the criminological gaze is structured and distorted, it is best to think of the discipline as an optic, as a lens through which the budding scientists peer down on their objects of study.
>
> (Young 2011:185)

During the last several decades, a number of researchers have described the range of gang subcultures that have become commonplace in US ghettoes and barrios as a response to the intersecting forces of economic, social and cultural marginalization inflicted on poor and minority communities during a period of deindustrialization, economic restructuring and globalization. The *New York Magazine* cover (Figure 2.1) is an excellent illustration from more than forty years ago of renewed journalistic attention being paid to the gang under an inflammatory headline. While there are disagreements as to who or what is responsible for "the gang," a variety of theoretical claims have been proposed, all of which give partial explanations for the continued proliferation of gangs in everyday life.

FIGURE 2.1 Cover of *New York Magazine*, March 27, 1972.
Source: Dan Wynn/*New York Magazine*.

As Young (2011) points out, every researcher has a gaze they bring to their studies. In most cases, however, especially in orthodox criminology, the gaze is unstated and the researcher writes as if from a neutral vantage point. This, of course, is impossible and one of the first obligations of the critical social scientist is to state frankly his or her preference for theory and how this will be used in the accompanying analysis and to what effect. This is precisely my goal in this chapter: to take the reader through the various theoretical contributions that have shaped my outlook, complete with the criticisms that I have found valid of the work. I have broken these perspectives into

four main clusters: Chicago School; sociological humanism and anomie; the Hobbesian alternative; and social reproductionism. I have
done so fully understanding that some of these theories and their
scholarly protagonists may overlap across different genres. Just as the
integration of history is crucial to any serious analysis of the gang so
too is theory, for all empirical data have to be interpreted, weighted
and ordered.

Gangs and the Chicago School

As is well known, Thomas and Znaniecki's (1920) early work on the
acculturation of Polish peasants to the urban environment of Chicago
first gave rise to the notion of social disorganization in the sociological literature. These early practitioners of Chicago urban sociology (known as the Chicago School) looked to the natural social
processes of norms and values to explain non-conformity, rejecting
both the individualistic pathological and rational choice view of
deviant behavior. In their view, rapid social change brought about by
technology, immigration and urbanization were the primary causes of
normative conflict or dissension, which arose when the institutions of
the community were insufficiently developed, non-existent or lacked
effectiveness. This disruption of society's imagined equilibrium was
termed social disorganization and was seen as a major reason for the
emergence of gangs.

Equally well known is that these Chicago School sociologists saw
the space of the city divided into concentric circles and the further
away from the center you resided the better off you were and the
more stable the environment. In the inner circle so-called interstitial,
transitional areas could be found, where the community of mostly
poor, working-class immigrants and migrants were caught in profound levels of flux with their institutions such as churches, schools,
social clubs, etc. somewhat in disarray. It is precisely in this socially
anomic environment that Thrasher's (1927) pioneering inquiry was
carried out.

Thrasher's research has stood the test of time not least for its
broad humanistic approach to the phenomenon, with his non-
delinquent definition of the gang still used today[1] by those not drawn

to tautological research or self-fulfilling prophesies. Thus, Thrasher's work is especially significant for the attention it pays to the meaning of gangs for those involved in these subcultures as well as those who observe them and the holistically layered complexity between these groups and the surrounding community. In Thrasher's work there is no fixation with violence, alcohol, drugs or various realms of deviance but rather a fascination with the gang as a site of diverse and creative forms of sociality for poor and marginalized youth adapting to those invisible areas of Chicago where the "other half" lived. This can be appreciated just by looking at the titles of his earlier chapters in his acclaimed work *The Gang: A Study of 1,313 Gangs in Chicago*: "The quest for new experience," "The movies and the dime novel," "The role of the romantic," "Playgrounds of the gang," "Junking and the railroads," "Wanderlust," "Race and nationality in the gang," and then finally "Gang warfare."

Certainly, Thrasher achieved as much a community study as a gang study. His analyses and empirical revelations are full of an appreciation for social processes set in an ecological context (albeit, as Hagedorn argues, Thrasher overlooks a key characteristic in Chicago's evolution: white supremacy – see Hagedorn 2006)[2] as he documents the city at a certain stage in its development, proceeding through the Chicago School imaginary of an evolutionary cycle of contact, conflict, accommodation, assimilation. But, of course, it is here at the point of change that Thrasher is found wanting, and the extraordinary insights he imparts become truncated by an ideological myopia that restricted the gaze when it came to recognizing the massive structural impediments to his assumptions about and expectations of an open society, summed up by Pfohl and Snodgrass as follows:

> In one grand sweep of sociological imagery, the Chicago theorists dismissed both the sentimental longings of the nativists and the structural critique of the radicals. By conceiving the negative consequences of rapid change as a deviant reaction of the naturally disorganized, rather than as a discontented reaction of the structurally or historically disadvantaged, the Chicago school contributed to a depoliticized image of social problems.
>
> (Pfohl 1989:143)

Instead of turning inward to find the causes of delinquency exclusively in local traditions, families, play groups and gangs, their interpretation might have turned outward to show political, economic and historical forces at work, which would have accounted for both social disorganization and the internal conditions, including delinquency. Needless to say, the interpretation as it stood left business and industry essentially immune from analysis, imputation, and responsibility in the causes of delinquency.

(Snodgrass 1976:10)

Although the emphasis on ecological space was novel and helped reinforce a view of gangs that was more Rousseauian than Hobbesian,[3] there were serious ideological blind spots within the Chicago societal vision that the critics above have powerfully underlined. It should come as no surprise that sociological studies housed in a private university founded by the largesse of oil magnate John D. Rockefeller should steer clear of any analysis of the overall impact of the corporate class on the city's evolution. Nonetheless, the pragmatic gang sociology that emerged, with its preference for multiple data sets, focus on the dynamic (if mechanistically interpreted) processes of urban development and a sensibility for what Matza would later champion as "naturalism", leaves us with a rich legacy that we need to claim, negate and extend.

Sociological humanism, the gang and the contradictions of capitalism

Thus, while the Chicago Schoolists opened the door for the systematic inquiry into the street gang, they left us short of a worldview and a theory that more adequately engaged the structural forces determining society's political economy, the ideologies reflective of the historically conditioned social antagonisms and the thorny issue of the meaning of urban change. It was one thing to link the gang to these tensions of societal anomie but quite another to see the phenomenon as indicative of the deep social fissures that made achievement of the American project impossible. By the end of the Depression, however,

Robert Merton shifted the Chicago-dominated discussion away from strict concerns about the "settled" versus "unsettled" nature of a community and instead launched his classic postulations on the contradictions between agency and structure that, he argued, resulted in the emergence of adaptive subcultures (Merton 1938), i.e. gangs.

Merton's thesis, in one of the most cited texts in American sociology, provided for a sharper focus on the relationship between structural and cultural properties such as class, ideology and, to a lesser extent, race and collective behavior. Greatly influenced by both Marx and Durkheim in his early years, he averred that while tensions between differentially empowered groups were common to most societies, it was a particular problem in the United States where members of the lower orders were supposed to be upwardly mobile, taking advantage of the socially approved avenues leading to the middle classes. The problem, he asserted, was the resulting tension between goals and means, especially when the lower classes do not have the life chances (something that nowadays would inevitably lead to a discussion of cultural capital) decreed in the imaginary "American Dream."

But Merton's contribution was a far cry from the mechanical interpretations of his work as contained in strain theory, still regarded as part of the canon of orthodox criminology. As Young has remarked, "Merton saw the Dream, namely as a cultural 'sop' which reduced the chances of rebellion against a system which systematically produced low rates of social mobility" (2011:92), i.e. the Dream was both a mystification and reification of US class ascendancy, a reading of capitalist ideology and culture not far removed from Marxists such as Lukacs. The main problem with Merton's schematic was that his delineation of the ideal-typical subcultural responses to the discord between culture and material reality was too suggestive of a utilitarian resolution, overlooking the propensity of youth to explore a mix of behaviors, norms and styles (or what Hebdige (1979) later called the bricolage).

In the post-World War II period, a number of researchers followed Merton's lead and formulated largely theoretical explanations for the continued discontent and alienation increasingly observed among lower-class youth.[4] This disaffection, later popularized through the cultural shock of rock and roll and film hits such as *Blackboard Jungle* (1953), *Rebel without a Cause* (1955), the *Wild One* (1955) and *West Side Story*

(1961), was responded to first by the likes of William Foot Whyte, and then by Albert Cohen, Richard Cloward, Lloyd Ohlin, David Matza and Carl Werthman, all of whom brought a more sustained humanism to the "optic," with which to contemplate delinquency, gangs and marginality. As Larkin (1979:47) later summed up this period:

> The youth of the 1950s lived in a context that on the one hand extolled youth as the ideal state of humanity, while on the other hand, resented the young for being youthful. Juvenile delinquency had become a serious problem. The 1960 White House Conference on Children has as its central focus the alienation and isolation of youth … The major issue was juvenile delinquency. The family was evidencing an inability to control its own young and the burden was falling ever harder on public authorities: teachers, counselors, social workers, and the police. Yet the adolescent "rebellion" was not a collective phenomenon, with the exception of the inner-city gangs.[5]

In 1943, thus, Whyte published his seminal book on "street corner society" based on a year of participant action observational research[6] while residing with a poor Italian-American family in a Boston "slum." Whyte's approach was radical for the time and included not only systematic observations and in situ interviews with a full range of social actors on the street, both gang and non-gang, but also his involvement in social advocacy movements with and on behalf of local residents. Whyte saw the gangs as reflective of the massive levels of disenfranchisement in capitalist society and ably applied the Weberian notion of "verstehen" (see also Ferrell 1997), careful to discern the range of behaviors (both deviant and non-deviant), the lived culture of a neighborhood, and the complex social networks in a poor area with high levels of social reciprocity. His classic work (which only received widespread attention seven years after its second edition was published) avoided pathologizing and typecasting his subjects. Instead he produced vivid, multi-dimensional, empathetic descriptions of them, stressing the energy and verve in their relationships, the inventiveness in their narratives and the structural contradictions they had to negotiate every day.

In specifically addressing the re-emerging gang phenomenon, Cohen (1955) employed concepts such as status frustration and the then voguish Freudian notion of reaction formation to describe and account for working-class youth's encounter with the hegemony of American adult middle-class ideals, ideology and practices that lay the foundation for much of the culture of institutionalized schooling. Cohen brilliantly explored the class-based assumptions of those condemning the wantonness and non-utilitarian attitudes of youth gang members and showed how humiliation, devaluation and social exclusion were what lay behind the panoply of behaviors often dismissed and categorized as "maladjustment." In many ways Cohen was hinting at the pained effects on youth of what later was called schooling's "hidden curriculum" (Anyon 1980), analyzed as an integral part of the ideological apparatus of contemporary capitalism. The success of his problematization of oppositional and perhaps irrational youth behavior was in contrast to the functionalism and unreflexive structuralism of the dominant Parsonian systems thinking of the day, within which capitalist social relations were normalized and reified. Unfortunately, the insights that Cohen provided on the cultural and psychological interpretations of the alienated were undermined by his overemphasis on the implicit negativity of so-called delinquent behavior, opening another door to the pathologization process discussed later in the chapter. As Fine (1991) has demonstrated, rejecting school could be as much about having a political consciousness of institutionalization and its regimes of tracking, surveillance and the curriculum culture that "kills the spirit" (see Loewen 1995).

A second important humanist intervention came from Cloward and Ohlin, who linked the phenomenon of gangs to the opportunity structure in a given neighborhood. Their work, in part an attempt to address the consternation and fear felt by the white upper-class Establishment toward the more expressive, multi-racial, post-war youth generations, sought to explain how working-class youth could be so resistant to their socially assigned roles and how the particular characteristics of a neighborhood's political economy and social structure could help resolve the deep-seated contradictions between objective realities and ideological representations.

Cloward and Ohlin's sociological location of inner-city youth pre-figured a debate that raged around the position of poor and minority youth during the urban resistances of the 1960s. As they stated:

> What remains in the community is a residual of "failures" – persons who have not succeeded in the search for higher socio-economic status. The old forms of social organization begin to break down, and with them opportunities for upward mobility diminish … Once again the young find themselves both cut off from avenues to higher status and free from external restraint. This is a period, then, in which we should expect a resurgence of violent modes of delinquent adaptation.
>
> (Cloward and Ohlin 1960:199)

However, their influential work did not simply become another hall-mark of "gang prevention best practices" as in today's parlance but rather the policy framework for Kennedy's war on poverty in 1961, leading to one of the United States' most effective and far-reaching interventions against the structural inequality of the twentieth cen-tury. The gang, therefore, was conceived as the symptom and harbin-ger of something much deeper within the current social order. Their work represented an attempt to grapple with the roots of the phe-nomenon, expanding outwards from the particular to the general, to reveal fundamental contradictions that needed to be addressed rather than some behaviors that needed to be controlled.

In this same radical reconsideration of the deviant, around the same time as Cohen, Cloward and Ohlin, Matza was arguing for the adolescent deviant/delinquent to be phenomenologically understood and situated in relationship to the normalized deviance of adult soci-ety and in particular to that of the parent class. Rather than dislodging youth from their embedded and contingent societal context Matza argued for a "rigorous humanism" and a methodological naturalism to see the world through the subject's eyes. As he eloquently states:

> Man [*sic*] participates in meaningful activity. He creates his real-ity, and that of the world around him, actively and strenuously. Man naturally – not supernaturally – transcends the existential

realms in which the conceptions of cause, force, and reactivity are easily applicable. Accordingly, a view that conceives man as object, methods that probe human behavior without concerning themselves with the meaning of behavior, cannot be regarded as naturalist.

(Matza 1969:8)

Thus, Matza was opposed to any pretense of determinism and essentialism in the delinquency encounter, be it gang or otherwise, and saw youth subcultures as self-imagined, often untenable (Young 2011) solutions (presaging the Birmingham School) to perceived marginality within a world suffused with opaque meanings, ambiguous practices and ironic outcomes. As such, there is an existentialism in Matza's sociology and criminology that emphasizes the free will and creativity of lower-class youth facing a world that was, and is, disturbingly absurd. In all of the humanists' research there is a sense of proximity to the researched and a degree of empathy which no doubt reflected the immigrant histories of most of these analysts and in the case of Cloward his unprivileged nativist upbringing.[7]

As the 1960s were drawing to a close, Werthman (1969), a student of Matza, advanced some of the clearest empirically based descriptions of urban gang behavior from within the labeling perspective. Based on his field studies in San Francisco of relations between the police and young black gang members, he discerned the performative processes by which identities, both deviant and mainstream, were constructed and how the "career paths" of gang youths were mutually constituted via the discriminatory attention of the social controllers. Werthman was critical of capitalist social relations and his prescient insights into the human dramas of the street resonate strongly with current criticisms of "stop and frisk" practices.

This humanist intervention vis-à-vis the gang, with its penchant for theory, represents a high point in gang studies. But like the Chicago School, in many ways, it did not sufficiently problematize the political economy and was always close to pastoral notions of the state and the liberal pretensions of capitalist democracy. Behind the humanism was a belief in the attainment of a "good society" with reasoned discourse, argument and counter-argument leading us toward a deeper understanding of the social problem and eventually to a solution for gangs that would not have to deal with the basic contradictions of structure. The unquestioned attainability of the social contract looms large and, of course, much of this discourse either presaged the 1960s or was written during this world-changing epoch. It is important to savor how dominant this humanist strain in gang studies was during this period, but also to remember the degree to which the pathologists were co-existing and how far we have moved now to this other end of the criminological spectrum.

Hobbesian renderings of the gang

Where and why did the pathological turn come in the academic rendering of the gang? Young (2011) argues that the anti-humanist turn in the US criminological construction of the "deviant" (of which the gang has been a major subject of study and debate) relates to the increasing influence of positivism in the social sciences, the rising social distance between the researcher and the researched due to the academy's professionalization and the domination of the United States in the field of international criminology. Meanwhile Wacquant (1997, 2002) traces the ongoing conservative turn to the lack of reflexivity among professional and professionalized researchers operating within a highly stratified university system and knowledge industry (Aronowitz 2000). In addition, of course, the dominance of positivism is linked to the neo-liberal political, economic and cultural sphere that for the last three decades has presided over the global political economy with the rejection of Keynesianism and welfare state models of governance. Practices and ideologies, thus, have tended to emulate those epistemologies and methodologies tied to the "dismal" science of economics. This is particularly the case in a US criminology that has so enthusiastically embraced such methods and perspectives probably more than any other discipline outside economics itself.

Perhaps reflecting the resurgence of middle-class white conservatism in the post-war United States, the criminological ideas of Toby (1957), Miller (1958), Yablonsky (1963) and Hirschi (1969) hold a special place in the rejection of the humanist treatment of gangs that has continued with gusto until today. This trend has been reinforced by the proliferation of criminal justice departments throughout much of the US system of higher education, with the numbers of criminal justice majors now rapidly outpacing both sociology and anthropology. Below I discuss five themes that link these treatments, underscoring the positions of both Young and Wacquant.

Social control

The Chicago School had strongly emphasized the importance of social control in relationship to the phenomenon of gangs and saw these subcultures as an indication of an area's social disorganization. Consequently, social control came from a Durkheimian imagination, one that viewed gangs and gang members in a broader relationship with the social whole and the specific ecological utilization and manifestation of urban social space. The pathologists, who mirror the correctionalists as described by Matza, started from a different understanding of control, space and place and focused on the relationship between an individual's self-control and his/her environment.

This is certainly true of Toby (1957) who argued for a strong containment theory (see Reckless 1961) vis-à-vis gangs and that it is the juvenile with the fewest "stakes in conformity" (see also Reiss 1951) who is most ready for what he termed "gang socialization." This Hobbesian worldview, positing that we are all naturally attracted to deviance and it is only our bonds, social contracts and agreements with societal institutions that restrain us is, of course, a thesis made famous by Hirschi years later (analyzed through his notions of attachment, involvement, belief and commitment). Thus Hirschi found, based on his data, that it was "the rational, calculational component in conformity and deviation" that was most important in predicting the onset of "delinquency" – rather than any Mertonian "strain" or Chicago School "culture."

Yablonsky took the pathological view to its extreme by diagnosing his subjects with sociopathic afflictions and tendencies, claiming that they were incapable of forming a gang but could establish a "near-group" for the purposes of violence. As Moore commented, noting the obsession with youth in a social science that had taken at face value Coleman's (1961) thesis in *Adolescent Society* that youth were "structurally isolated":

> Yablonsky has the most adult-free approach. In his attempt to account for violent gangs, he sees that they share many features with the "pseudo-community" of "paranoids" … Yablonsky's conceptualization has been widely criticized; all we need do here is point to it as a case of extreme focus on youth and pathology in gang research.
>
> (Moore and García 1978:49)

Miller is somewhat different to other pathologists with his focus on the class and its values as the cause of gang delinquency. Thus, Miller saw gangs emerging from the normative criminogenic culture of the lower classes and pointed to its unchangeable and generalizable nature that produces the following "concerns": trouble, toughness, smartness, excitement, fate, autonomy.

It is hard, however, to understand why these traits are so particular to the lower class since in disparate contexts they are equally apparent in the middle and upper classes. Further, what is meant by the lower class, since Miller's view of class as a concept is hard to discern. Is the class related to the organization of the means of production? Is it a social stratum arbitrarily defined by some form of income segmentation? Is it defined by occupation or perhaps through residency? The answers do not readily appear in Miller's work and one can only assume he never felt compelled to answer such an obvious question.

Deviant deficits

Deviants, for the pathologists, are riddled with deficits. They lack bonds to conforming adults, a commitment to the middle-class values of school, a consciousness that allows them to form collective organizations and possess a self-condemning attitude to life that will always see them in the lower classes. There really is not too much variation among this deviant class and it is not surprising that most pathologists called for increasing the range of punishments for such youth or at least recognizing that social mobility is not for them, nor should it be.

Consequently, the class structure of society is what it is although it is rarely mentioned as an analytical concept or theme that is tied to society's structuring. The pathologists contrast the negativity of the gang delinquent to the positivity of what Hirschi called "conventional society" such that no other interpretation of the negative behavior is attempted. It is simply a property that is assumed and given by the researcher such as "law violating acts" (Miller 1958) or, with Hirschi (1969), that seems to be more akin to the ambiguous notion of a delinquent role. The deficit model as an ideology thus resonates strongly with the Western colonial model, i.e. the observer views him or herself as neutral and somehow above race, class and gendered constructions of knowledge, morality and the norms of epistemology. This deficit model goes a long way in gang research and heavily underpins much of the funded research carried on in the present day.

Absence of contradiction

Nowhere in the pathologists' work do we see any of the ironies, paradoxes, latent functions and contradictions that the humanists were consumed by. This absence is quite apparent in Hirschi who, based on an extremely long self-report survey with school-age youth in Northern California (that he felt was not tainted by all manner of concealment, as is typical in surveys), found that there was no relationship between social class and this ambiguous concept of delinquency. Although Hirschi notes the objective reality that most of the incarcerated come from the lowest social strata he is loath to find the "findings" somewhat contradictory and counter-intuitive. Similarly, Miller, a trained anthropologist, utilizing a staid conception of "culture," which he seems to equate with values, assumes the class of his research subjects to be sealed off from the general culture of capitalism with its invasive messages of conformity around the themes of consumerism, work, mobility, national superiority and anti-communism. How could this be, after World War II, in the middle of a Fordist America, the Korean War and the McCarthyism that ran through much of the 1950s?

But for pathologists the emphasis must always be on the problems of "adjustment" for individuals who fail to fit in with the "norms" of the mainstream regardless of whether those norms are ultimately contingent on the power arrangements that socially order our experiences of race, gender, class and age. In a complete rejection of the work of Mills, who argued that for sociology to have meaning we must move from the inner world of humans to the outer world of power, domination, oppression and resistance, i.e. from personal problems to social issues, the pathologists search for a resolution to their data sets through insider-talk, as far removed from the contradictory lives of human beings as possible. Young frames this issue of the avoidance of contradiction, drawing on Mills' critique of Parsons, as follows:

> He [Mills] distinguishes semantics and syntax: semantics are words about reality, syntax are words in relation to each other … Thus typologies have a reality of their own, concepts chatter with each other, the academician ponders over subdivisions without questioning what is being divided.
>
> (Young 2011:6)

"America" is the world

It might be assumed that somewhere researchers would look at the world they describe each day in their writings and wonder if it's the same the world over. Alas, the rituals of solipsism rarely jolted the consciousness of the pathologists, who presumed that what prevails in the United States must be the case everywhere.[8] I presume in the 1950s, with the United States famously asserting its economic, military and political superiority, it was difficult for provincial white middle-class US researchers to imagine they came from anywhere in particular other than the institution that trained them. It was a gaze on the world that comes naturally from a privileged vantage point, as numerous critics of the domain assumptions in social science have long averred (e.g. Gouldner, Mills, Haraway, Foucault, Williams, etc.). Claims from a particular situated knowledge, therefore, flowed and gushed effortlessly, ordering "crimes," devising "categories" of behavior, and delineating between normal and deviant traits with little reference to history, ideology, culture (as in meaning-making) or politics. Such constructions were well represented in professional journals in the late 1950s, were much less in vogue during the 1960s, but came back strongly during the Nixon era and continue to saturate US-based academic journals, books and conference proceedings.

The presumed need for generalization

While some aspects of the pathological gaze have purchase on why gangs might emerge over time it is surely in reference to the dynamics and processes at the level of the social that must receive most of our criminological and sociological attentions. For example, the painstaking studies of Oscar Lewis (1965) and his assertion that a "culture of poverty" as observed in highly marginalized and oppressed sections of the working and sub-working class help us understand how violence is learned and perhaps passed on from generation to generation. Or perhaps the theory of youth subcultures that states that groups emerge from both the agency and the adaptation of youth as they respond to their perceived structural powerlessness (see Thrasher) provides insights into the proliferation of such groups in a highly stratified, hierarchical society. But the scientistic compulsion to generalize, usually based on surveys of dubious validity and levels of representation, or the propensity of positivistic researchers to make *pronunciamentos* about deviant subjects with whom they have little social contact or cultural appreciation, sometimes not even speaking the language of the subpopulation, is at the least misleading and at the worst a contribution to the reproduction of elite-based power and social control. As one leading criminologist has commented on the more recent work of Hirschi (and Gottfredson's) which claims to have discovered a "General Theory of Crime":

> The justice of that society, or the role of the state as a criminogenic agent, or the context of society in global processes is not part of the general theory. If the theory really wanted to be a "general theory", a much wider world of crime and normative tensions would need to be observed.

> (Morrison 2006:226)

The five themes that run through the pathological school strongly characterize this approach to the gang and are taught as the norms of research in many if not all criminal justice colleges in the United States. Competing paradigms and the sociology of knowledge from which they emerge are rarely discussed; thus it is not surprising to encounter graduate students at hugely attended criminology and criminal justice conferences in the United States who have only a cursory understanding of the contours of this long debate regarding the position of the street gang in US society and, with the mass export of this pathological paradigm, the same observation might be made in many other societies. Thus there is no mention of class in this school and certainly no consideration of the political economy, but instead a healthy regard for the chosen pathways of the individual and the ever-troubling prevalence of criminal transgressions by the almost naturally criminogenic lower orders predictably found in the same criminogenic environments. It is Hobbes writ large and makes sense that the coercive state and its harsh laws of social control have become strong accompaniments of this influential gaze.

Social reproductionism and the gang

And so on to social reproductionism and the return of a discourse seeking to place gang social behavior in a more structured context and, in particular, account for the proliferation of the gang in the post-1980s period. For much of the 1960s and 1970s there was a lull in the empirical and theoretical research on gangs with the exception of Klein's work at the turn of the decade (see Klein 1971) and the national gang study by Miller in 1975. Those two works reinforced the pathological claims about gangs, tying their definitions to the commitment of delinquency (Klein) and violence (Miller). Hence there seemed to be little of the Chicago School or 1950s humanism until Moore entered the fray at the end of the decade (Moore and García 1978) with her pioneering, ethnographic collaborative study of Chicano gang members set in the California barrio and prison system. There was a tremendous difference between these researchers, with Klein pursuing a more positivistic psychological path while Miller continued with his conservative anthropological outlook compared to Moore's grounded historical approach that emphasized the gang's "habitat" and an inductive mode of inquiry that carefully considered cultural traditions, age-graded self-organization and the contextual politics of a colonized subpopulation.

Together this research heralded a trend that has continued to the present that I have called social reproductionist, a sociological concept conceived in the work of Marx vis-à-vis the reproduction of the working class and later used to great effect by Bourdieu (see for example *Distinction: A Social Critique of the Study of Taste* (1978), in which he tries to understand how the class system reproduces itself through a combination of structured socialization and subjective dispositions (i.e. the habitus)). An excellent example of social reproduction at work is the research of Bourgois, whose ethnography of a drug gang in Spanish Harlem led him to conclude:

> Contradictorily, therefore, the street culture of resistance is predicated on the destruction of its participants and the community harboring them. In other words, although street culture emerges out of a personal search for dignity and a rejection of racism and subjugation, it ultimately becomes an active agent in personal degradation and community ruin.
>
> (Bourgois 1995:9)

Bourgois' assertion is a classic rendition of the social reproduction paradigm, as members of the lower classes are observed to make a rod for their own backs. Thus while they expressively and symbolically resist the values, norms and ideologies of the dominant class/race culture, they do so only to substantively reproduce them. This perspective, also theoretically and empirically contained in the studies of Willis (1977), Macleod (1995), Fordham (1996) and Ogbu (1978), among others, was prevalent in debates on the nature and trajectory of the so-called emergent "underclass" that raged during the early 1990s (for critiques see, *inter alia*, Di Leonardo 1998, Wacquant 1997, Scott 1985, Reed 1992). This discourse had an important impact on the ways inner-city gangs were imagined, interpreted and causally conceived.[9] While the gang–underclass–social reproduction literature has many contributors, there are three distinct perspectives that I have assembled for further discussion below: (1) gangs as typological constructs; (2) gangs as post-industrial organizations; and (3) gangs as quasi-institutions.

Gangs as typological constructs

According to Klein, the appearance of the underclass was the main cause behind the "astounding proliferation of U.S. street gangs" (Klein 1995:205) during the late 1980s and early 1990s. In his work and that of many of his associates we see an attempt to systematize the knowledge of gangs by reducing them to criminological constructs and fitting them into one or other organizational model such as traditional, neo-traditional, etc.[10] His data, most of which come from surveys or reports from intermediaries, such as social workers or field workers, completing interviews in criminal justice settings (what Hagedorn pejoratively calls "jail house criminology"), contain little ethnographic observation or first-hand life histories that derive from a trusted or knowing relationship between the researcher and the researched (Miller (2001) is an exception in this school). Thus, there is no accounting for the historically conditioned specifics of the research setting or the subjectivities and culture of the subjects. This model is an easily replicable positivistic approach that objectifies gangs and gang members and has been popular in circles of US orthodox criminology, making its way readily across the Atlantic where moral panics over gangs are well underway (see Hallsworth 2013, Hallsworth and Young 2008).

As Moore (Moore and García 1978) some time ago pointed out, such research is highly problematic since it posits deductively an ideal-typical construct on an objective reality, which, in the case of gangs and most "deviants," eschews the intrinsic problems of identification, representation and recognition. In essence, it reduces a complex, holistic social problem to an identifiable, measurable and quantifiable one that can be grasped by the outsider in the service of social control (Becker 1963) and well-funded investigation.

While Klein has long argued against the gang repression model, which typifies US militarized social control efforts in the more recent period, he is also against a form of pastoral outreach that will only unintentionally lead to the gang reinforcing its negative gang identity. Thus, we are left with another version of "correctionalism" that starts from the deficits of the research subject(s) (particularly if they are adjudged to be members of the underclass) and the criminogenic nature of the social animal.

In this kind of research, if we borrow from Young, it is the (forensic or clinical) psychologist's optic that holds sway – identifying, proportioning, selecting and distilling behavioral properties of the group and transforming them into objects of study and dissemination. This structuralist (in terms of organization) approach, proceeding from a non-inductionist, anti-reflexive bias, lays the groundwork for the bureaucratic, repressive policies supposedly opposed by the social scientist. It is no coincidence that Klein's 1971 gang definition was a departure from gang research in the past and was one of the first definitions to make the gang *ipso facto* criminogenic (supported by Miller in 1975).

Gangs as post-industrial organizations

Jankowski (1991), in contrast, offered a different reading of the underclass–gang relationship. Based on his multi-site, bicoastal field research, Jankowski concluded that enduring gangs are first and foremost sophisticated organizations rationally responding to economic and social deprivation; integrated into the community; and largely containing members who typically boast defiant individualist characteristics. For Jankowski, a gang is distinguished from other delinquent groups to the extent that it is:

> an organized social system that ... plans and provides not only for the social and economic services of its members, but also for its own maintenance as an organization.
>
> (1991:29)

According to Jankowski, the key to a gang's longevity is the strength of its dialectical relationship with the community. If the gang consistently goes against the accepted norms of the local neighborhood, then the residents will no longer tolerate the gang's operations and will begin to provide intelligence reports to anti-gang law enforcement agencies and generally be complicit in the state's attempts to eradicate the group. Members of the neighborhood, therefore, engage in a calculating cost–benefit analysis and decide whether to accept the range of gang-related services, i.e. protection, illicit economic access, sponsored social gatherings, and so on.

Venkatesh (1997, 2000), in a different though related vein, argues that certain contemporary gangs in Chicago, far from settling for their fatalistic trajectory, have also actively engaged the American Dream with varying levels of success. In his study of black gangs in a housing project, he describes their myriad efforts to respond to their social and economic disenfranchisement through their own forms of illicit capital accumulation, joining with other community associations to enhance the quality of life of their impoverished neighborhood. This process he describes as corporatization, a term he uses to explain the range of social and economic interdependencies between the gang and the community. One of his major contributions is the novel analysis of the way the community is reconstituted through what he calls "built social space," a concept that merges Chicago School ecology with the neo-Marxist spatial theories of Lefebvre (1971).

While both Jankowski and Venkatesh advance our understanding of gangs without necessarily endorsing a pathologizing[11] research path, they both consider the phenomenon emblematic of pragmatic, marginalized social groups responding to and socially reproducing their said environment. The group and its actors are intensely rational, albeit engaged in a series of relationships with a system that is highly irrational (if the end goal of that system is a social order built on democratic principles). But gangs and gang members need not be rational and there is much in gang life that is non-reflective, an observation made by Thrasher, particularly with his emphasis on spontaneity. Further, the construction of agency, while present, has no transformative properties, for the gang imagination is always confined within the possibilities of the status quo, thereby always reproducing oppressive economic and social relations.

Gangs as quasi-institutions

Commenting both on the Chicano gangs of East Los Angeles and on their African-American counterparts in Milwaukee, Moore (1991) contrasts gangs in her 1980s research to those of the past, using the underclass as a primary marker of difference:

> It is also important to remember that these [contemporary gangs] are overwhelmingly black and Hispanic youth. They are not the ethnic Europeans of the gangs of the 1920s, whose marginality lasted only one generation. Nor are they the working class youth of so many studies, but rather they are increasingly a fraction of the urban underclass. In short, when we talk about gangs we are talking about quasi-institutionalized structures within the poorer minority communities.

The underclass paradigm was applied both to young inner-city blacks in the rust-belts of the Mid-West (Hagedorn 1988) and to Latino/as in the so-called booming metropolises of the West (Moore 1991, Vigil 1988), leading to a consensus that these subcultures both directly and indirectly reproduce behaviors and value systems that are oppositional to those of the dominant culture yet ensure the continuance of a system of oppression and subordination.

The gang, therefore, functions as a form of quasi-institution in post-industrial society, filling the social cracks of a racist, sexist and class-based structure that only guarantees the multi-marginalization (Vigil 1988) and social invisibility of the barrio and ghetto poor. For Vigil, a confederate of both Moore and Hagedorn, gangs provide a set of values and practices that produce a form of street socialization within which youth can be raised as an alternative to the middle-class ideals of regular families. This condition emerges from the colonized experiences of the poor, subordinated by the racist structuring of the United States and held in place by institutions that discriminate and make manifest a modern form of white supremacy now expanded through the mass incarceration of poor blacks and Latino/as.

Hagedorn similarly argues strongly for the quasi-institutional model and in his most recent intervention (Hagedorn 2015) postulates that this extends to reproduced ideals of organized crime *à la* the Mafia where gangs have begun to emulate this infamous ethnic Italian capitalist enterprise, or as Bell (1960) referred to it "as an American way of life." According to Hagedorn, there is plenty of imagination in the gangs as well as structure, but it is overdetermined by the capitalist ethos of profit seeking.[12] Hagedorn posits that there is definitely a mis-recognition of gangs by outsiders, especially the corrupted law enforcement Establishment and politicians committed to top-down social control and the maintenance of the elite-inspired racial and class structure of cities like Chicago, now reinforced by the politics of neo-liberal globalization. Together these forces and processes conspire to massively expand urbanized poverty and permanently divide cities across race and class lines policed by the increasingly politicized, punitive systems of criminal justice.

While this assertion of gangs as institutions is provocative, and there is definitely some evidence of this evolution, there is a tendency to pathologize their permanence and to underappreciate the contradictions within the institutionalized gang's values, ideologies and practices. Further, there is a tendency toward cultural and economic determinism in gang studies using the underclass concept as if it were a catch-all variable (Sullivan 1989). Certainly, if the underclass is to retain any explanatory power (one hears few references to it nowadays) it must be constantly re-examined in light of changing local, national and global conditions, which should be analyzed as part of a contingent and reflexive relationship between gangs and the external society, alongside the changing agency of social actors. This is equally true of a concept that is increasingly used to explain the newly emerging gang structures such as the "precariat"[13] (Standing 2012).

Finally, across the gamut of perspectives that endorse the processes of social reproduction there needs to be a much stronger and more coherent light shone on two critical properties of the current society. One is the nature and practice of the state, if for no other reason than that the criminal justice system and its attendant surveillance networks and legal apparatuses comprise a huge state and non-state network of social control institutions and labor forces that select, manufacture and contain "Others" at a rate and with an intensity that smacks far more of authoritarianism than of democracy. The second property is the class nature of society. The absence of such an analysis is glaring in so many gang studies, particularly if social reproduction is a dominant theme with some of its origins in Marxism and neo-Marxism. Far too often social reproductionists seem to argue that gangs are consciously and unconsciously complicit in capitalist state designs regarding the control and exploitation of the subordinate and subaltern classes. However, I am not convinced of the complete absence of a counter-hegemonic dynamic within the field of gangs, or that we should settle for the assumption of the assured victory of neo-colonialism and its various forms of domination in ghetto, barrio and other transnational urban and suburban domains. We have not long ago experienced the extraordinary uprisings of the Arab Spring or the various Occupy movements – all of which occurred with participants drawn from across the lower- and middle-class spectrums of the respective societies at historical moments that trained observers had least expected.

Conclusion

In this chapter I have discussed the range of theses that make up the bulk of gang theory, providing a critical reading of their major claims and outlining some of the problems with each approach, particularly the absence of any thoroughgoing class analysis of the gang in capitalist society. This engagement with the gang literature does not pretend to be exhaustive and its less grandiose aim is to take the reader through an appreciation of gang theory as it pertains to a critical discourse of society that is conceived as an ongoing, unfinished and highly contradictory project. My conceptual framework borrows unashamedly from the analyses of Young (2011) who advises us to see theoretical frameworks in the form of gazes and optics through which scholars look at micro, meso and macro processes of deviance construction and control. I have attempted to designate these optics by themes that are a major aspect or inspiration behind their claims. As a critical scholar I am more partial, of course, to a Rousseauian worldview of social order and social change than theories that derive from a Hobbesian perspective. For the latter I assume will support the status quo and be dismissive of the inherent contradictions within our currently ordered capitalist society that leaves the door open to possibilities of progressive social movement and change. At the same time, I am also critical of a social reproductionist perspective that forecloses on the possibility of a transformative gang agency.

For me, it is a humanist ambiguity and skepticism towards dominance that best approximates a critical perspective on gangs, recognizing the pitfalls of social reproduction but keeping alive the possibility that meanings are constantly being created and there is much going on in these subterranean worlds and cultures that defy the outsider's rational approach to data collection and systematic inquiry. In the next chapter I will enter the next stage on this odyssey toward a critical gang theory and outline the meanings and claims of yet another gaze, or what I call situated resistance.

Notes

1 Thrasher defined the gang as: "an interstitial group originally formed spontaneously and then integrated through conflict … the result of this collective behavior is the development of tradition, unreflective internal structure, esprit de corps, solidarity, morale, group awareness and attachment to a local territory" (1927:46). See his non-pathological rendering of the phenomenon, especially the last sentence: "The gang develops as a response to society. The social group of which the gang boy is a member has failed to provide organized and supervised activities adequate to absorb his interests and exhaust his energies. An active boy without an outlet for his energies is a restless boy – seeking satisfactions he cannot name, willing to experiment, curious about this and that, eager to escape whatever surveillance is placed upon him. *The gang solves his problem, offering him what society has failed to provide*" (1927:178).

2 The race riots in Chicago of 1919 were one of the major expressions of race conflict at the time, started by white gangs invading black neighborhoods in the South Side.

3 The Rousseauian/Hobbesian dichotomy is often used in the social sciences to emphasize the liberal/conservative divide in basic notions of humankind. For Rousseau our state of nature was relatively harmonious, and we are capable of creating a social contract from which our collective freedom and self-determination can be obtained. In contrast, Hobbes sees our natural state as one of a war of all against all. For Hobbes, who wrote during and after the English Civil War of 1642–1651, we are faced by "continual fear and danger of violent death," with "the life of man, solitary, poor, nasty, brutish, and short," therefore a strong government or state is needed to protect us from ourselves. Sound familiar?

4 NB the Zoot Suit riots in Los Angeles occurred in 1943, before the end of the war, but presaged a major growth in resistant youth subcultures amid

the tensions of race and class relations in US urban areas. See Alvarez (2008) and Gilbert's (1986) analysis of ongoing moral panics over youth deviance as they become a market force in the epoch of mass consumerism.

5 It is instructive to remember that New York state was the first state to start trying juveniles as adults in 1962 under the Family Court Act. Here is what the *New York Times* Editorial Board said recently about this reversal of juvenile justice reform in the home of juvenile justice reform:

> At the time, lawmakers were unable to agree on the age at which offenders should be declared adults; they set it temporarily at 16, pending further hearings. But as often happens with public policy, inertia set in and "temporary" became permanent … The result is that New York channels nearly 40,000 adolescents a year into the criminal courts – most of them charged with nonviolent crimes like fare-beating in the subways, marijuana possession and shoplifting. The consequences have been especially disastrous for black and Latino young people, who are overrepresented among those arrested and disproportionately at risk of having their lives ruined by encounters with the criminal justice system. (*New York Times* Editorial Board, 2014)

6 A precursor to the now popular action research model in the social sciences.

7 It is worth mentioning the radicalizing life history experiences of these researchers. Whyte was the son of academics who grew up in the Bronxville section of New York; traveling to Germany during the Depression with his parents he witnessed the rise of National Socialism. As a young adult he professed an early interest in the empowerment of the disenfranchised and later published numerous works on labor and worker cooperatives. Matza was born in the Bronx, was deeply affected by a brother killed at the end of World War II and lived through and participated both in the anti-Vietnam War and the Free Speech movements in Berkeley. Cloward meanwhile had first-hand experience of deviant US soldiers imprisoned during the Korean War, played a leading role in the Mobilization for Youth, the student occupation of Columbia University and the anti-poverty movements of the 1960s and was the target of a vengeful assault by McCarthyistic forces that almost ended his tenure bid at Columbia. Merton was born into a humble Philadelphia household, lived through the Depression and World War II, felt the intense attention of the FBI under McCarthyism and lived with an adopted Anglicized name to cope with the realities of anti-Semitism. Finally, Cohen, also from modest beginnings in Boston, served in World War II in the Philippines and later suffered the indignity of discrimination after being repeatedly rejected from full-time work in the Academy due to his Jewish ethnicity.

8 In the multi-polarized world to which we are now accustomed with the extraordinary planetary flow of capital, labor, goods and cultures and the proximity between social worlds massively narrowed by the Internet, it would seem impossible to maintain such a non-reflexive posture.

9 This class, identified famously by Wilson (1987), using a term borrowed both from Myrdal (1944) and Glasgow (1981), was said to consist primarily of urban residents within census tracts where poverty rates exceeded 40 percent. For Wilson, the extent of the underclass was determined by four variables: the out-migration of the middle-class; the shift in industrial modes from manufacturing to service; the segregation of minorities; and the failure of the educational system. In short order, not least because of the ideological war being waged on the poor, the underclass notion took on a life of its own, both in social scientific and popular media discourses. In many respects, the underclass was a combination of what Spitzer (1975) referred to as two kinds of surplus populations, social dynamite and social junk.

10 Klein along with his collaborator Maxson (see Klein and Maxson 1996) found four types of patterned gang structures in the United States which they identified as traditional, neo-traditional, compressed and specialty. Later Klein also talked about the "autonomous gang" (Klein 1995), which he found to be one of the most prevalent as the influence of the traditional gang seemed to wane. These typologies have had a great deal of influence on gang research and are used in multiple settings including all across Europe via the so-called "Eurogang Project" (Decker and Weerman 2005). In fact the "Eurogang Project" took pride in the fact that its participants (gang researchers from various disciplines across Europe) could come to a consensus on what a gang looks like and concluded that it was: "any durable street-oriented youth group whose involvement in illegal activity is a part of its identity" (Van Gemert and Fleischer 2005). The mind boggles at the level of pathological designation given to groups of youth across Europe by this type of research.

11 While Jankowski clearly sees gangs as highly instrumentalist and its members characterized by their defiant individualism, both of which are forms of pathology, my interpretation of his work is that his chief emphasis is on the social pathology of the environment to which certain community members are responding rationally. In this sense I do not see his work as furthering pathologizing research.

12 For Hagedorn the gang has many causes and is clearly the result of society's massive contradictions being worked out by social actors now operating on a global stage. While sometimes there is an oversimplification of the background causes of the gang in his work (which is the case with his use of the concept "underclass") at other times he is more cautious and sees multiple causes springing from capitalism's global crisis and the lack of internal remedies or possible resolutions without the intervention of a new social order. In this sense the capitalist ethos of the gang is one of its overdeterminations, where the gang itself is a living contradiction of capitalism.

13 Standing's concept of the precariat is important to grasp in this debate. It comes from his combining "proletariat" with "precarious" and refers to late modern, neo-liberal capitalism in which secure jobs have become

increasingly rare and the world is filled with unemployment, under-employment and work aligned to flexible, global production. In terms of the class hierarchy the precariat are below manual workers (who have some form of security) and are "flanked" by the unemployed. They generally work on temporary contracts and are essentially expendable. They lack all seven types of security that come with more fixed employment conditions, i.e. labor market security, which provides adequate income-earning opportunities; employment security, which gives protection against dismissal; job security or the ability to obtain a niche in the labor market; work security, which allows protection against injury and illness; skill security, or the opportunity to learn and acquire work-related skills; income security or the ability to acquire a stable income over time; and representative security such as trade unions (see Standing 2011:10).

3
GANGS AND SITUATED RESISTANCE

Agency, structure, culture and politics

> The basic tendency of the naturalist study of serial life has been to question and criticize a conception of pathology and, increasingly, to purge it from the discipline of sociology.
>
> (Matza 1969:42)

I come into gang theory thus from a rich legacy of Chicago School and humanist sociology that includes drawing on the contributions from more recent social reproductionists. To summarize the major themes I would note the following bodies of knowledge that I principally draw upon to arrive at a critique of gang orthodoxies and, as Matza proposes (above), to "purge" pathology from our inquiries. From the Chicago School I take the commitment to community context and the dynamism of social processes; from the humanists the importance of naturalism and empathy in social inquiry and the recognition of the paradoxes and ironies between the dominant and subordinate classes; and from the social reproductionists their foregrounding of race and the importance of structure. However, we need to go further and develop working concepts of resistance and agency in gang research which draw more overtly on the critical traditions in social science, particularly those which have been influenced by

FIGURE 3.1 Ticket to a dance in New York City organized by Zulu Nation in 1996.
Source: Street Organization archives.

class-based and neo-Marxist paradigms of social action. At the same time, I insist that ambivalence and contradiction not be lost in our understandings and interpretations of the praxes of gang subcultures and street organizations. Failure to pay close attention to the complex, often misrecognized ways in which historical structures are mediated can leave us complicit in what Cacho (2012) calls the "social death" of criminalized and vulnerable populations.

Resistance, subcultures and the street organization

Based on the assumption that gang members live within a bounded social ecology, complete with its bleak socio-economic landscapes and cultural contexts, the notion of youth resistance has predictably limited currency. This position is summed up by Moore when she concludes: "Defiance and resistance are, in effect, an energetic spinning of the wheels: but not revolutionary" (1991:43). But what do we make of the lower-class gang that is not so hermetically sealed off from the rest of society (as Young has theorized)?[1] What emerges when the street gang is not so homogeneously underclass but a mix of proletarian and sub-proletarian elements with an ideology aimed at dismantling the barriers to its own isolation?

With such questions consistently emerging from and eventually guiding our ethnographic work (see Chapter 5) the significance of expanding the notion of gang resistance can be appreciated. Such considerations prompted us (Barrios and I) to develop an alternative definition of youth subcultural street behavior that we called a street organization, defined as:

> a group formed largely by youth and adults of a marginalized social class which aims to provide its members with a resistant identity, an opportunity to be individually and collectively empowered, a voice to speak back to and challenge the dominant culture, a refuge from the stresses and strains of barrio or ghetto life and a spiritual enclave within which its own sacred rituals can be generated and practiced.
>
> (Brotherton and Barrios 2004:23)

Clearly, such a definition is in complete opposition to that which is used in orthodox criminology (e.g. Klein and Miller) and is much closer to the non-pathological constructions first demonstrated in the work of Thrasher. However, this definition contains elements which privilege agency and struggle and do not settle for the condemning passivity of the usual criminogenic varieties, especially those that are employed by law enforcement agencies. But what then of theory?

Of necessity, once we rethought the definition of the gang we were dealing with in such a radical and foundational way it meant that we were straying way beyond the boundaries of most criminological discourse. In fact, we were moving much closer to the neo-Marxist renderings of youth styles and subcultures as found in the Birmingham School during the 1970s in England, some of the more

TABLE 3.1 Comparative approaches to youth subcultures and street gangs

Source	USA models	Birmingham School	Situated resistance
Methodology	Early humanistic–naturalist models of Chicago sociology giving way to criminal justice positivism, privileging notions of measurement, causality, rational action and the research practices of empiricism	Strong emphasis on cultural criticism and neo-Marxist interpretative, heuristic paradigms where in situ studies are the exception	Plurality of methods, drawing from Chicago naturalist traditions, British neo-Marxist culturalism and contemporary trends in cultural criminology
Class values	Lower-class, proletarian and sub-proletarian (i.e. underclass)	Specific to the working-class and middle-class history of the subculture	Working-class and sub-proletarian, strongly infused with specific racial and ethnic experiences
Relation to mainstream or dominant class; structure	Adaptive and/or rejectionist	Subversive and magically oppositional but never transformative	Subversive, partly adaptive, partly oppositional, intentionally transformative
Observable deviance from the prototypical mainstream	Mainly delinquent, involving group organized fighting, crime, drugs and other anti-social behaviors	Heavily aesthetic and stylistic, some drug use, some fighting	Stylistic, political and ideological, members recruited from both working and sub-working classes
Historical contingency (i.e. does the analysis take pains to dialectically and historically situate the phenomena?)	Mostly transhistorical or ahistorical, however there are exceptions, such as the work of Hagedorn (the black underclass) and Moore and Vigil (the Latino underclass)	Rooted in specific historical conditions	Highly historical, shaped by discrete resistances from below and social control processes from above

Representational forms	Socially organized, displays of turf allegiance, some later attention to attire and both body and verbal language	Wide range of symbolism involving music, attire and language	Wide range of symbolism involving music, graffiti, physical and verbal language, attire and written texts
Gender	Mostly male-centered, little attention paid to gang females. When focused on females generally seen as auxiliaries or sex objects. Theoretical and empirical exceptions on the contradictions of gendered empowerment more recently are Moore, Miller, Quicker, Nurge and Mendoza-Denton	Mostly male-centered with some attention paid to gendering, e.g. Willis. McRobbie is major exception offering a critical feminist approach within this school	Effort to include the voices of females within the groups as well as from the perspectives of family members. Draws on some critical feminist perspectives in both theory and methods
Race and ethnicity	Early gang research: little attention paid to race. In the 1970s more focus on segregation and gangs and neo-colonialism. Essentialism of the underclass discourse undermines studies of the class–race dialectic	Attention to race through style and moral panics. The race–class dialectic different to the United States with class overdetermining race in youth subcultures	Emphasis on history of colonialism and neo-colonialism in racial formation and the gang. More attention to race–ethnic nationalism as forms of resistance to socio-cultural subjugation and institutional discrimination

Source: adapted from a table that appears in David C. Brotherton and Luis Barrios. 2011. *Banished to the Homeland: Social Exclusion, Resistance and the Dominican Deportee.* New York: Columbia University Press. Reproduced with kind permission from Columbia University Press.

fecund renditions of social movements theory coming out of the United States and Europe (e.g. Castells 1997), the radical anthropological work on social dissent by researchers such as Scott (1985), the leftist post-industrial sociology of Touraine (1988) and Bauman (2004), the performance studies approach of Conquergood (2013) and the critical interdisciplinary perspectives of cultural criminology (see Young 2011, Hayward *et al.* 2010, Hamm 1993). Below I borrow and extend from my previous work to compare, review and reconsider the range of youth subcultural modes and models typically employed in the United States, the Birmingham School studies, and the conception of gang theory I am calling situated resistance.

From Table 3.1, we see that the situated resistance model is in striking contrast to most US mainstream gang paradigms but also differs from the more radical perspectives of the Birmingham School (see Hall *et al.* 1975, Hebdige 1979, *inter alia*). However, to recap, the philosophical and methodological differences between the situated resistance approach and that of orthodox criminology are primarily concerned with three areas: the role of history; the acceptance of positivism; and the conception of agency, whereas the contrast with the Birmingham School is mainly centered on the notion of agency.

Orthodox criminology and situated resistance

Orthodox gang treatments rarely involve an analysis of the subjects situated in any historical context. To this extent, gang members are typically seen as transhistorical, as if the processes they make possible can occur without some recognition of the epoch in which such groups emerge and develop or any grounded reference to the reproducing social structures in which these social actors are embedded. Even in the best of the orthodox gang treatments such as Thrasher (1927) there is no mention of capitalist social relations or of the roots of the global pushes and pulls that were creating the cultural conflicts (i.e. social disorganization) that gangs were supposedly reflecting (see also McDonald 1999). In contrast, I am arguing that all gang subjects both make and are made by historical forces (using a traditional Marxist concept of materialism) and that it is essential to locate our studies in such an historical and political economic framework to understand more fully the contexts of action, the meaning webs of culture and the contradictions of social and institutional settings (e.g. schools, prisons, the family, the church, etc.).

Second, the orthodox criminological approaches revere the methods of positivism. Rarely are the wide-ranging and long-standing epistemological debates on the ideological nature of social scientific truth claims, the asymmetrical relationships between the observer and the observed, or the politics of grant-financed research allowed to enter into the discourse. With few exceptions, gang criminology languishes in a time warp, incorporating the worst traditions of empiricism without a shred of reflexivity or critical engagement with the received wisdom of causality. Against this, I advocate a multi-tiered research project, drawing on a plurality of traditions from the naturalist Chicago School of Thrasher to the neo-Marxist critiques of the Birmingham School to the radical reflexivity of the cultural criminologists. Adopting such an approach does not mean throwing out rational positivism per se but does require a more critical and discerning appropriation of it, starting with the understanding that "social facts" are cultural texts and have to be seen in relationship to the political economy of language, thought, action and emotions.

Third, in most orthodox accounts of gangs there is little that deviates from either liberal or conservative versions of social reproduction. It is clear from my research that gang members can be as conscious of their actions and their structural contexts as any other social actor. Further, their individual and group praxes can be extremely contentious, subverting hegemonic norms in a variety of overt and covert ways from intergenerational underground manifestos and subaltern spiritual rituals to spoken counter-narratives and non-verbal interactional performances.

The Birmingham School and the situated resistance approach

While the Birmingham School celebrates the notion of subcultural agency through style, its adherents failed to attribute anything transformative to such behavior. Part of the problem with this interpretation for US subcultures is that much of the explanation for subcultural development is located in the tensions between adults and youth and that many subcultures express the contradictory need to both rebel against parental cultures and at the same time maintain many of the class traditions which parents themselves embody (see S. Cohen 1972, Willis 1977). Thus, Hall *et al.* (1975) state that the subcultural, while it is stylistically oppositional, should not be mistaken for the counter-cultural, which is more consciously political, ideological and organized. As Hebdige (1979:138) argued, "I have tried to avoid the temptation to portray subculture (as some writers influenced by Marcuse were once prone to do) as the repository of 'Truth,' to locate in its forms some obscure, revolutionary potential."

In contrast, I argue for a greater appreciation of transformative agency based on three considerations. First, that the subcultural in late modernity has become more autonomous[2] and that social movements are rapidly emerging in a range of local and transnational guises as youth, in particular, rebel against the global corporatization of culture, time, space, production and social relations (see Castells 1997). A hallmark of this period, therefore, is the widespread emergence of "spaces of hope" developed by youth and oppressed peoples out of traditional social interactions but also, of course, through the extraordinary proliferation of the new informational highways. Such movements are fueled by an eclectic mix of ideologies, affective logics and contestational positions, from humanist socialism and communism to anarchism, liberation theology and situationism. In the following quote from the compilation *We Are Everywhere: The Irresistible Rise of Global Anticapitalism* (Notes from Nowhere 2003), we read the anonymous authors' Port Huron-like statement on their resistance motives:

> Resisting together, our hope is reignited: hope because we have the power to reclaim memory from those who would impose oblivion, hope because we are more powerful than they can possibly imagine, hope because history is ours when we make it with our own hands.

> (Notes from Nowhere 2003)

The second consideration, important in the US context, is that many contemporary youth subcultures come out of the *hybridization* of street and prison cultures, especially in this period of mass incarceration for people of color, the working class and the poor. Consequently, the structuration of these groups, in terms of their organizational, ideological and representational practices, can be much more revolutionary than the "playful" acts of the street, reflecting the exponential growth in interlocking regimes of punishment, torture and social control that are now commonplace in the nation's incarcerated and civil societies (see Parenti 1999, Christie 1993, Gilmore 2007, Welch 2004).

The third consideration, which again is of primary importance in understanding street subcultures in the United States, relates to the intergenerational exclusion of certain communities. I argue that while such long-term processes of structured exclusion produce the spaces for street socialization (as Vigil and others cogently argue), such socialization does not have to be accommodationist or social reproductionist. Rather, under certain conditions a more politically resistant and socially transformative street subculture can take root complete with its own trenchant critiques of power relations (Brotherton and Barrios 2004), alternative "transcripts" (Scott 1985), creative subjectivities (McDonald 1999), ritualized performances and languages (Conquergood 1997), and models of self-organization that ensure a continuous flow of street/prison rebels, resistors and radicals (Esteva 2003). Let me now break down the notion of situated resistance into component parts to understand how it might be applied to different settings and, in particular, what I mean by the term situated.

Situated spaces

The spaces occupied by street gangs are highly charged, sociopolitical domains (Conquergood 1997). These are largely public spaces where the state and its agents have created a plethora of interlocking legal devices to control the autonomous behavior of the working class and the poor. Gangs seek to eke out spaces for themselves, sometimes in competition with other groups but often in competition with policing authority. Further, these spaces also exist across physical and symbolic borders. Gangs today are local, national and transnational. They communicate across state lines, between the prison and the street, across national boundaries and oceans and have globalized pretensions (although, of course, not all of them). It is imperative to understand the construction of spaces over time to grasp the meanings and practices of gangs and gang life. Any theory of the gang that does not seek to theorize the space in which the gang exists will be necessarily flawed and will only describe a gang outside of space, as in the cardboard cut-out versions of much typecast gang criminology, which largely fails to think in terms of the political economy of space or the contours and practices of place-making. Consequently, a spatial imaginary of urban grids conceived and managed by the dominant class-race structure is the norm. Contested space is neither well documented or theorized, although Conquergood and Zilberg's work are major exceptions and point the way forward to broadening approaches to space and the gang by considering, for example, gangs in relationship to: (1) institutionalized versus non-institutionalized space; (2) incarcerated versus free space; (3) exiled versus citizenship space; and (4) public versus private space.

Situated cultures

Most gang criminological studies treat culture as something that is tied to structure and usually amounts to not much more than a discourse on values, i.e. class, race/ethnic and/or gendered values. In my work, a culturalist approach is critical to the research project, for I am primarily interested in the meanings attached to a panoply of behaviors that I view as individual and collective interpretations of material circumstances and traditions, the rehearsed and self-created symbols of everyday life and the rites and rituals that characterize, organize and give meaning to gang life as members interact among themselves, and with the surrounding community and outside world. Culture, therefore, is made, lived and mediated. It is, as Conquergood argued, a verb not a noun. Consequently, a theory of gangs must see this culture as a rich assemblage of properties and processes in production, in flux and in context. It should be represented and interpreted in a way that highlights its various influences and connections not as an example of exotica or self-contained deviance but as an outgrowth of struggle for social autonomy as well as social reproduction.

Importantly gang culture needs to be considered as the expressivity of a subaltern population that has physical, textual and virtual dimensions. The cultural and symbolic repertoire of such groups is located within a colonized and post-colonized set of relations that circumscribe its liminality, i.e. groups are positioned between internal and external borders, low and high cultures and linguistic structures (see Mendoza-Denton 2008). As adherents of the Birmingham School emphasized, youth subcultures intersect strongly with and are infused by a range of values, ideologies and norms from below and from above, e.g. they are simultaneously influenced by the commodified seductions of the leisure industry and youth marketing as well as by the social obligations of their parents and peers. Such subcultures take from these cultural vistas a range of meanings and symbolic attachments that have to be appropriated, interpreted, reincorporated, engaged and arranged through a process of bricolage that provides individual and collective meanings not just routinized action.

Some examples of this situated culture might be as follows. In our work with the Almighty Latin King and Queen Nation (ALKQN) there were members who had been raised by their parents with distinct memories and traditions of 1960s radicalism that included the dynamic movements of the Young Lords and the Black Panthers. The radical, oppositional narratives from this period were handed down to the children, who saw their reinvention and application in the groups that they now belonged to. Similarly, in the research of Mendoza-Denton in Northern California the north/south Latino/a gang divide she describes as "hemispheric localism" speaks to the situated legacies of post-colonial displacement, not as something that is simply the outgrowth of gang enmities. Finally, Vigil emphasizes the continuing cultural importance for the style, identity and self-representation of West Coast gang members of the "cholo" (historically an indigenous Mexican that is also part Indian) – an interpretation of historical memory that is more grounded than the unproblematized archetype generally assumed to signify the Chicano/a gang presence. All of these are examples of a dynamic, fluid yet situated culture that can be further illustrated through dance, poetry, music, political and cultural writings, graffiti, etc., all of which constitute part of the gang's subaltern cultural literacy and memory.

Situated politics

> There is no doubt whatsoever that the Chicano youth of this
> district, gang members and squares alike, were deeply involved
> in Chicano militancy in the late 1960s. Cesar Chavez held his
> famous marches in 1966. Reies Tijerina was organizing the land
> grant claimants in Texas and New Mexico. The Brown Berets
> and the militant college youth group (UMAS, later MECHA)
> was organized in 1967. The East Los Angeles high schools pro-
> test blowouts occurred in 1968. Street demonstrations, pro-
> test meetings, and militant propaganda against the overkill of
> Chicanos in the Vietnam war began in 1969. Clover was a cen-
> ter of this Movimiento activity, yet this powerful resurgence
> of ideology is never mentioned as a condition for the project's
> experimentally-induced changes in group cohesiveness.
>
> (Moore and García 1978:44)

As Moore intones, frequently missing from gang research is a thor-
ough consideration of the asymmetrical power relations played out
in different dimensions of politics, even though the gang is often
represented as a barometer of the class, race and gendered nature of
society. Dawley similarly comments on his experience as a community organizer with the black gangs of Chicago in the 1960s:

> There were more programs, even a national coalition with
> similar street organizations,[3] and as in all of the other activ-
> ities, blacks controlled and whites helped as new partnerships
> were built into programs before their concept became more
> widely accepted. Furthermore, while trying to create oppor-
> tunity for individuals to develop potential, CVL [Conservative
> Vice Lords] Inc. at the same time was trying to change "the
> system" – a strategy of economic, educational, and political
> development.
>
> (Dawley 1992 [1973]:190)

Within gang worlds, therefore, there are multiple ways in which
organized as well as spontaneous politics can be discerned: community

struggles (see Chapter 1) often form part of a gang's etiology, political tensions representing different ideologies can also be viewed within the development processes of various gangs and, of course, it is readily apparent how the gang becomes the subject/object of outside social constructions played out within the shifting politics of law enforcement and the related moral panics over drugs, immigration, class tensions and race/ethnic Otherness.

Thus, in situated politics we are contemplating both the politics of gang empowerment and gang control that extends beyond the notion of exchange relationships (e.g. as in the work of Jankowski) and comes closer to a treatment of subaltern power relations as seen in the work of Conquergood and Scott or to social movements as viewed in the research of Castells, McAdam, Tarrow and Touraine, among others, and European youth studies in the recent contributions of Feixa and Palmas. Consequently, a more critical treatment would see the gangs in relationship to a politics of the street in which material, spatial and symbolic power systems are constituted and reconstituted over time. The work of Pleyers is particularly helpful here as this research documents emotionally charged social movements in response to the politics of hyper-marginality and super-exploitation within and across global capitalist power grids.

Pleyers, like his mentor Touraine, sees a return of the actor via new forms of politics outside the traditional organizations of the working and middle classes (e.g. the world social forums of grassroots organizations). Gangs can also be injected with this force field of political desire in which imagined states of freedom, autonomy and self-empowerment are pursued in a world designed to produce a surplus class and generations of wasted lives (Bauman 2004). I argue, therefore, that gangs under certain conditions represent a form of what Solnit (2010) calls "survival politics" given that these groups now exist in the chaos, militarization and destruction engendered by global capitalism. Our task is to ask and answer whether such groups can contain and sustain the moral affinities of the poor and articulate (however inadequately) the levels of frustration, humiliation and otherness known expressly by those in the shadowed society.[4] Is there a politics of spiritualism in gangs that draws on the syncretic religiosity of their race/ethnic histories? Does anti-colonialism feature in their political outlook, given the subjugation of their communities and peoples? Is there a politics against the collective experience of mass incarceration? Such questions will be addressed in the rest of the chapter and will be taken up in Chapter 5.

Situated crime and violence

While we must take into consideration the involvement of gangs in the two properties with which they are most associated by the dominant culture it is important that we do so not at the expense of all the various other properties, meanings and characteristics of the gang that distract us from seeing its all-sidedness. From a critical left-realist perspective (Lea and Young 1984), it has long been emphasized that as researchers we cannot ignore the degree to which organized street youth can victimize their own communities (i.e. what is the evidence that this is occurring through organized rather than spontaneous groups and individuals?). What form does this take and in what precise contexts do such actions arise? In other words, we must be careful not to pick up the habit of fetishizing and reifying certain transgressive behavior, which is strongly represented within the purview of so many orthodox criminological and criminal justice journals and bodies of work.[5]

In this critical notion of situated criminal action I am concerned with extant social, political and economic power relations in a specific neighborhood, the other cultures of crime and transgression in that neighborhood and the levels of marginalization felt and experienced by youth that help explain the involvement (or lack thereof) of gangs in criminal acts and their actual (not purported) relationship to systems of criminal opportunity. Klein (1995) argues that street gangs are unlikely to become good at organized crime; Taylor (1999) said he found a number of "corporatized" drug gangs in Detroit; Hagedorn (2015) is convinced that a putative Latino mafia was in the imagination of certain street groups in Chicago; while recent reports from Honduras suggest horrendous levels of victimization and extortion by ubiquitous street gangs operating in an essentially failed state, post-conflict situation (Robles 2014).

Research in this area is undoubtedly important and needs to be continued to not only understand if and how these groups are changing, the truth behind the various claims, and the conditions under which such changes are taking place but also to agree on a set of responses that will not exacerbate the situation through logics of control and the multiple processes that amplify deviance and deepen the suffering of vulnerable communities.

What is needed are both short-term rapid assessment research interventions that can provide good data for policies that are called for immediately plus long-term grounded, ethnographic research of the kind that Curtis (1998) has been doing in New York for many years. While it is crucial to fully explore criminal action in gangs through a resistance paradigm I am careful not to idealize the actions of those riding in the boxcar of the system (as Zinn would have it!). Furthermore, we must always be cognizant of the comparative treatments by the dominant society of those who engage in direct versus indirect violence without denying the deleterious effects on communities already weakened by intracommunal violence, be it intra- or inter-gang or simply gang-related, as it feeds into spiralling systems of repression from the outside while undermining the bonds of solidarity and possibilities for socio-political action on the inside. Consequently the appearance and semblance of crime and violence in relation to the gang must be politicized and not just viewed through the lens of behaviorism, legal rationalism or epiphenomenal data gathering.

Situated organizations

What models of organizations do gangs adopt in different socio-geographical terrains? Where does the knowledge come from to create such models? Do the models change over time? What influences the shape and character of the organization? The usual criminological approach is to suggest that gangs fit a certain typology. One frequently adopted approach in the research, for example, is that gangs vary but their organizational capabilities are relatively weak, usually undermined by internal status conflicts, but they may be observed along a grid of "traditional," "social" and "non-traditional" organizations (e.g. Klein). Another perspective posits that as an organization they are much stronger and more resilient (e.g. Jankowski), ideally meeting the rational economic and political needs of poor youth in poor communities. Still others (e.g. Hallsworth 2013) see the purported structure of the gang to be a social construction of powerful outsiders who imagine the group to be top-down and hierarchical, much like their own occupational model.

Nonetheless, it is primarily Hagedorn (2008, 2015) who insists that the gang as a self-contained entity which he analyzes through organizations theory, is entropic and not homeostatic and prone to instability due to: the frailty of its leadership structure; tendencies toward self-aggrandizement and elitism; the constant pressures of law enforcement; and the influences of prison gang leaders who are increasingly exercising control on the streets (as an unintentional consequence of mass incarceration). Certainly, it is possible that gang entropy might be the case in Chicago, and perhaps given the decrease in gang-related homicides nationwide (although such statistics are fraught with definitional and methodological flaws amid the politics of law enforcement – see Katz and Jackson-Jacobs 2003) this is a more generalizable observation. However, Hagedorn (and others) also argue (as stated earlier) that the gang is a quasi-institution filling the cracks (Jankowski 2003) in the political economy and the social welfare state and sustained by the long-term societal strictures of racial ordering. Thus, a certain stability and longevity has also been observed in gangs, particularly as so many of them have become intergenerational, a phenomenon often related to the seemingly intractable problem of poverty, particularly in the United States.

While I do not wish to argue here against these other perspectives, for if the claim is made it is the researcher's task to prove it, but rather I simply request that given the extreme instability of current society it is important to consider other modes of gang organization which develop under certain conditions. Consequently, in previous work with the ALKQN (and other groups) in New York City, which we carried out at the end of the 1990s and have continued by following the progress of some of these groups in other parts of the world, we devised a table of organizational characteristics and properties of the ALKQN that saw the gang from a completely different organizational perspective, which we termed the "empowerment model."

Essentially in our work we argued that the gang was a hybrid organization in this form, borrowing both from gang and other models

TABLE 3.2 Empowerment models used in the ALKQN's reform phase (Brotherton and Barrios 2004:151)

Radical political models	Spiritual models	Self-help models	Other models
Black Panthers; Young Lords; Puerto Rican Socialist Party	Judaism; Christianism (Roman Catholics and Protestants); African-originated religions (e.g. Yoruba/Santeria, and Palo)	Alcoholics Anonymous; Alternatives to Violence Program	Orthodox Jewish Community; Black Civil Rights Movement

Source: David C. Brotherton and Luis Barrios. 2011. *Banished to the Homeland: Social Exclusion, Resistance and the Dominican Deportee*. New York: Columbia University Press. Reproduced with kind permission from Columbia University Press.

of organized collective behavior normally dismissed by the orthodox gaze. But, as we see above, there were and are a range of influences on the gang that if recognized can be a powerful point of entrée for outsiders to work with such groups and come to terms with their social, political and cultural aspirations rather than the one-dimensional criminal aspect which has been the default position in academia and in the social control industry.

Situated societal responses

It is widely assumed that gangs are always reacted to negatively by society but this is far from the case and the differing reactions to gangs heavily influence the development of the phenomenon. Thus, although gangs are widely apparent through much of the United States' capitalist history and are increasingly emerging in different parts of the world under the global impact of neo-liberalism they have nonetheless been met with divergent patterns of societal reaction.

First, the political nature of the society within which gangs emerge matters a great deal. In New York under the mayoralty of John Lindsay in the 1970s there used to be a thriving "Roundtable of

Youth" sponsored by the mayor's office that met regularly at Gracie Mansion (the mayor's residence) to humanistically address the city's gang problem. Compare this approach to gangs with the adoption of 'zero tolerance' in the 1990s by the Giuliani administration. This draconian policy to combat a variety of transgressive behavior while adroitly avoiding the roots of poverty and discrimination was aided and abetted by the essentialistic notions of "Broken Windows Theory" (see Wilson and Kelling 1982) and swiftly exported to the rest of the world. In my recent work in Spain, I saw sharply contrasting reactions to the gang in the more authoritarian social control environment of the capital Madrid, which borrowed heavily from the US models of gang repression and containment, and in the more liberal civil society culture of Barcelona (especially with the city's long history of resistance to fascism). In Barcelona the authorities paid more attention to the alternative academic work originating with the Street Organization Project in New York (see Brotherton and Barrios 2004) and the gang–academic collaborations in Barcelona, Genoa and Quito (see Feixa *et al.* 2006, Palmas 2014, Cerbino 2010). The consequences for gang control and inter-group conflict were remarkably different (see Chapter 6). As Palmas (2014:147) concludes (translated from the Spanish by the original author):

> We have designated this work and desire, the political and social construction (of gangs) through two grand institutional strategies or logics of action in the field: gangs "in" and gangs "out," with the first one being anthropofagic and the latter anthropoemic. These two logics were experienced both in Barcelona and in Madrid. The distinction between them depends on power relations between institutions and positions in the field, between the right hand and the left hand of the State and the quality of warrior capital on one hand and pastoral capital on the other.

In other words the state and society, drawing on both Levi-Strauss and Bauman, adopt an exclusionary and/or an inclusionary rhetoric and set of practices vis-à-vis the gang and its base community. These

approaches are not simply binary ones but, as Young (1999) has force-
fully demonstrated, happen at the same time and represent different
state and non-state actors struggling over competing paradigms in the
post-Keynesian epoch. We see this same contradictory approach in
many European contexts but perhaps it is most evident in developing
nations such as El Salvador where the "zero tolerance" (called "mano
dura") approach of the state is linked to the anti-communist cleansing agents of the paramilitaries with devastatingly pernicious consequences for civil society and public order (Zilberg 2011, Levinson
2008).

Therefore, the epoch in which gangs become noticed and make
their presence felt is critical. For example, are we in an epoch of
criminal justice reform and decarceration or in the present period of
punishment and coercive social control?[6] Are we in the middle of a
moral panic against the immigrant amid an economic crisis or living
through a period of economic expansion when immigrant labor is
more economically desirable? Is this an era when white domination
of the political process appears to be less threatened, or the current
situation in the United States (for example) when non-white populations are voting in greater numbers and conservative, pro-nativist
political power is more broadly contested? Are we living through a
period of heightened anxiety due to fears of "terrorism" and other
presumed threats to public and national security or do we reside in
a relatively peaceful epoch when the results of imperial endeavors
seemed to be more manageable (however illusorily)?

What of resistance?

How do we bring all these areas of study together in relationship to
the concept of resistance? All of the above fields of action include
moments and situations for gangs and their members when collective meanings are developed in specific contexts (hence situated).
Behind these meanings, which are social, political, cultural, performative, organizational and spatial, etc., is a notion of possibility that
fuels social action and is the dialectical opposite of fatalism and the
socially determined set of conditions that is said to be evidence of

pragmatism and social reproduction. Alexander (2010:171) says this about the embrace of the gang identity by youth:

> Psychologists have long observed that when people feel hopelessly stigmatized, a powerful coping strategy – often the only apparent route to self-esteem – is embracing one's stigmatized identity ... Indeed, the act of embracing one's stigma is never merely a psychological maneuver, it is a political act – an act of resistance and defiance in a society that seeks to demean a group based on an inalterable trait.

Resistance, then, is made manifest at the level of social action but it is also an ongoing, opaque, unspoken process active both in our thoughts and in our emotions. It does not need to be romanticized and idealized to show the Rousseauian elements of urban primitives, as is often the counter-claim made by social scientific pathologists. Rather, we have to be open to recognizing those different forms and moments of refusal and agency that are deeply embedded in community contexts and histories that we do not always understand, recognize or even see. Within gang worlds there are layers of concealment and alternative modes of signification as bespeaks subaltern subcultures, but their misrecognition does not mean that we resort to misrepresenting them in order to satisfy an arbitrary need for social measurement or the fetishization of social order.

In gang cultures we see lower-class youth (mostly) aspiring to levels of self-organization and autonomy as part of a collective survival mechanism within a world that is confusing, oppressive and disenchanting yet highly reflexive. In the current period of late liquid modernity with unremittingly exploitative systems of the political economy, seen particularly in the falling or stagnant rates of social mobility, the gang assumes the function of a social refuge and cultural commune with multiple levels of resistance, modes of expressivity and meaning systems (Castells 1997). These subterranean semiotic structures of alternative street grids, grammars of a different socialization process, rituals of subordinate spiritualities, and knowledge that are key to enlightenment and empowerment in many groups, make for a complex compendium of self-originated scripts. Thus these resistance modalities can appear both organized and inchoate responses to an invasive, punishing rather than nurturing state. In this security state (Hallsworth and Lea 2011) it is clearly the purveyors of warrior capital who are calling the shots while the supporters of pastoral capital struggle in vain to put some rationality back into expanding, interlocking systems of exclusion, cruelty and carceral continuity. What is key, however, is whether this resistance has the potential to become transformative – subverting structures of domination and reinforcing the will and desire to rebel, dissent and imagine a different kind of (sub)world. In an earlier work I conceptualized my working notion of resistance as follows:

> My understanding of gang resistances gives particular weight to actions inspired by the kind of agency that has been termed "projective" (Emirbayer and Mische, 1998), that is, future-oriented. Such resistance begins with small oppositional gestures that are aimed at existing power relations as they have been conceived, broadly, in both the Foucauldian and Weberian traditions. Over time these gestures, however discrete, evolve into a set of actions that are transformative both in terms of the self and the life worlds of actors. At the more general level, we might also describe such agency/resistance as the conscious and/or unconscious opposition of individuals and groups to structural constraints, be they in the form of institutional values and treatments or the micro–macro processes of cultural, physical, economic and social subjugation.
>
> (Brotherton 2007:59)

Conclusion

In this chapter, I have briefly sketched the dominant paradigms in sociology and criminology that have sought to address the gang phenomenon. My concern has been to show the pathway to a resistance approach which has characterized my work over the last two decades and has been applied to "gangs" in various settings from New York to Los Angeles to Madrid, Barcelona, Quito and Santo Domingo (see Chapter 6). I argue that although resistance practices within gangs are often occluded by perspectives that privilege adaptation and social reproduction we must go beyond these veils of social scientific concealment to get closer to these other "truths" of the subaltern sub-worlds.

These resistance practices illustrate the extent to which youth groups differ substantially not only from the widely held conservative notions of the gang as pathological deviants but also from more liberal conceptions of the gang as an oppositional culture. I argue that once we recognize the existence of such resistances we can link them to a growing literature in the politics of contestation and self-transformation outside of criminology. On the other hand, if we limit ourselves to narrow versions of youth deviance, we obscure and sometimes completely misread the motives, styles, imaginations and organizations of oppressed peoples as they make the everyday.

Notes

1 That is, what happens when gang populations are economically excluded by the mainstream but culturally included by capitalism's corporate media and its consumerist ideology? In contrast to Young's radical interpretation of the relationship between consumerist cultures and ghetto residents are the treatments of orthodox criminologists of similar processes (e.g. Klein 1995, Decker and Curry 2003, etc.). According to such mainstream researchers, gang subculture has spilled into the nation's mass culture and is fueling the spread of US urban gangs in rural, suburban and non-US geographic domains. In this contagion model of gangs, taking its metaphors from medical science and public health discourses, we read of "gangs plaguing neighborhoods," of "gang risk factors" and of "gang resilience factors." Anthropologically it is close also to Mary Douglas' (1966) discussion of pollution and taboo in primitive and modern societies. In the following, Douglas (p.3) explains how rituals of purity and impurity are related to our attempts to create social order: "the ideal order of society is guarded by dangers which threaten transgressors. These danger-beliefs are as much threats which one man uses to coerce another as dangers which he himself fears to incur by his own lapses from righteousness … The whole universe is harnessed to men's attempts to force one another into good citizenship. Thus we find that certain moral values are upheld and certain social rules defined by beliefs in dangerous contagion."

2 Of course, this is arguable, given the level at which the state has effected laws and social control regulations to manage purported risks to bourgeois society. But these controls are primarily coercive, employing different forms of "warrior capital" (Palmas 2014) and ideological penetrations to

discipline, contain and sometimes to eradicate. These controls, together with an intense commodification of society, produce a general animus to be free from the banalization of everyday life. At the same time vast numbers of youth are economically excluded as the pastoral state retreats and capitalism cannibalizes itself. The end result is that subcultural groups proliferate as a punishing society ends any pretense of reintegration. In so doing they seek more autonomy from the dominant society and often gain it despite the incursions of the state.

3 This quote from Dawley's 1973 text is the first time the gang has been referred to as a street organization according to my knowledge of the literature.

4 For example, most people will never know what it is like to be incarcerated and to live one's life as a marked person (Pager 2003, Goffman 2014). Yet for hundreds of thousands in the shadowed society this experience is quite normative and is the rule rather than the exception.

5 I am thinking here of the bulk of studies that fall under the rubric of situated crime analysis or rational choice approaches to crime or certain pseudo-psychological studies of violence that operate from such pathological notions as the lack of impulse control, etc.

6 Luca Palmas, writing from Spain and Italy, refers to this as the state's role in producing both "warrior capital" and "pastoral capital" and likens it to Bourdieu's analysis of the left and right hand of the state in effecting social control in the interests of capitalism (see Palmas 2014).

4

STUDYING THE GANG CRITICALLY

Very few tell in detail what a juvenile delinquent does in his daily round of activity and what he thinks about himself, society, and his activities … One consequence [of his insufficiency] is the construction of faulty or inadequate theories. Just as we need precise anatomical description of animals before we can begin to theorize and experiment with their physiological and biochemical functioning, just so we need precise and detailed descriptions of social anatomy before we know just what phenomena are present to be theorized about … We do not … [then] have enough studies of deviant behavior … [or of] enough kinds of deviant behavior. Above all, we do not have enough studies in which the person doing the research has achieved close contact with those he studies, so that he can become aware of the complex and manifold character of the deviant activity … If … [the researcher] … is to get an accurate and complete account of what deviants do … he must spend at least some time observing them in their natural habitat as they go about their ordinary activities.

(Becker 1960:166–170, quoted in Matza 1969:40)

FIGURE 4.1 Antonio Fernandez (formerly King Tone of the Latin Kings and Queens) 1996. © Steve Hart 2014. Originally published in David C. Brotherton and Luis Barrios. 2004. *The Almighty Latin King and Queen Nation: Street Politics and the Transformation of an Inner City Gang.* New York: Columbia University Press. Reproduced with kind permission from Columbia University Press.

The majority of studies of youth gangs are achieved in the grand tradition of positivistic social science. Taking natural science as the paradigm of good research, a premium is placed on the value neutrality of the observer, the scientific rigor of the methodology, the unpolluted character of the data and the generalizability of the findings, all with the aim of proving or disproving ideology-free testable hypotheses. In this vein US criminology has seen gang studies move increasingly away from the interpretive, holistic and probing approaches of earlier Chicago School analyses (as quoted above) to the certitude of survey-based truth claims, "jail house criminology" and an assortment of studies whose findings reflect the race, class and gendered position of the investigators and their largely uncritical domain assumptions. As noted criminologist Jock Young has commented:

> What we need is an ethnographic method which can deal with reflexivity, contradiction, tentativeness, change of opinion,

> posturing and concealment. A method, which is sensitive to the
> way people, write and rewrite their personal narratives. Our
> problems will not be solved by a fake scientificity but by a
> critical ethnography honed to the potentialities of human cre-
> ativity and meaning.
>
> (Young 2004)

In this chapter I argue for a critical, anti-colonial ethnography
which is best suited to study subaltern groups and their "hard to
reach" populations whose lifestyles, "habitats" and purported characteristics are highly stigmatized and pathologized by the larger society.
Such an approach is based on the premise that all social and cultural
phenomena emerge out of tensions between the agents and interests
of those who seek to control everyday life and those who have little option but to resist this relationship of domination. Drawing on
the diverse methodological and theoretical work of researchers from
across the disciplinary divide (such as Geertz, De Certeau, Whyte,
Katz, Conquergood, Young, Mendoza-Denton, Fine, Ferrell, Scott
and Clifford) and my own experiences in the field over two decades I argue for a mode of social inquiry that takes seriously Mills'
(1959:225) advice:

> Before you go through with any piece of work, no matter how
> indirectly or occasionally, orient it to the central and continu-
> ing task of understanding the structure and the drift, the shap-
> ing and the meanings of your own period, the terrible and the
> magnificent world of human society.

Such research at a minimum:

(1) is committed to the provision of multiple forms of data, ana-
    lyses and theoretical constructions designed to critically engage,
    understand, humanize and holistically analyze subjects while
    resisting the dominant tropes of a society that pathologizes,
    devalues and obscures the humanity of these same subjects;
(2) is based on the ongoing dialogical relationship between the
    investigator(s) and the investigated, such that the research subjects

are presumed to be active, historical agents embedded in structured contexts and contingent situations; and

(3) produces knowledge that potentially contributes to social reform, self-empowerment and social justice.

Critical gang ethnography

If traditional, modernist ethnography is about studying the "folkways" of a community, painstakingly describing its everyday rhythms, its complex systems of social interactions, its relationship with the broader society and the different meaning systems that cultures and subcultures develop, then critical ethnography problematizes each of these notions, situating them within the asymmetrical power relations of a globalized capitalism within which we are all situated. A critical practice of ethnography is tied to excavating "the political underpinnings of all modes of representation, including the scientific" (Conquergood 2013: 81) and instead of asking "what is," it asks, "what could be" (Thomas 1993:4), as was the distinguishing feature of critical theory itself.

Further, it does not take at face value the meanings of an action, speech term or observation but is always aware of the ironies within these spheres of "meaning-making" that speak to the contradictions and the symbolic and hidden meanings within the data. This distinction in methodological practice and epistemology is part of the general crisis of representation in the social sciences (Marcus and Fischer 1986), which in large measure occurred with the decline of imperial and colonial power after World War II. The critical turn has had a powerfully radicalizing effect on the legitimacy and assumed authority of social science research, which had primarily accepted unproblematically a research practice and epistemology of enlightenment based on the privileged nature of the text and assumed role of the author. While this post-colonial (and often postmodern) critique has had a great deal of currency in disciplines such as anthropology and sociology it has had less impact on the US version of criminology so long dominated by the criminal justice industry, and has been particularly resisted by a criminology common in gang studies.[1]

As important as this critique of what passes for much gang research is, a host of questions still remain for those aiming to attain a more consciously reflexive and political orientation to the praxis of gang ethnography. For example, how do we do this research without becoming the "zoo keepers" of the deviants (Young 1971)? How do we resist adopting the gaze of the colonizer and/or the middle-class paternalist? Or how do we prevent ourselves going "native" and los- ing all sense of perspective? These are some of the central questions with which we are confronted regardless of our good intentions and rigorous opposition to the dominant paradigms of a social science always constructed and conceived from above.

In the following I expound upon six methodological areas that have been at the core of much of the critical ethnographic research I have been engaged in, hoping to avoid what I have referred to as the "social scientific safari"[2]: (1) the fallacy of the neutral observer; (2) researching from somewhere; (3) principles of collaboration, entrée and field work praxes; (4) data for a holistic study; (5) represent- ing and (w)riting; and (6) converting knowledge into power, not oppression.

The fallacy of the neutral observer

The critical approach recognizes that the world is intrinsically unfair and that the material, ideological and cultural structures are heavily stacked against the subjects/participants. Therefore, when the sub- jects act or speak they do so from a peripheral position that makes attempts to hear and understand them difficult. No matter how one tries to objectively experience and portray the setting or engage subjects through interviews we always have an impact on the envir- onment and vice versa (see Maher 1997). One cannot divorce our presence from our thinking and feeling, or what Galeano calls the need to realize that we all engage in "senti-pensante" (feeling/think- ing) rather than being varieties of the fragmented Cartesian binary that orthodox social science usually maintains. As Galeano explains:

> Why does one write, if not to put one's pieces together? From the moment we enter school or church, education chops us into pieces: it teaches us to divorce soul from body and mind from heart. The fishermen of the Colombian Coast must be learned doctors

FIGURE 4.2 My research partner Luis Barrios baptizes a Latin Queen in his Methodist church in Harlem with King Tone, the leader of the New York ALKQN at the time, pouring the sacred water over her head in 1997. © Steve Hart 2014. Originally published in David C. Brotherton and Luis Barrios. 2004. *The Almighty Latin King and Queen Nation: Street Politics and the Transformation of an Inner City Gang.* New York: Columbia University Press. Reproduced with kind permission from Columbia University Press.

> of ethics and morality, for they invented the word *sentipensante*, feeling-thinking, to define language that speaks the truth.
>
> (Galeano 1998:32)

Thus ethnographic researchers are always part of the scene, always in a processual relationship with the subjects, negotiating positions, stances and strategies. They are thus embodied and embedded in the data that interacts with and through us, with the research act of observing and recording always a matter of interpretation.[3] Further, we are not simply looking on but rather we are rupturing (whether wittingly or unwittingly) the normal patterns of life, often as we record those external ruptures that come from state agents arresting and engaging members of the subordinate class.

Obviously the researcher tries to be hyper-observant but bodies of knowledge, codes of action, rituals, symbols and practices are not self-evident, coming neatly packaged with labels. So many meanings are frequently missed due to mis- and non-recognition or privileging different dimensions of the activity and perceived reality. The only remedy for this is time spent in the field to become increasingly acquainted with the terrain, the culture and the community, accepting that such co-presence necessitates proximity to the subjects. This intimate, intrinsic relationship requires an immersion into the group and its terrain that is appreciated in the methodological notions of action research, participant observation and "edge work," and fundamentally contradicts the presumed and prescribed separation of the researcher from the researched (for good examples of these research methods in gang studies see Black 2010, Vigil 1988, 2007, Weide 2014, Maher 1997, Durán 2013). To this end I agree with those who argue that to get close to the naturalist meanings of the subjects, e.g. to have the possibility of the subjugated knowledges of the group or subculture revealed, the researcher has to be fully engaged and committed to the subject(s) yet open to different possibilities, contradictions and ambivalences in the encounter, in the making of everyday life (Schutz 1967).

Of course this is a risky, precarious endeavor and the pinnacle of power or location from whence the researcher normally descends, speaks or observes is at stake, but that is the price of doing research that does not promote what Conquergood called "epistemic violence" both to the researched subjects and/or the community. For example, how do we access "them" when "they" are so cut off from our own life-worlds? How do we trust what "they" tell us since most of us do not naturally, organically live in their life-worlds? How do we gain their confidence, relate to us their "insider" knowledges when they have little reason to trust outsiders who boast both the "expert" knowledge and status that reinforces lines of social hierarchy and cultural value? And how do we overcome or even recognize our own biases, given the power of hegemonic discourses in which these subjects are often judged to be inferior, pathological, remorseless and incorrigible (e.g. Bennett *et al.* 1996, Yablonsky 1963, Fleischer 1998).?[4]

Therefore we must remain mindful that we come from some-where and that we are always positioned and situated. However, at the same time that there is a point of departure from which we speak, observe and interact through our experiences of race/ethnicity, gen-der, class and age, these identities and signifiers do not amount to a fixed impenetrable location in the social and economic borderlands. Rather it is our obligation to recognize that borders bleed (Trinh 1991), and the task of the ethnographer is to record and enter this zone of complex meaning-making, transgression and liminality, to share layered social actions, to reciprocate, to experience and to co-perform with the researched population through worked out processes of social solidarity, mutual respect and recognition.[5] Such praxis might be seen as the ethnographer's political statement, a form of ethnographic activism and a way to demonstrate the right of all of us to have a voice in this contested space we call society – a space that is at once home to the researched but also a watched terrain, a sur-veilled habitat constantly being policed, Othered and exoticized (Di Leonardo 1998). In short, a space made to feel off limits and beyond our scope of "verstehen" (see Ferrell 1997).

Researching from somewhere

One of the first projects of critical ethnography is to recognize where we come from to assist us as we negotiate a way into a community or group. Further it is important to come to terms with the fact that our research and our site is not always chosen by us but rather it is chosen for us because of who we are. In Figure 4.3, of my father's East End (London) shop taken at the turn of the twentieth cen-tury, is represented much of my identity. I was born in that building, raised in that environment and socialized by the traditions of artisans handed down through generations of my family. If I am interested in the marginalized and fascinated by the cultures of inner-city popula-tions it has a lot to do with that sepia-colored photograph taken by someone more than a century ago. I make this point because all too often in research of subaltern populations the investigator appears to have dropped from another planet, such is his or her relationship with the researched population, and it is frequently the case that the

FIGURE 4.3 My father's shop on Commercial Road, Stepney, in the heart of the East End of London, taken around 1910 with my grandfather and great grandfather. Image courtesy of David C. Brotherton.

investigator reveals nothing about him or herself to the subjects. In fact, there are many esteemed and well-funded researchers who have never seen nor met any of the research subjects. In the studies I have long been involved in my praxis is quite the opposite and I take great pains to explain to the group or members of the subculture over time who or what I represent in history.

Therefore, to do critical ethnography with gangs is to move consciously and reflexively from the center to the periphery, to establish a trusted location in the community under study that becomes accepted and natural to the study's participants. As I already explained, the concept of situated space is crucial in such studies and this includes the situated place/space in which research is carried out. While it is true that many gang ethnographers try to do their research in the habitat of the subjects with interviews, for example, in the homes of research participants as well as in public spaces where the subject feels comfortable and not under threat, if there is a neutral zone that can be found or at least a space that offers the subjects protection and reassurance of the study's legitimacy, this is preferable.

In my own experience of carrying out gang research in different terrains on the East and West Coasts of the United States as well as in Europe, the Caribbean and Latin America, I have found the choice of location for this research to be quite critical to the success of the project. In San Francisco many of my fieldwork interviews were done in parks, public high schools and the homes of the subjects; in the Dominican Republic they occurred in public spaces that included restaurants but also within the confines of property belonging to a radical political party where some of the members regularly assembled. In New York, where many of the most revealing, detailed and richly textured interviews were performed, we were fortunate to have access to a church that provided a regular space to the group's members and represented a symbolic counter-space to a society that was increasingly attempting to control the group on almost every level, spatially, culturally, politically, etc.

Consequently, such considerations as research space combined with the identities, personalities and skills of the researchers, the stated versus perceived auspices of the research and the stated versus practiced methods of the researchers are key to a study's integrity and its ultimate success not only in the eyes of the researcher but in the eyes of the researched. The importance of this combination of subjective and objective factors was critical to the quality of our experience with various youth street subcultures during the late 1990s in New York City and allowed us to establish what we called "The Street Organization Project" in 1997 where we produced several substantially innovative pieces of work (including articles, books and photographic exhibits) along with well attended, highly inclusive national and international conferences and a range of interventions (from academic presentations, to community workshops and policy recommendations).

How did we achieve this without engaging in "fables of acceptance" (Di Leonardo 1998:23)? As stated earlier, one way we did this was through a church that became the site where the group's members could meet to discuss their own affairs but also to convene with trusted members of the community who were interested in further-ing the radical political project that the group was now embarking upon. The church, then, became the project's research and political hub in the community and was perceived quite differently to the academic center of the study that was still located at the college. This enabled the subjects to approach the inquiry not as something from a distance and external but almost as an internal project and as an integral endeavor of the group and of the community (i.e. not just as the tolerable idea of outsiders motivated by some vague commitment to social justice at best and at worst careerism and self-promotion). In a sense, it became over time "their" project as well as ours and a sanc-tuary that everyone looked forward to utilizing since this was where they could achieve respect and validation, feelings that were all too uncommon in their daily lives.

A second issue in addressing the distance between the researcher and the researched is the degree to which we reveal our other iden-tities to the subjects. In our research we have always embraced this principle and find that a holistic knowledge of ourselves both solidi-fies and demystifies the relationship. For example, Luis Barrios, my co-principal investigator and a priest at the church, was a noted leader of the Latino/a community with a long history in the community's struggle for social justice. He is also bilingual and bicultural and shared many of the experiences of immigration, social exclusion and oppression that featured in the accounts of the group's members and their families. In time he became an important confidante to both the leadership and the rank-and-file, with his blessings and sermons helping the group to legitimate itself to the public while his spir-itual and political analyses contributed to the group's development and progress. Moreover, Barrios went through the struggle with the group and this was his way of doing "edge work."[6] He was, therefore, not detached, in that social scientific, value-neutral sense, but was a partisan in the quest for knowledge and societal respect.

My role was quite different. I revealed to the group my own his-tory of struggle in the labor movement and my own lower-class ori-gins and this allowed them to see me outside of my middle-class academic status and professional persona. In addition, I stayed with the group across time and place, day after day, and did not opine negatively or disrespectfully about the group to the media or other agencies, even though I was frequently asked for interviews since the group was often in the public eye. At the same time I explained that my research role was to stand back and observe the proceedings with a little more distance though at all times I was expected to be there "when it counted." This is not to imply that the group's members did not test me on various occasions and on one occasion, in particular, my intentions were vigorously questioned as I was called upon to respond to the perceived transgression of another colleague whose actions had angered the group. The other field researchers did something similar, judiciously revealing their own historical narratives of shared oppression, not in any heroic, self-aggrandizing way but as a shared, human experience, mark of respect and discernible point from which empathy could be understood and accepted. We also had the collaboration (see Chapter 5) of the group's leaders, with the President Antonio Fernandez encouraging the group to grant us access to all their meetings as well as individual interviews while his influential "lieutenant" Hector Torres constantly discussed with us the group's development and helped to secure our entrée across multiple sites of the group's activities in real time.

In addition, there were several other bilingual researchers (male and female) who would hang out at various locations for extensive periods of time with different branches of the same group, after the local leadership had granted them permission. Some leaderships were more welcoming than others but all of the different branches required an extensive amount of time to "accept" our intrusion in their private and public lives. Ultimately, we managed to successfully have multiple field sites running concurrently, all located deep within the group's respective neighborhoods. This allowed us to see comparatively and holistically (see later in this chapter) what was happening across the group, between the group and other groups and between the group and the community, all of which increased our breadth of knowledge as well as our legitimacy. For, in the latter case, it demonstrated our ongoing commitment and our genuine interest in trying to understand the group in all its profundity.

The act of collaboration

> unless community participants are actively involved in both research and its uses ... both the research and its ultimate uses tend to be highly suspect. While this can be termed politicization, the alternative is not very pleasant either. Unless the community is involved, so-called objective research will almost inevitably be politicized beyond the researcher's control.
>
> (Moore and García 1978:10)

The third issue is a commitment to the practice of collaborative research as briefly elaborated in the quote from Joan Moore (above). Fundamentally, this is the formation of a relationship with the subjects/participants that is transparent, mutually respectful, built on trust and with benefits that both parties can understand in intrinsic ways. Why is this important for a critical research method? First, we need to be accountable for what we say about communities that have much less formal cultural power than we do. Second, because we cannot get close to these communities and subcultures without their consent and cultural guidance. Third, we need the help of the researched in designing the study, in coming up with questions that only they would know to ask while addressing issues appropriately in a language that is understandable and will provoke a response. Fourth, we need to think of constructive ways to redistribute the knowledge back into the community so that the community can utilize and claim this knowledge about itself for itself (see Moore's quote above). Fifth, we need to think of research as mutually empowering, of being able to offer opportunities on both sides of the line, and to provide a means by which marginalized communities can think differently about themselves in order to gain more resources as well as to counter the criminalizing gaze to which they have long been subjected. Sixth, we need to be aware of what such communities can teach us about ourselves.[7] And finally, we need to be open to collaboration outside of the community and be prepared to consult with a range of researchers who can bring different levels of expertise to the data.

FIGURE 4.4 A photograph of myself and my colleague, Luis Barrios, with male and female leaders of the ALKQN in 1997 before a universal meeting. © Steve Hart 2014. Originally published in David C. Brotherton and Luis Barrios. 2004. *The Almighty Latin King and Queen Nation: Street Politics and the Transformation of an Inner City Gang.* New York: Columbia University Press. Reproduced with kind permission from Columbia University Press.

Holistic data

> I would argue that rather than see all human meaning as modeled on one type of code, we need to see social life as containing many different kinds of meaningfulness, incarnate in different practices and forms, layered and overlapping, connecting up in complex ways.
>
> (Willis 2000:22)

If one of the basic tenets of critical ethnography is to humanize the research subjects it is incumbent upon us to collect data that more

FIGURE 4.5 A blown-up photo of King Blood at an ALKQN meeting held to commemorate his birthday in 1997 (photo anonymous). Image courtesy of Antonio Fernandez.

fully explores the environmental contexts in which the groups and the subjects make their lives as well as what constitutes the subjects' multiple identities, practices and social obligations/relationships. This basic reconceptualization of these "deviant" social actors as subcultural participants struggling for cultural meanings within massively unequal social, economic and cultural power relations compels us to develop an "ethnographic imagination" similar to the one advocated by Paul Willis (above). An imagination that goes far beyond the research parameters normally conceived in most gang projects.

Consequently, in conceiving of the contradictory agency of gang members on the streets, in institutions such as schools, prisons and work places, in their respective families, across and between local and

national borders, etc., we inevitably discover that their life-worlds
are constantly in flux and not at all the assemblage of properties and
characteristics we had previously conceived or the cardboard cut out
aggregate of behaviors privileged in most orthodox gang treatments –
now, more than ever, drawn from surveys. Consider, for example,
the following characteristics of gangs and their members that I have
observed over two decades:

members routinely enter and leave gangs;
members go through different periods of development within
   gangs;
gangs themselves change across time;
laws toward gangs change across time;
gang styles go from the margins to the mainstream;
some gangs become intergenerational while others simply
   disappear;
some predominantly male gangs are run by women;
some hyper-masculine prison gangs allow gay and transgender
   members;
some gangs which formally only allow members of a certain race
   include members from a variety of races;
some gangs have overtly political doctrines while others
   have none;
gangs of various descriptions are increasingly found in countries
   across the developing and developed world.

Thus, considering the vast variations between gangs across space
and time, how do we begin to understand or even compare their
internal and external meaning systems? How do these systems relate
to different societal reactions across a variety of contexts? Such questions can only be answered by the collection and analysis of multiple forms of data, many of which we do not know exist before the
research begins. This variability within and across the groups can be
gleaned from some examples of findings from my own research.

(1) Although the home of graffiti is considered to be New York, with
    the massive growth of this street aesthetic during the 1970s (see
    Cooper and Chalfant 2009 [1984]), this practice was not deemed

that significant to the street groups we studied in New York City in the 1990s. Meanwhile, on the West Coast the Latino gangs were incredibly attached to their street texts and proudly used them as territorial markers for purposes of what Conquergood terms "affirmation through negation" as the group competed spatially, physically and symbolically with other gangs.

(2) On the West Coast groups produced little in terms of gang-related internal texts, but on the East Coast these were a fundamental means of self- and group expression through manifestos, poems, photographs (see above King Blood), essays, rap lyrics, etc.

(3) On the East Coast we encountered a vibrant oral subculture, with members regularly performing different forms of oratory via individual testimonies or public demonstrations of their commitment to the group, all of which had little of comparison on the West Coast – although similar practices were observed in Europe and in Latin America.

(4) On the West Coast the females in the groups were largely subordinate to the males and had little relative autonomy whereas on the East Coast female members were far more organized and expressed themselves through their own manifestos, meetings, activities and different forms of representation.

Once the researcher taps into this deep reservoir of both collective and individual practices and bodies of knowledge, which can take the forms of art, counter-memory, oral history, prison/street narratives, physical gestures, physical encounters, the particularities of language, clothing, figurative representations, etc., a complexly layered life-world emerges, which has been accessed not just through the usual practices of observation and formal interview exchanges but through the subject's inner eye. These myriad practices, some of which are ritualized and rehearsed while others are more extemporaneous and not all necessarily understood at the time; their significance as cultural forms may not immediately become apparent. Nonetheless they all belong to the congealed, multi-level, historical experience of the group that we are attempting to capture.

It should be evident that limiting our research to prescribed, readily acceptable and available data severely reduces our ability to

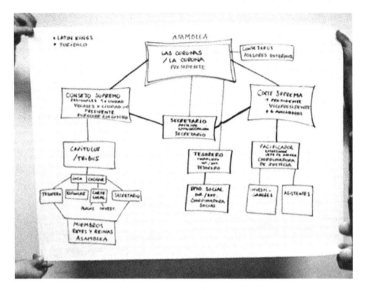

FIGURE 4.6 A photo taken by the Ecuadorian section of the ALKQN as they prepare for a ceremony marking the group as a legitimate non-profit organization in 2007. Image courtesy of Mauro Cerbino.

appreciate the wide-ranging realms of self-expression and creativity of these subcultures and what Willis (2000:24) calls their "object-ive possibilities." It also closes us off from the array of situations and environments in which the group performs and both the new and the old identities (both individual and collective) change and develop. I maintain that these are critical questions and issues that only a hol-istic approach to the group can enable us to contemplate, answer and address.

(Re)presenting and (w)riting the under-represented

But de Certeau's aphorism, "what the map cuts up, the story cuts across," also points to transgressive travel between two different domains of knowledge: one official, objective, and abstract – "the map"; the other one practical, embodied, and popular – "the story." This promiscuous traffic between different ways of

knowing carries the most radical promise of performance studies research. Performance studies struggles to open the space
between analysis and action, and to pull the pin on the binary
opposition between theory and practice. This embrace of different ways of knowing is radical because it cuts to the root of
how knowledge is organized in the academy.

(Conquergood 2002:141)

How do we resist reproducing the dominant culture's pathological,
exoticizing and negatively deviant categorizations of such groups
and its limitless web of assumptions that normalizes "our difference"
from "them"? This is an important and complicated question that de
Certeau is alluding to in the quote above and, based on my experience, our success in this endeavor depends on: (1) the degree to
which we are committed to a humanistic study of the group; (2) our
willingness to represent the group through various mediums and art
forms; (3) our practices of *reflexivity*; (4) writing and (5) the importance of theory.

Humanizing the subjects

By now it should be clear that my approach is to show the subjects
(both individuals and groups) in all their multi-dimensional aspects
and contradictoriness, being careful to situate them in deeply social
and historical contexts. To do this means to let the subjects speak
candidly, authentically and truthfully and to draw on as many voices
as possible, always recognizing the problem of concealment but then
also the likelihood of revelation and the various forms that "penetrations" take (Willis 1977) as subjects make "lived assessments of their
possibilities" (Willis 2000:34) within their imaginaries.

In so doing we show the different positionalities of members and
their associates and, if done with strong powers of observation, noting
both patterns and changes, latent and manifest functions, the vocabularies of motives that describe action and the array of outcomes, be
they intentional or not, will contribute to a humanizing research that
does not have to privilege the text over the people.

Multiple data with multiple analyses

Just as we are committed to holistic data sets so we must be prepared for multiple types of analysis. Of course fine-tuned, rigorous descriptive analysis is of necessity but we must constantly think about the types of data collected and their need for specialized treatments, even if it means recruiting other analysts. For example the socio-linguist approach of Mendoza-Denton (2008), the performative, semiotic view of Conquergood (1997), our own recourse to social movement theory (Brotherton and Barrios 2004), Zilberg's (2011) social geographic excavations, Miller's (2001) and Maher's (1997) interpretation of feminist ethnography, DeCesare's (2013) photographic forays and Willis' (1977, 2000) socio-symbolic reading of cultural production all provide different, fresh, innovative contributions to reveal more well-rounded lived experiences of groups and their members. Thus we must refuse to be methodological prisoners of the data, but rather use a radical inductive approach that does not recoil from crossing disciplinary boundaries but at the same is careful not to be dilettantish, borrowing analytical techniques that are not well understood or sufficiently processed.

Reflexivity and representation

I have already argued that reflexivity is a sine qua non of this kind of research, but implementing this is not easy, especially in writing up our accounts either in the present or in the past. It is difficult to reveal the effects and impacts of research as it passes through us, as we become moved by the events or actions, but it is critically important to show this side of the study relationship otherwise we have become supremely privileged. For our arguments may appear sound, with the subjects making appearances to fit the frames, but the "truths" on display will be suspect. I have encountered this on multiple occasions as events in the field sometimes turn into their opposites and our expectations are suddenly dashed. At the same time, however, it is precisely at such points when we are confronted with the unexpected that our observational and analytical abilities become most needed and our real commitment to remain within this bracketed existence is most tested.

(W)riting

Where possible we try to write with energy, verve and clarity. Rejecting the desiccated, neutral expositions of mainstream criminology/sociology we write against the dominant currents that police our disciplines, creating practices and products of the social scientific safari. Of course, this is easier said than done but it is something to be aimed for rather than settling for the pedestrian prose that passes for most social scientific writing. One way to do this is to look to great writers and artists to learn how they wrote with imagination, experimentation and style (e.g. Galeano, Agee and Evans, Mills, etc.)

Further we try to capture not simply the fixed and one-dimensional but the transcendental, the counter-intuitive, the soulful, the accidental as well as the epiphenomena of the quotidian. Mindful that we live in a period when "all that is solid melts into air," this culture and political economy of extreme liquidity should influence our writing as we experiment with new and old vocabularies to capture figures moving through life, filled with hopes, disappointments, fears and certainties. With my own students in the field I advise them to write ethnography bearing the following in mind:

> People suffer and enjoy life, so feel their pain and learn to appreciate how life is laughed at and enthusiastically created at the margins despite the obstacles.
>
> Do not elide unless you have to. It is safer to err on the side of caution and create "thick descriptions" as a habit, playing with the prose to evoke and reproduce the aura of the scene and the existentiality of the moment.
>
> Use your pen to create a canvas. It is a given that this messy web of interactions, histories, and stated and unstated vocabularies of motives is difficult to conceive on paper, and will necessarily be an act of creativity.
>
> Use your pen to perform. For example, when describing graffiti think of the rush flowing through the veins of perpetrators; in a meeting imagine the front stage/back stage antics, as you listen to discourses and utterances remember the symbolic violence that often frames them and the resistances that might contradict the norms of social reproduction.

When writing of injustice tell it like it is. Find your voice, your style, your angle, your scream. You can always edit!

Theory development

While we all have theories about these groups, some of which are learned in the academy and some which emerge out of new experiences in the field, as critical ethnographers our obligation is to be open to counter-intuitive data, confounding experiences, a set of realities that sometimes conform to our theories and sometimes completely contradict them, but it is our stretch for theory at all times that is crucial for the furtherance of the study.

In our New York study, we paid attention to Burawoy's notion of extended case study – the idea that theory needs to be developed and extended in the face of anomalous outcomes rather than simply rejected (see also Snow *et al.* 2003). In our case there was little in the gang literature that talked about political gangs or about gang politics so we had to go to other perspectives to find out how we might think theoretically about this movement on the streets. As critical ethnographers we are not wedded to a set of theories but rather to the subjects, the community, etc., and we need to be contemplative of all manner of theoretical explanations for the rational/irrational, hidden/opaque social and cultural processes. Consequently, theory drives the project and then the data drive the theory. As Willis (2000:114) makes clear:

> To repeat and clarify: the original elements of a "theoretical confession" [i.e. the stated theoretical questions and conundrums being pursued through the ethnographic project] are not tightly structured positions looking merely for exemplification (the hallmark of pointless field work, merely the flip side of empiricism). They are the nagging issues which drive a curiosity within an overall theoretical sensibility of a particular kind.

As a research practice to further the goal of theory development we would have regular debriefing sessions among all the field workers, about once every two weeks. During these sessions we would summarize the data and then discuss patterns, contradictions and anomalies we were witnessing. Following these discussions we would try to see how theory might come close to explaining our experiences or not. Over the course of the project such discussions and probings produce a substantial amount of analysis that become key to theory development in the final instance.

Using research knowledge for social reform and empowerment

Thinking carefully about de Certeau's comment above (Conquergood 2002) prompts us to ask how we translate knowledge "about" into knowledge "for" and be true to one of our main principles: to return our research back to its social source so that it becomes shared knowledge. Such knowledge can increase the reflexivity of the subjects, enabling them and their communities to more cogently name the systems, apparatuses and practices that foster and justify the structures that bind and contain or the habitus that deepen processes of social reproduction rather than social resistance. But what's the reality? How is this possible?

In our last two major projects there are several good examples of this recuperation process and I am glad to report that the knowledge, analyses and theories gained have been diffused in a manner that underscores the principle of reciprocity in critical research. Below I briefly describe three of these contestational processes that were direct results of the interventions.

The concept of the street organization

We came up with the concept of the "street organization" early in the research to supplant the highly pejorative and pathological term "gang." By the 1990s this latter term had lost most of its sociological meaning and was being used in both popular culture and criminology as an ill-defined deviant youth grouping of the lower class unproblematically linked to the dominant class's various moral crusades against drugs, terrorism, the poor, immigrants and so forth. Our replacement concept, complete with sharply contrasting ideal-typical properties, was adopted by various subcultures to counter the gang label, i.e. the ALKQN, the Ñetas, La Familia and Zulu Nation among others. The

ALKQN in fact used the term during their press conferences in the late 1990s to answer the usual question from journalists regarding why the group was no longer a gang. But the concept has gone much further and has entered the more general discourse on these groups. For example, in various policy and intervention efforts to stem the intra-group violence in sites as diverse as Baltimore and Chicago in the United States, London, Barcelona and Genoa in Europe and Quito and Santo Domingo in Latin America, the concept of "street organization" often replaces "the gang." Increasingly in more critical sociological and criminological accounts researchers have invoked the street organiza-tion concept and even in political discourses, for example statements by Louis Farrakhan, we note the use of this anti-hegemonic concept.

This rupture of the hegemonic process is important and helps to break those loops of signification that sustain pathological cat-egories of identification and essentializing properties of subaltern populations.

Dangerous truths as contraband

In our 2004 edition of the ALKQN book we wrote that we hoped to see this text used as a tool to show the levels of self-organization, resistance practices and modes of symbolic representation that reflect alternative modes of political empowerment usually dismissed as threatening or made invisible by the dominant culture's power to erase and diminish oppositional behavior. But we did not expect the work to have such a reach with its presence now well established among a range of street subcultures, advocates for the poor and prison inmates. In fact, currently the book is considered "contraband" by prison authorities and viewed as dangerous literature for the incar-cerated population despite its being a well-regarded social scientific text. For such a scholarly intervention to be feared and regarded as subversive to authorities in a total institution must mean that our inquiry has joined those lists of other "dangerous truths" deemed too unsettling for structures which already have extraordinary levels of power and control over both behavior and thought. Such a develop-ment points to the book's counter-hegemonic critical content which, I suppose, is one of the best reviews one can receive.

Voices of the powerless strike back transnationally

In our most recent work on deportation, which included a number of testimonies about the influence of street organizations, this most vulnerable of populations caught between nation states has been able to utilize the narratives of lives in exile to defend themselves against further persecution and provide immigration lawyers with fine textured accounts to bolster their legal arguments for relief in the US courts of appeal. The result has been that the work is now widely used in the US immigration courts, while it has resonated strongly with Latino activists who see the research as confirmation of the extraordinary levels of criminalization and social exclusion that their communities have withstood for so many years, particularly during the last two decades. In this dissemination process, we see a commitment to making the invisible visible and the capacity for these highly marginalized voices to become powerful, unsettling narratives placing the deportee in a deeply troubling global context (since the deportee is now part of a worldwide adoption of the "deportation regime" (see De Genova and Preutz 2010)). Thus, instead of these testimonies stopping at the page of the academic they begin to circulate among a world of counter-memories and counter-signifiers that contribute to a growing movement to halt the mass exile of members of a social class now deemed surplus to US needs and caught in the racialized judicial flows and apparatuses of the "crimmigration" system (Brotherton and Barrios 2011, Stumpf 2006).

Conclusion

> Sparks of dangerous sensuality may sometimes fly from bikers or street buskers, or from their flinty clashes with authorities – but as such groups and situations become the subject matter of criminology, those sparks are snuffed out, or fanned into flame, by method.
>
> (Hayward *et al.* 2010)

In the above I have summarized briefly some of the major methodological lessons drawn from my work and that of others committed to critical research projects with "gang" and related "deviant" sub-groups. There is, of course, much more to say on this, but for now I have made a case based on concrete experiences in the field that can act as signposts and principles of engagement for future and current researchers to avoid, as the cultural criminologists above aver, the "dangerous sensuality" that is such a part of the gang terrain being "snuffed out."

Suffice it to say that the power dynamic between the researcher and the researched is of inestimable importance and any skirting this relationship will necessarily lead to a much less ambitious, probing and counter-hegemonic project than that which is intended. At the same time the road to hell is paved with good intentions and no amount of empathy and solidarity with the oppressed will be enough for the production of a powerful piece of social science that stands up to the inevitable charges of partisan scholarship and non-objective approaches to the subject. Nonetheless, there is truth in the stories we tell; or rather there are "truths", but we need to craft them and reveal them with both care and precision for them to be believable to more than just a few. At the same time, we must always aim to bring together both the background and the foreground of the phenomenon we are studying and locate it historically as well as in the confines and contingencies of the broader society. As the Comaroffs have warned us:

> We require good grounds for claiming the non-existence of a system or a structure – the fact that we are unable to discern one at first blush is hardly proof that it is not there.
>
> (Comaroff and Comaroff 1992:24)

Notes

1 A version I have already described as often characterized by a theoretically thin positivism suffused with the discourses of rational choice that eschew the cultural, the structural and the historical (see earlier chapters).
2 See Brotherton (2013) and my call for "ethnographic activism."
3 The late folklorist Alan Lomax is a perfect example of this inevitable process. He recorded countless blues artists but he knew what he was looking for; he knew these art forms existed and he knew he had to preserve them for posterity. For him it was both an artistic and a political commitment and he did his best to get recordings that were as authentic as possible and

then to archive them and interpret them, leaving them for us to appreciate in their purest form. Without his thinking and feeling about this subject our cultural knowledge would be that much poorer today.

4 As I write an interesting debate is ensuing over the publication of Goffman's (2013) *On the Run*, which some have called another example of the "jungle book trope" (Rios 2012).

5 It should not come as a surprise that those who carry out such research are frequently denounced by social control agents for their empathy with these marginalized populations. This usually takes the form of academic banishment, physical threats and sometimes violence, institutional redbaiting and claims of enabling the deviance/deviants to develop.

6 The notion of edgework relates to what Lyng (1990) calls the corporeal transaction engaged in by the ethnographer working with subjects in high risk bodily transgressions, e.g. bungee jumping, illegal speed racing, graffiti writing and so on. The ALKQN definitely engaged in a lot of transgressions in their physical dealings with the police who harassed them constantly. Barrios, who had a long history of civil disobedience, was often on hand during such confrontations, which I consider a form of "edgework." Part of the allure of the group in the barrio was its refusal to be intimidated by the state and Barrios chose to be in solidarity with this position through his physical presence and experience.

7 One way we did this was by employing the leader of the group as a consultant on the project as well as some of his or her most trusted aides.

5

IMAGINING GANGS

From folk devils to objects of desire

> In the public sphere, the label gang is a thickly layered represen-
> tational screen onto which powerful and contradictory images
> are projected. The term gang powerfully cathects and conjures
> middle class fears and anxieties about social disorder, disinte-
> gration and chaos, that are made palpable in these demonized
> figures of inscrutable, unproductive, predatory, pathological
> alien Others lurking in urban shadows and margins, outside
> the community of decent people.
>
> (Conquergood 1991:4)

Conquergood spent much time with the Chicago Latin Kings
during the 1980s and 1990s, one of the largest street gangs in the
United States, and in the above he reflects with great poignancy on
the class and race-based processes of demonization and criminalization that he witnessed at close hand. He was unusual for a student of
gangs since he actually knew many of the human subjects he wrote
about and was able to express through articulate academic prose how
it felt to be the subject/object of the extraordinary social control
pressures and state-sponsored measures that come with the territory
of pathologizing the urban Other in late modern America. Such

FIGURE 5.1 Photo from the South Bronx gang documentary *Flying Cut Sleeves* (Fecher and Chalfant 1993). Image courtesy of Rita Fecher and Henry Chalfant.

processes, however, do not simply belong to the present but have a long history, as we saw in Chapter 1, and have been commented upon by social reformers and researchers stretching back through much of this and the latter part of the last century. Pointing to the penchant for exaggerating the prevalence of gang-related deviance, turning it into a spectacle of outsized, threatening behavior of the lower orders, the elite-owned media has rarely resisted the temptation. Nearly 100 years ago the sociologist Frederic Thrasher made this prescient pre-semiotic observation under the heading "Spectacular Crimes and Crime Waves":

> Gang raids which involve large losses, and murders perpetrated in the execution of gang wars possess a spectacular quality which have given the impression that the United States in general and Chicago in particular are being deluged in a great crime wave. The truth, however, is that the so-called "crime-wave" is a state

of mind. Crime is an ever-present reality. It is the attention and the interest of the public which moves in waves. While certain spectacular crimes, such as gang murders, have become more frequent due to internecine warfare among beer gangs, there has been no general increase and there is no reason to believe that Chicago is the "crime center of the United States" or the "murder capital of the world." These impressions are created through improved means of communication and modern journalistic technique.

(Thrasher 1927:211)

In this chapter I discuss different ways youth gangs have been represented through the various mediums and discourses of the dominant culture, but I also deal with an opposing trend that has not been given sufficient attention in the literature. Thus, drawing on an array of critical perspectives aimed at reimagining deviance and its socially constructed folk devils I address the mechanisms behind the prevalence of gang images as the assemblages of the usually presumed pathological properties of the dangerous classes as well as their casting as objects of desire and commodification.

Gangs and moral panics

Societies appear to be subject, every now and then, to periods of moral panic. A condition, episode, person or group of persons emerges to become defined as a threat to societal values and interests; its nature is presented in a stylized and stereotypical fashion by the mass media; the moral barricades are manned by editors, bishops, politicians and other right-thinking people; socially accredited experts pronounce their diagnoses and solutions; ways of coping are evolved or (more often) resorted to; the condition then disappears, submerges or deteriorates and becomes more visible. Sometimes the object of the panic is quite novel and at other times it is something which has been in existence long enough, but suddenly appears in the limelight. Sometimes the panic passes over and is forgotten, except in folklore and collective memory; at other times it has more serious and long-lasting repercussions and might produce such changes as those in legal and social policy or even in the way the society conceives itself.

(S. Cohen 1972:9)

So begins Stanley Cohen in his classic early work *Folk Devils and Moral Panics*. If we are to discuss the image-making machinery around gangs we must begin with the concept of moral panics. The emergence of moral panics and their persistency in a highly mediated, networked society raises a host of questions, only some of which have been the subject of research. Cohen's definition, above, has stood the test of time notwithstanding the important critique by McRobbie and Thornton (1995) that we need to constantly revisit the concept to take into account society's increasing reflexivity and media heterogeneity (particularly now with social media) and the continuous rather than episodic array of moral panics we are subjected to.

Cohen's transactional study of the social construction of England's "mods and rockers" in the 1960s drew on deviance, subcultural and collective behavior theories as well as the studies of disasters. He combined these theories and methodological frameworks to set up a sequential analysis to account for the historical emergence of this new "social type" constituted by a stratum of working-class youth chafing at their situated limitations within the expanding capitalism of the early 1960s, i.e. amid the illusory promises and contradictions of mass consumption, full employment and the "never had it so good" *pronunciamentos* of the then British Conservative Prime Minister Harold Macmillan. Cohen's nuanced account was broken down into *the inventory*, i.e. a sociological accounting of the scene in which folk devils emerge both as a spectacle and as a new "social type", including the manufacturing of news about the phenomenon; *the reaction*, which includes the various opinions about the phenomenon from different social actors and the policies enacted to socially control it; and finally *the impact* of the phenomenon on society and the theoretical explanations for the ongoing emergence and continuity of other "folk devils." Along with Jock Young's groundbreaking book *Drug-takers*, this early research set the stage for a welter of youth studies (including the Birmingham School) that saw in the moral panic a combined if uneven dialectical process of social ordering, ideological promulgation and symbolic production that resonates powerfully with the ways gangs have been viewed, engaged, controlled, stigmatized and generally reacted to across various sections of society. In particular, during the more recent neo-liberal era of rising inequalities, heightened regimes of punishment and relentless dynamics of social exclusion (and, however contradictorily it may seem, cultural inclusion – see Young 1999, 2011), a number of studies, particularly in the United States, have homed in more directly on the gangs and the moral panics connection, showing how structured economic, social and cultural power relations and the interwoven mechanisms of social control from the selective application of legal "norms" to the inculcation of colonized tropes play out in this process.

For example, Chambliss in the late 1950s sought to explain the differential societal reactions to two high school gangs, "the Saints" and the "Roughnecks", and concluded that "The answer lies in the class structure of American society and the control of legal institutions by those at the top of the class structure." Moore (1991, Moore and García 1978) referred to the process of Chicano gang stereotypification in Los Angeles as a case of "cognitive purification" similar to Douglas' (1982) argument about society's need to cleanse and guard against social dirt. Zatz (1987: 129) similarly looked at Chicano gangs in the South-West United States and found that their images were filled with the racial codes and class assumptions of the dominant society that built on anti-immigrant sentiment and the fear of the gang predator for instrumentalist policing purposes.

> I suggest that the image of gangs, and especially of Chicano gangs, as violent converged with that of Mexicans and Chicanos as "different" to create the threat of disorder. In addition, it was in the interests of the police department to discover the "gang problem" and build an even greater sense of threat so as to acquire federal funding of a specialized unit.

McCorkle and Miethe (2002) in their textbook account of the gang panic in Nevada during the 1990s asked how the repeated discovery of gangs has continually affected social policy leading to enormous and unnecessary economic and criminological costs. Gilbert (1986) wondered about the intermittent appearance of moral outrage over deviant youth culture, often tied to the confirmed sightings of gangs, and the profit-based needs of a youth culture industry shaped in particular by film and television's growing influence over our taste buds (see later in this chapter). Meanwhile Kelley (1994:209), reflecting on the post-Rodney King era of Los Angeles, concludes:

> The construction of the "ghetto" as a living nightmare and "gangstas" as products of that nightmare has given rise to what I call a new "Ghettocentric" identity in which the specific class, race, and gendered experiences in late capitalist urban centers coalesce to create a new identity – "Nigga."

Of course, this is not to say that gangs and their practices are simply a social fiction or that the very real problems that gangs may bring to economically marginalized communities, and their penchant for self-destructive behavior, is not worthy of our ethical and political attention. But there is nothing essentialistic about this phenomenon and it certainly cannot be understood without a careful analysis of the barrage of emotionally-charged symbols, signs and discourses that purport to discover, describe and diagnose the gang outside of its broader socio-cultural attachments, its socio-political contents and the meanings it possesses for the subjects who may produce it (Phillips 1999).

As many social scientific commentators have argued, the moral panic over gangs in the most recent period has powerfully contributed to the current situation regarding Black, Latino/a and poor youth in general being submitted to what Alexander calls the "new Jim Crow" (2010:4), "a stunningly comprehensive and well-disguised system of racialized social control" of mass incarceration, punishment, and premature social and physical death. Wacquant (2007) similarly has described these embodied processes and socio-economic outcomes as part and parcel of a new market-determined capitalism with its violently imposed penal state targeting the "underclass" and largely replacing the welfare state, all done in the service of intensified capital accumulation by white elites. Sassen (2014a), more recently, argues that this global process of hyper-exploitation of human beings and the environment characterized by the increased domination of the world economy particularly by predatory finance capital leads to a range of brutal expulsions, displacements and unparalleled imprisonments. In reference to new types of gangs springing up in cities that are equally new frontier zones, she says, "there is also a kind of public-making work that can produce disruptive narratives, and make legible the local and the silenced" (Sassen 2014b:3). In summarizing research on the gang suppression model undertaken in the United States (Greene and Pranis 2007:37) the authors conclude:

> The current preoccupation with gangs is a distraction from very real problems of crime and violence that afflict too many communities. Gangs do not drive crime rates, and aggressive suppression tactics simply make the situation worse by alienating local residents and trapping youth in the criminal justice system. Our review of the research found no evidence that gang enforcement strategies have achieved meaningful reductions in violence, but ample proof that science-based social service interventions can curb delinquency.

Thus, the gang is one of the many polymorphous enemies utilized to organize and rationalize this shift in society's resources and priorities such that extraordinary measures of social control are requested, implemented and made acceptable as part of the dialectic of population management and the disciplining of the working and sub-working classes. This occurs, *nota bene*, within the overall development of the capitalist state and capitalist society's means of production and exchange (Rusche and Kirchheimer 1968 [1939], Melossi and Pavarini 1981). The constant demonization of the gang, therefore, not only reflects the colonial gaze of the dominant society vis-à-vis the primitives and the misbegotten, or a handy "distraction" for the general public away from the business as usual of corporate theft and other skullduggeries (see Will *et al.* 2013), but a massive shift in the balance of class forces. To invoke the Gramscian analysis of Hall *et al.* (1978), it is an outgrowth of the ideological war for position that ruling elites have to wage to gain the kinds of consensus and the levels of legitimate authority to rule in a certain way under (un)certain conditions.[1]

Gang imaginaries and their consequences

Consequently most images and what might be called the imaginary of the gang[2] are carefully chosen to arouse and depict the gang as a thing-in-itself, separate from any community. As such it represents a floating signifier of threat that can have multiple connotations. Ewen and Ewen (2008:489), in their extraordinary study of the historical and systematic prevalence of typecasting in US and Western European society, note that: "It is at the crossroads between law enforcement and typecasting that the relationship between stereotype and power is most visible." An excellent example of this process is surely the racial profiling so evident in the "stop and frisk" campaigns in New York City carried out during the last decade, in which over 800,000 mostly African-American and Latinos were required to be physically searched by the police every year. Often the auspices for "tossing" the subjects was that they were suspected gang members, "the bad guys" in police parlance, and another reminder of the depth of social Darwinism in the criminogenic imagination of the state's control agents (see Fagan 2010).

While thinking about these processes at the transactional level is instructive, consider at another level the degree of organization involved in such a long-standing policy. Just imagine the amount of resources harnessed and expended, the ideological contents behind the training, the occupational culture that emerges, the range of social practices required, the variety of social actors who participate and are affected, the larger impact on community relations, the difficult to measure social consequences for all those targeted. It is virtually impossible to imagine the possibility that 800,000 white middle-class youth and adults would ever be treated in the same way in their own neighborhoods. As Chambliss concluded, the social and class structure simply would not allow it. Yet it is the norm in so many cities that are policed in this class-based, racialized way as a matter of course and the image below goes some way to explain how and why it happens through a gang imaginary.

Recently, an organized, voluntary group calling itself the "Association of Gang Investigators" held its eighth annual training conference in New York City and its twenty-third annual conference in Anaheim, California (see www.nagia.org). It is interesting to think about the notion of a group calling itself the "gang investigators." What gives them the authority to describe themselves in this way? Who are they? How did they arise? What is their mission in life? What do they do? A little researching on the web as well as talking to subjects who have participated in their various conferences over the years provides some insight into the way such an imaginary has developed and what it constitutes both ideologically and symbolically. According to the association's self-publicity and that of its affiliates, the original organization began, as one might presume, in California in the late 1970s, but became a national organization in 1998. Currently it is active in twenty-three states with 20,000 members and its mission is to reduce:

> the threats of gang violence by increasing public awareness, training, monitoring legislative efforts, intelligence dissemination and prevention, intervention, suppression and re-entry efforts.

Of course, it matters a great deal what the association's members consider to be a gang and so the definition provided on its website is instructive:

> A group or association of three or more persons who may have a common identifying sign, symbol or name and who individually or collectively engage in, or have engaged in, criminal activity which creates an atmosphere of fear and intimidation. Criminal activity includes juvenile acts that, if committed by an adult, would be a crime.

The group has set itself up as not merely the arbiter of information on gangs but the definer of the gang, the monitor of the gang, the warning system of the gang, the legislative watchdog of the gang and a market mechanism by which the gang is sold as a favored commodity to the surveillance/security industry, which is now a multi-billion dollar enterprise in the United States and beyond. They are, in short, both the control agents and the moral entrepreneurs of the gang.

We see from just this example, and the dozens of such websites throughout the United States where self-proclaimed gang experts organize and sell their specialized knowledge and experience, that all the negative, exoticising tropes of the social imaginary deemed characteristic of gangs, i.e. fear, violence, intimidation, dangerous collective organization, symbols of trouble and "youth," are there to be discovered in groups with as few as three people![3] If a self-selected socially organized group could be devised to intentionally and unintentionally invent and then inflate the existence of the pathological gang, creating the self-fulfilling prophecy and phantasy of a gang epidemic, this would be it. I would argue that in this enabling climate such organized groups yield tremendous power in naming and defining the purported enemy, growing exponentially as part of the self-styled, unregulated, semi-state apparatuses that support the overall growth and prevalence of the surveillance state in a range of countries in both the developed and developing world. They function as originators, conduits and reinforcers of the same kinds of uncontested police-based knowledge, with often devastating results for human rights and the democratic pretensions of society. Contemplate the following instances of corruption, police abuse and general global proliferation of the militarized state on the backs of the anti-gang crusades:

In 2013, the former director of the Department of Homeland Security (DHS) Michael Chertoff was cited in a successful class action lawsuit filed by Latino immigrant plaintiffs in federal court. The plaintiffs complained of being racially profiled by Immigration and Customs Enforcement (ICE) under the direction of DHS in 2007. ICE is now the largest law enforcement agency in the United States and had raided more than 100 homes in the early morning on Long Island, looking for violent deportable immigrants all purportedly belonging to gangs. Of the 120 picked up only twenty-three had any relationship with gangs. Of the more than 100 officers employed (drafted mainly from Texas and Oklahoma) only a handful were trained in gang "intelligence." Most of the officers stated they had learned about gangs through the Internet or had participated in a single workshop provided by gang police. The *New York Times* reported on the Federal Court ruling:

> In a series of raids in suburban New York in 2006 and 2007, agents of Immigration and Customs Enforcement burst into private homes in the dead of night, without warrants, looking for undocumented immigrants, often in the wrong houses. They pounded on doors, terrorized innocent residents, ineptly drew guns on police officers who were supposed to be their partners, and found hardly any of the gang members they were hunting. It was a stunning display of aggression and incompetence.
>
> (*New York Times* Editorial Board, 2013)

In 1998 the Rampart precinct of the Los Angeles Police Department, which boasted the city's biggest gang unit called CRASH (Community Resources Against Street Hoodlums), was under investigation for corruption, including stealing and dealing narcotics, bank robbery, framing of suspects, planting of evidence, unprovoked shootings, etc. More than seventy officers were investigated; twenty-four were found guilty, 140 civil lawsuits against the city were filed and settlements amounting to $125 million were paid out. It was one of the largest cases of police misconduct in US history and as Tom Hayden (2004:102), a California State Senator at the time who participated in the investigation, concluded:

> In essence, Rampart symbolized sanctioned aggression against gang members who were stigmatized as a class, as aliens from another planet without the rights belonging to other Americans.

In the 1990s the Street Crimes Unit (SCU) in New York City, whose motto was "we own the night", was heavily in action against a range of the city's "gangs," carrying out Mayor Giuliani's ubiquitous zero tolerance policy toward social disorder in the city's "high-crime neighborhoods." The unit (having grown to almost 400 members in 2000 from 100 in 1994) was eventually disbanded in 2002 after multiple unexplained killings of innocent victims such as Amadou Diallo and Patrick Dorismond. Although the SCU is now a thing of the past it was succeeded by the NYPD's "stop and frisk" policy. Hayden's (2004:108) comment on the tactics and thinking behind such policing is prescient:

> This was about gang-profiling more than racial profiling. The rationale was that against an elusive, invisible "terrorist" enemy it was necessary to take preemptive action to bend the laws and procedures in order to capture the teenage predators who often proved too difficult to catch in the felonious act. Paramilitarism became the dirty secret of a dirty war against an allegedly dirty enemy. Middle-class leadership looked away.[4]

In 1999, a federal judge shut down a secret anti-gang unit in the Chicago Police Department for engaging in the physical abuse and torture of prisoners in order to extract confessions. A year later five officers from another gang unit were charged with running a cocaine ring, causing the whole unit to be overhauled. In 2011 a gang member in Chicago filed a lawsuit against a gang unit for picking up young gang members in one neighborhood then transporting them to another neighborhood in enemy territory as a way to extract information via humiliation, intimidation and punishment. The plaintiff provided documentary evidence from YouTube and claimed it was a common practice in the Chicago area, leading to physical beatings and worse. There are similar claims in many other "gang" cities.

In 1997 New York's Board of Education ordered a special investigation of the infiltration of the city's schools by gangs, following a sensationalized scoop by the tabloid *New York Post* exposing the presence of a Latin King as a member of a public school security team. The investigation found little evidence of any systematic gang infiltration but the story played a significant role in the run-up to the mayoral election by completely negating the charges made by Ruth Messinger, a Democratic challenger to Mayor Giuliani, after she exposed the crisis of school funding and overcrowding in many of the city's poorest communities. In 1998, Mayor Giuliani ordered the NYPD to take complete control of the city's public school security system, leading to what the New York Civil Liberties Union (2012) calls "the over-policing of New York City's schools," which "paired with school zero tolerance policies, drives youth directly towards the juvenile and criminal justice systems," i.e. the now infamous schools-to-prison pipeline. Currently there are more than 5,000 school safety agents and 190 armed police officers in the school system, compared to 3,100 guidance counselors.

In 2012 the Center for Constitutional Rights in Oakland, California, filed a lawsuit against the state's maximum-security correctional facility at Pelican Bay charging the institution with practicing torture. The facility was established in 1989 to deal with the threats posed by prison gangs in an attempt to isolate the leaders of gangs and prevent the proliferation of their networks. The prison is infamous due to its Secure Housing Unit (SHU) where hundreds of purported gang members are in solitary confinement, housed in windowless 7.6 foot x 11.6 foot cells for 22.5 hours a day. According to the lawsuit, more than 500 inmates have been held in these conditions for more than a decade. Many of the inmates are simply categorized as "gang associates," i.e. they have been seen in the company of gang members but there is no proof that they are actually in a gang. In 2011 four inmates from different gangs launched a hunger strike at the inhumane conditions. The strike spread to more than 30,000 inmates throughout the California system. There has been no significant decrease in gang organization in the prison system as a result of these isolation measures. The hunger strikers are making the following five basic demands:

- eliminate group punishments for individual rules violations;
- abolish the debriefing policy, and modify active/inactive gang status criteria;
- comply with the recommendations of the US Commission on Safety and Abuse in Prisons (2006) regarding an end to long-term solitary confinement;
- provide adequate food;
- expand and provide constructive programs and privileges for indefinite SHU inmates.

Tom Ammiamo, Chair of the California State Assembly on Public Safety, stated:

> We cannot sit by and watch our state pour money into a system that the U.S. Supreme Court has declared does not provide constitutionally acceptable conditions of confinement and that statistics show has failed to increase public safety.
>
> (Law 2013)

In El Salvador, the anthropologist Zilberg describes the effects of the zero tolerance strategy toward gangs, imported from the United States and known as "mano dura" (iron fist in English), as part of a transnational "neo-liberal securityscape" in the region. This process and its dynamics mark the historical contours of the relationship between the United States and El Salvador, which she now describes as the "politics of simultaneity." US gang members are deported in their thousands back to dependent, very poor Central American nations which adopt US-conceived and financed anti-gang measures, producing massive destabilizing effects and severely undermining national sovereignty and any possibility for democratic growth. The result of the United States' export of its social problems is a rapid increase in the crime rate, the explosion of the prison population and the further ratcheting up of the gang repression apparatuses that converge with the country's past US-sponsored anti-communist political and militarized crusades, with the same bloody results. Zilberg (2011:238) concludes:

> The disappearance of the communist challenge and with it the triumph of neoliberalism as the dominant order between the United States and El Salvador coincided with the signing of a new social contract in El Salvador. Indeed, the appearance of the gang member as a "new criminal type" in the immediate post-civil war period bears a particular relationship to the emergence of "democracy" in El Salvador as the form and discourse of political legitimacy … Rene Girard argued that the loss of distinction between former enemies leads to a "mimetic crisis." This structural crisis, he says, can only be resolved through a

unanimous antipathy toward a common enemy. A scapegoat, then, is always necessary to the beginning of a system. Across their entwined histories, it seems that El Salvador and the United States have both needed an other – a "contemporary savage" – against which to define themselves, be it the figure of the native, the communist, or in this case, the gangster … However, zero-tolerance strategies … cannot resolve the crisis precisely because they emulate the sacrificial form itself and are therefore subject to "compulsive repetition disorder."

Donna DeCesare (2013:143), in her prize-winning photo journalistic work titled "Unsettled" (much of which documents the rise of the Central American gangs in Los Angeles and then in El Salvador and Guatemala after the mass deportations referred to above) cites a colleague working for the United States Agency for International Development (USAID) in efforts at youth reform:

> "We had a window of opportunity back then [after the peace accord that brought an end to the civil war]. But the great mistake was Mano Dura … They filled the jails like tins of sardines – three times capacity. Obviously there was inter-gang violence" … But what most exasperated my friend was the Salvadoran government's subsequent decision to segregate the gangs not only within cellblocks but also eventually by prison. This effectively gave specific gangs control over entire prisons, fomenting a level of criminality and group cohesion that contributed to the nightmare of violence in which El Salvador now finds itself.

Gang talk

> Gang talk, I will argue, is a catastrophe discourse about gangs constructed by those who do not live gang realities but have a vested interest in gang lives and gang worlds. Gang talk is thus a discourse that reflects what, following Lefebvre, I propose to term representations of the street not street representations as gang members produce them.
>
> (Hallsworth 2013:1)

Does the panic around gangs lead to a specifically structured language that Hallsworth and Young (2008) first called "gang talk"? Do such gang talk and gang images now have a global reach enabling social control and media agencies to collude in creating a universal symbolic product that merges with their vested interests? What does the moral focus on the gang problem tell us about deeper ideological shifts in the power structure and the enactment of both latent and manifest political/economic agendas (Hall *et al.* 1978, Conquergood 1991)? Such questions have been repeatedly asked by a number of critical students of the gang and none more so than the criminologist Hallsworth, whose research has primarily focused on the discovery of gangs in England during the last decade, the home, not coincidentally of course, of both Cohen's and Young's work and the site of a long tradition of critical criminology.

Hallsworth argues that the current dominant gang discourse, with its largely pathological tropes lending themselves to repressive social control policies, is a language unto itself with a "determinate structure." Borrowing from Wittgenstein and invoking the notion of the gang imaginary (see above), he says that gang talk is a "discourse of power; it represents a way of framing the world in terms such that those producing gang talk can comprehend it" (Hallsworth 2013:2).

Thus we have gang talkers who make claims about the gangs and the gang world that bear little resemblance to the claims made by gang members themselves. This process essentially produces a "control fantasy that reveals the predilections, anxieties and desires of gang talkers more than the truth of the street it aspires to represent" (Hallsworth 2013:3). This symbolic and linguistic feedback loop, which is similar in many respects to the moral panic argument of Cohen and Young, involves a range of mutually reinforcing social actors: media workers, politicians, social workers, social scientists, teachers, police and civil servants. The phenomenon has several facets or "reinforcing tropes" according to Hallsworth, in his almost satirical analysis of the English variety of gang discovery:

> Novelty: They were not here but now they are and we have never seen their like before.

Proliferation: They were few but now there are many. Now they are a Multitude.

Organization: Until recently they were disorganized but now they are organized and organizing.

Weaponization: Their violence was once manageable but as they organize they appropriate and possess ever more terrifying "weapons of choice."

Penetration: They may emerge in particular areas but over time they expand to penetrate and colonize new settings.

Monstrousness: Gang members may look like "normal" people but they are essentially different. Here be monsters.

Such a process of demonizing gang talk can be seen in various socio-geographical and political settings. It is clearly present in the United States, El Salvador and the United Kingdom, but even in Spain, which has had little street gang history, Palmas alerts us to this in his convincing multi-year, in situ research of the comparative forms of social reaction to street gangs in Madrid and Barcelona from 2006 to 2013 (Palmas 2014). Borrowing from Bauman, he likens the range of responses to the gang, which varies from integration to exclusion, to societal responses to the "foreigner" or what Bauman calls the anthropophagic and anthropoemic. What is unique about Palmas' study is that he documents a model of repression imported from the United States that was employed first in Madrid and is contrasted with a more progressive policy of conversion/normalization initiated in Barcelona (and also in Genoa, Italy).[5] In 2011, the reformist policy in Barcelona was ended amid a political-economic crisis that saw youth unemployment mushroom to 55 percent and the provincial government pass into the hands of the politically and culturally conservative CIU nationalist party ("Convergència i Unió" in Catalan).

Palmas argues that in the Spanish case warrior capital won out over pastoral capital in the politics of social control, ushering in a more unified, less contested version of social expulsion as the dominant theme in the socially bulimic dialectics of a precarious late modernity (Young 2011). He also makes plain that Spain was not simply at war with the gangs but with the new Latino/a immigrants who were struggling to establish their economic foothold and post-colonial identities in a Southern Europe now facing sharply reduced rates of social mobility and racial/ethnic "tolerance." Further, he relates the now normative practice of "gang talk" to the neo-liberal transformation of the city and of its public spaces:

> The aim is to build an intimidating environment and the establishment of preventive repression. Delgado (2007) talks about the new social hygiene in the urban environment that has to be transformed into a theme park, immersed in good behavior and without any trace of conflict and the foul character of social inequality.
>
> (Palmas 2014:35)

Gang desire and commodification

> Gangs are a genuine commodity produced by the brand of Spain.
>
> (Palmas 2014:36)

Thus far, in this chapter, I have emphasized the symbolic Othering of gangs and gang members as part of the largely moral crusades against poor and minority communities in the struggle to maintain a certain social and class domination of urban areas and of society in general. But there is another side to this process of symbolic exploitation that is critically important to address to more fully understand the complexities and contradictions of the wars being waged against the street gang in terrains generally characterized by high rates of relative deprivation, blocked opportunity structures and a politics of vindictiveness toward the marginalized, variously described as "brutal" (Sassen 2014a), "cruel" (Giroux 2012) and "pernicious" (Wacquant 1997). For gangs are not only a putatively dangerous entity like "social dynamite" (Spitzer 1975) to be controlled; they also function as a desire and as a commodity to be bought, sold and exchanged at various levels of the cultural and political economy.

To grasp this, we need to understand that behind the so-called rational calculation of social policy, particularly in its most coercive forms, lies a pleasure (Pfohl 1989) in these rituals of control and domination. Or, as Phillips argues, such policy constitutes a semiotic animus and a performance (Butler 1993, Conquergood 1991) that is contextualized and bounded by a "late capitalist consumer culture" (Phillips 1999:32).

Gangs as the seductive "Other"

> In ways that we do not easily or willingly define, the gangster speaks for us, expressing that part of the American psyche which rejects the qualities and the demands of modern life, which rejects "Americanism" itself.
>
> (Warshow 1970, quoted in Kelley 1994)

The world is seductive and erotic, argued Bataille (1986, see also Jenks 2003); full of taboos, acts of transgression and self-destructive urges. It is also a spectacle (DeBord 1994) in which we all play a role whether wittingly or unwittingly. Gangs perfectly fit into this world with its "hall of mirrors" (Ferrell 1999) as an amalgam of purported behaviors and lifestyles that contravene the predictability, boredom and mundaneness of the everyday. The gang as a milieu for transgressiveness speaks to youth and others who chafe at the thought of remaining bound forever by and to the "straight" life.

Such deviance, therefore, is what Katz (1988) calls "seductive" and is particularly attractive to youth who want to play the role of the "bad ass" and acquire the status of such a street identity or feel the respect that comes with enlisting in groups of street royalty who may control territory, have access to large social circles of the same or opposite sex, provide camaraderie and function as a pseudo-family. Often such attributes of the gang are portrayed as properties pure and simple that subjects wish for as in some marginal utility curve. Desire, however, is much more complex than this rational-choice-constructed relationship and might be better understood as the active negation of the things we cannot normally be or do (see Warshow quote above).

Presdee (2001) calls this the carnival of crime (borrowing from Bakhtin[6]) and, since there are so many activities in the life-world of gangs that are performative, e.g. as they participate in the spontaneous, unpredictable dramas of the street, appear in an ongoing social control play involving the police and others in the criminal justice system, or get portrayed in myriad spectacles distributed through the mass media from news dailies to popular films, the application of this concept is appropriate. For Presdee, in a world that has insufficient outlets, such as the carnivals of yore during pre- or early capitalism, the lower classes (particularly the youth) grow weary of the constant appeals for restraint and sobriety and go in search of opportunities to perform, transgress and act out at different levels. He includes gang membership as one of these opportunities and certainly the action of the street, the time spent hanging out rather than consuming or working, and the creative rituals of self-organization, communication and representation can all be appreciated through a carnivalesque frame:

> The basic premise of my argument is straightforward, without a partly licensed carnival forum to satisfy our second life it emerges more haphazardly, unrehearsed and often unannounced … However, by being incomplete they do not manage to balance the paradoxes that Bakhtin's carnival does and without coherence it is relatively easy to separate the unpalatable or savage performances from the acts of pleasant social entertainment.
>
> (Presdee 2001:39)

Gangs as commodified culture

Presdee, however, is also clear that such acts are incomplete aspects of the street carnival phenomenon and are prone to commodification, with the gang as no exception. In fact its commodification has yielded vast profits to a host of powerful expropriators. Gangsta rap is an excellent example of the way deviant gang culture has been appropriated by the mainstream corporate entertainment industry; then there are gangsta styles in clothing, a gangsta genre in films (as already noted), the gangsta as raw material in the global social control industry and the gangsta as art, seen in the process by which graffiti has moved from being the epitome of low culture, as marginalized youth "bombed" urban spaces, train cars and various cityscapes, to become a prized fixture in high cultural circles and auction houses. Kelley (1994:191) opines:

For other consumers of gangsta rap, such as middle-class white males, the genre unintentionally serves the same role as Blaxploitation films of the 1970s or, for that matter, gangster films of any generation. It attracts listeners for whom "the ghetto" is a place of adventure, unbridled violence, erotic fantasy, and/or an imaginary alternative to suburban boredom.

This appropriation by the market of the archetypal deviant Other is difficult and almost impossible to resist and it cannot be otherwise. The boundaries between the subcultural and mass popular culture are more porous than ever and the financial desire to expropriate and transform virtually any practice into a commodity is inexhaustible in today's market-driven social and economic life. Further, as Flores (2000:17) reminds us, these processes of symbolic inversion are continuous in relationships between so-called high and low cultures:

> This dependence and this secret desire for what is excluded and disdained go to account for the deepest irony of popular culture, that "what is socially peripheral is so frequently central."

A visit to YouTube or a viewing of any one of the hundreds of music videos with gang-related motifs, e.g. advertisements for the globally successful South Korean singer Psy, who transforms facile "gangsta" themes into pure entertainment, shows the power of the market and the seemingly irreversible processes of commodification. In such processes various facets of the gang signifier are simply captured and fed back to the mass market eagerly awaiting such products. Nothing is left of the authentic subculture in this other form of cultural production and commodity fetishization; with its original meanings lost it is not even a copy of a copy.

Conclusion

Essentially, the stereotyping of gang-related inner-city populations is a favored practice of societal elites and the politicians and scribes who serve their interests, as they seek social space from and cultural control over the "dangerous classes." What many of the studies have found is that the violent, bestial and primitivistic imagery of gang youths have been constant themes in crime and community reports and play a powerful role in constructing the symbolic reality for a mass audience, most of whom have little real contact with actual gang members. Such reporting has been an effective tool in fueling if not creating "moral panics" at various stages of the economic cycle and translated into successive waves of anti-gang legislation at local, state and federal levels.

Thus, around such populist concerns as urban decay, rising immigrant populations, juvenile crime, the drugs culture, failing public schools and youth immorality, gangs have been "tagged" (Young 1971) as a leading contributory factor rather than as a primary symptom of a broader set of structural contradictions. In Erikson's (1966) terms, the use of such "enemies" is an effort by the dominant order to restore society's social boundaries by ensuring that the threatening Other is managed and brought into line. At the same time gang images and cultural products are heavily commodified, coopted and recirculated. We see this in the production of gang graffiti, gang clothing and styles and gang-inspired rap and assorted hip-hop.

Is it not time to really make research (all of it), intellectual study and contemplation part of society's manifold responses to one of the social conundrums of our times, the continuity and discontinuity of the street gang? This task is particularly urgent, as the phenomenon of the gang can no longer be simply imagined within the grid of street-corner life in Chicago, Los Angeles or New York. Rather, it has become a highly adaptive and plastic social configuration manifesting itself both in objective reality and in the fictions of social controllers on the global stage. These issues will be taken up in the next, penultimate chapter.

Notes

1 Of course, we know how precarious, unstable and unsustainable these conditions are for vast sections of both lower- and middle-class society, with rates of immiseration, social immobility and mass unemployment reflected in extraordinary rates of mass incarceration and mass migrations. Such profoundly unstable conditions, *nota bene*, are the roots of the recent 'Occupy' movements and uprisings in the United States, Europe and the Middle East (see Castells 2012).

2 By imaginary I am referring to the social imaginary, the ways in which human beings imagine the world to be through its symbolic dimensions. It draws on the work of Castoriadis (1987 [1975]) who stated that "the imaginary of the society … creates for each historical period its singular way of living, seeing and making its own existence." Thus our imaginary is a creative, interactive process producing an historical construct that enables us to represent collective life. I also see the social imaginary as something linked to social phantasy, which is heavily predicated on both social fear and desire.

3 At least with Cohen's mods and rockers the general public were reacting to hundreds of youth descending on beaches and seaside shopping streets on particular days of the year; here we have these highly nebulous groups somehow judged to be presenting serious threats to the social order by control agents whose knowledge and authority comes from other control agents.

4 This reference to the gangs as "terrorists" comes from a comment made by Los Angeles Police Commissioner William Bratton early in his tenure. Bratton was and is a proponent of the infamous "broken windows" policy regarding the maintenance of social order. However, Bratton was firmly against the notoriously indiscriminate Operation Hammer anti-gang policy pursued by former LAPD Commissioner Darryl Gates, which served to alienate poor minority communities from the police department.

5 It should be said that the Barcelona model, which was enacted through local legislation in 2006, actually worked and led to a marked reduction in inter-group violence. This is in contrast to the Madrid policy, which saw an increase in violent incidents between these types of street groups.

6 "Carnival celebrates temporary liberation from the prevailing truth of the established order" (Bakhtin 1984:109).

6

REFLECTIONS FROM THE FIELD

> Many criminologists, like U.S. journalists in the Iraq war, have become embedded in the law enforcement bureaucracies … waging war on gangs, drugs, and terror, practicing a kind of domestic orientalism.
>
> (Hagedorn 2008:134)

How do we avoid the domestic orientalism of the gang that Hagedorn describes? I argue that it is imperative to understand gangs through the eyes of the participants, much as has been advocated by some of sociology's and criminology's leading researchers of deviance for most of the last century. This involves thinking seriously about what gang members tell us about their life's chances, their daily practices, the meanings attached to their subcultures and the contexts in which all this takes place. For example, what does making the crown, as the young Latin Kings do in Figure 6.1, signify and mean to the subjects? My aim in this closing part of the book is to reflect on the twenty years or more of gang research during which I have established relationships with subjects related directly or indirectly to these subcultures in multiple locales. From San Francisco, California to New York City; from Santo Domingo, Dominican Republic to

FIGURE 6.1 Latin Kings making a crown circa 1996. © Steve Hart 2014. Originally published in David C. Brotherton and Luis Barrios. 2004. *The Almighty Latin King and Queen Nation: Street Politics and the Transformation of an Inner City Gang.* New York: Columbia University Press. Reproduced with kind permission from Columbia University Press.

London, UK and from Barcelona, Spain to Quito, Ecuador I have observed and listened to youth and adults as they make sense of a society that it seems impossible to accept is organizing itself rationally, equitably and effectively. We seem to be in a world that the author and political commentator Eduardo Galeano once called upside down, in reference to the need for a "looking glass school" that would teach students to turn the world the right way up. It is also a world that Saskia Sassen (2014b) reminds us is being savagely sorted.

> The upside-down world rewards in reverse: it scorns hon-
> esty, punishes work, prizes lack of scruples, and feeds canni-
> balism. Its professors slander nature: injustice, they say, is a law
> of nature. Milton Friedman teaches us about the "natural rate
> of unemployment." Studying Richard Hernstein and Charles
> Murray, we learn that blacks remain on the lowest rungs of

the social ladder by "natural" law. From John D. Rockefeller's lectures, we know his success was due to the fact that "nature" rewards the fittest and punishes the useless: more than a century later, the owners of the world continue to believe Charles Darwin wrote his books in their honor.

(Galeano 1998:5)

In keeping with the book's premise of providing a critical gaze on the subject of gangs I will be focusing on my own comparative experiences while drawing on a wide body of research, including that coming from gang researchers tired of the worn-out concepts and findings of traditional gang empiricism. Such researchers have embarked on new journeys into the field, bringing a richness and depth to an area of study desperately needing new ideas, new data and new ways of interpreting a world in constant flux, despite the creaking structures of power that maintain those processes of social exclusion guaranteed to reproduce the gang.

Gangs as a last refuge in the age of neo-liberalism

Thomas Piketty's latest economic findings about the devastating consequences of the continuing concentration of wealth and the threats to democracy in a society that guarantees less and less social mobility have been widely debated in the media, reminding us all how fragile the political economy and the social peace really is. As Piketty (2014) shows, capital if left to its own devices naturally tends toward rising inequality, and the contemporary world boasts a level of concentrated wealth that is close to that of the "gilded age" of the early twentieth century. But, as Harvey argues, this process does not emerge without enormous struggles taking place between the classes. It is this power imbalance between labor and capital that is essentially at work and at the heart of neo-liberal economic policy and politics around the globe.

The steady decline in labor's share of national income since the 1970s derived from the declining political and economic power of labor as capital mobilized technologies, unemployment, off-shoring and anti-labor politics (such as those of Margaret Thatcher and Ronald Reagan) to crush all opposition.

(Harvey 2014)

This massive increase in inequality simply affirms what so many researchers of American daily life have been seeing for years, and clearly relates to Merton's 1930s thesis that subcultures will emerge as youth struggle to balance the growing contradictions between the mainstream goals of a society's governing ideology and the formal and informal means of achieving those goals. It was two of Merton's students, Cloward and Cohen, who went on to discuss some of the results of these jarring contradictions and their relationship to the gang phenomenon through their notions of blocked opportunity structures and reaction formation (albeit based on little data).

Certainly, in the present era of glaring conspicuous affluence at one end of the social continuum while at the other we are confronted daily with the depressing spectacle of stagnant and falling life chances experienced by millions, and the emergence of this strange, liquid phenomenon called the "precariat" (Standing 2012), the application of such subcultural theories should be a constant – be they revised and extended (Burawoy 1998) or not. However, we need to apply and situate these theories (and other insights from across the disciplinary divide) not only within those data that reflect the daily, holistic lives of these groups and their surrounding communities (see Chapter 4) but within the broader political, social, economic and cultural domain. It is imperative to incorporate in our thinking, design and analyses those currents initiated by and on behalf of elites (e.g. in pursuit of what former President Bush once referred to as the "New World Order") not as impenetrable structures but as sites and processes, as material conditions which the lower orders react to, mediate, infuse with their own agency and at times even succeed in rejecting, bringing about a new world order. These structural contingencies of the gang are essential to contemplate and ponder[1] and, as Mills would argue, connect our data to the "big picture." For without them being taken into account the vicissitudes of gang life and gang formations become overly local affairs located in the type of depoliticized notion of "society" that is the hallmark of so much orthodox sociology and criminology.

Looking back and thinking forward

One of the major themes that I have observed and heard over the years working with gang members is the experience of the social divide that is their lot. Twenty years ago, while working in the Mission District of San Francisco with Vietnamese, African-American, Mexican, Chicano and Central American gang members, the economic refrain most commonly heard was the lack of jobs, due, in part, to a recession then gripping California. However, many of these youth were also fleeing from much worse situations in the countries of their birth. They had seen and felt the brutalities of civil war in El Salvador, Nicaragua and Guatemala, experienced the inhuman treatment of the Mexican state and its federal police (i.e. torture) or remembered coming to the West Coast as refugees from South-East Asia with a fragmented family and barely a suitcase of belongings. The native-born subjects meanwhile spoke of family trajectories moving up from the South in search of work, or escaping Jim Crow in a previous generation and now facing a daunting educational and economic future in the midst of the raging crack trade now besieging their community.

Gangs for many of these youth were a way to fit in, a process of settlement somewhat akin to the notion of "segmented assimilation" (Portes and Zhou 1993). They often referred to gangs as a normal part of street socialization, similar to the observations of Vigil and others. Some of the gangs functioned like intergenerational quasi-institutions (Hagedorn 2008) while others had only recently been established (for example Filipino and Vietnamese youth gangs) and were busy building their street reputations. Those youth coming from Central America also faced the opposition of other gang youth in long-established Latino neighborhoods, to which they developed their own organizations almost as a defensive measure similar to the way gangs such as the Mara Salvatrucha emerged in Los Angeles. Back then I wrote that the gang was part of a complex inter-ethnic youth identity process, as I observed mainly male lower-class gang members claiming their symbolic and physical territories, defending the honor of their affiliated groups in ritualized challenges that frequently led to injury and sometimes death. This was, after all, the era of tit-for-tat drive-by shootings and brawls in and around schools that often saw their security guards in action on most days of the week (see Brotherton 1992).

The public schools were dealing with these youth through a mixture of containment and expulsion. In one school where I spent a year they had a special section in the basement where those with the most transgressions were normally housed, under the rationale they had learning difficulties and exhibited inappropriate behavior. Many of them were in various gangs and the class was run by an active bodybuilder who acquired grants to buy a range of the most recent bodybuilding equipment:

> People come in here, some of them complain that there's no academics getting done. I don't give a shit about academics; they can burn their books for all I care. These kids are not ready for that. That's what I tell them, otherwise they wouldn't be here.
>
> (Mr. A., the Special Education teacher,
> May 8, 1992 in Brotherton 1992)

Mr. A. unofficially called his program "Pump City" while the students and some other teachers referred to it as the "San Quentin" track. Mr. A. reasoned that if the youth could at least take pride in their bodies and develop some self-discipline they might not need the gangs anymore and could avoid the predictable trajectory from "juvie" to the "big house" (i.e. San Quentin, the infamous state penitentiary across the San Francisco Bay). In reality there was very little learning going on and the program succeeded in keeping some of these youth in school and provided at least a sanctuary from their usual risk-filled lives on the streets.

Field Notes: (5/16/92)

I enter the front doors of an inner city public high school. Standing there are two hall guards looking self-assuredly at the pockets of student cutters, truants and "hallway hangers," grouped on the school steps outside. The guards' job is to keep them out and prevent them from disturbing the social calm of the school during class periods. I nod to one of them, Leroy, a well-built, African-American ex-college football player whom I have come to know over the last two years.

"How's it going?" I ask

"The usual, keeping the animals in their cages."

"Anything happen today?"

"No, nothing major. It's been pretty quiet. A couple of fights lunch time, that's about it."

I walk on, ascending the hallway stairs that lead to a large open space, architecturally designed to accommodate the throngs of students and teachers who fill the area between class times before fanning out to their assigned rooms. Approaching me is the Dean of Boys, a tall, middle-aged Latino. He patrols the school's corridors and its outside perimeter usually every hour, trying to gather wayward students.

"Back again?" he says

"'Fraid so," I answer, "Not finished yet. All quiet today?"

"Yep, so far so good. Although you don't wanna speak too soon. Know what I mean?"

"Yeah, I do. Well, I've just gotta check on Mr. A.'s class, see what's up."

I proceed on, making a right through another set of doors that open into a corridor whose walls are covered in graffiti. On my left, sitting on a wooden pew are three Latino youth, two of whom I interviewed about three weeks before.

"How's it going Dave?" says J., an ebullient 10th grader who looks very stoned. "Off to see Mr. A.?"

"Yeah, thought I'd see what's happening today. Everything OK?"

"Pretty good I'd say."

"Yeah, see what you mean," I respond. J. laughs and the other two youth join in the joke, taking it as a reference to their lunch time marijuana smoking rituals.

I walk on toward the end of the corridor and outside Mr. A.'s room a private security guard is sitting on a bench. On either side of him are two youths, one African-American and the other Latino. They all seem to be talking at the same time. The two students are acting out an event that occurred that day at the school, something to do with the police, a student and an outsider. The guard looks at me, recognizes me as the one who's always hanging around the corridors and nods.

"Is anyone in?" I ask.

"Yeah, just knock, there's a whole bunch of 'em in there. You know how it is."

I simply smile. I am now at the door of Pump City, the name given by Mr. A. to his special education classroom. Inside, the area is divided into three very different spaces. Immediately behind the door is Mr. A.'s office. It contains his desk, filing cabinets with all his charges' psychological evaluations, several chairs and desks, a Coke machine, a closet, a large window behind Mr. A.'s desk that looks out onto the "special ed" classroom and a door that takes you there. The classroom is equipped with a 30" television screen, a VCR and a stereo system. There are desks and chairs for about 20 students and Charles, the teaching assistant, will normally be there supervising six or seven legitimate "special ed" students plus an equal number of students who are cutting other classes.

Two big, heavy doors lead from this classroom to a small hallway, across from which is a weight room. This is what gives this class its name, Pump City. The name is emblazoned in bold letters across the front of the gym.

Someone opens the door after I knock two or three times. Sitting at his desk is Mr. A. The scene reminds me of the last part of "Apocalypse Now" when Marlon Brando is discovered in his surrealistic lair, being catered to by the mysterious mountain people.

"How's it going?" Mr. A. bellows to me. "Come to check out the crazies?"

Two African-American female students are braiding Mr. A.'s hair. Mr. A. is a larger than life Italian-American, extremely muscular, covered in tattoos and dressed in hip street/prison garb. The two females are busily chatting to each other while carefully pulling on his sparse locks, gently layering one strand over the other in the current popular fashion. The usual boundaries between students and teachers do not hold for Pump City.

Sitting on a couple of desks I recognize four youths from the Los Locos street gang. I know them quite well since I have interviewed them extensively over the past six months. Flaco and Pancho, both wearing their gang t-shirts, nod towards me and each one in turn holds out his hand for the routine "homeboy" hand shake. After several complicated movements in which our palms, fingers and fists move across each other, I take a seat. Flaco and Pancho carry on their conversation in Spanish.

"It's going crazy round here again. The girls beat up some white chick this morning. Mitchell comes in after getting beaten up in the park. And now the gangsters are outside going for it. Who the fuck wants to do this job? What crazy mother fucker can say it's worth it?"

Meanwhile, upstairs in the mainstream part of the school, the teachers did their best to bring down a reported drop-out rate of 50 percent,[2] always struggling to cope with one budget crisis after another. Many of the teachers, however, had little training in how to deal with youth in the gang subcultures and could easily succumb to the pressures of the moral panic around both immigrants and gangs that was prevalent in California during this time (Brotherton 1996b). A lucky few students managed to graduate on time, making it to a community college or perhaps to a state university with the odd, highly motivated youth getting into UC Berkeley after taking some college prep classes and receiving special mentoring during the summer months.

Unlike most gang researchers, however, I was also able to interview a number of females involved in these groups (Brotherton 1994), some of whom were developing their own independent organizations. Such gang females had largely been overlooked in the literature with their presence and subcultural roles dismissed by male social scientists (see Campbell 1991 for an excellent counter). I found the females to be reflective and insightful, and certainly not opposed to the possibilities of a formal education if only there could be learning material that spoke to them and their experiences. If only they had teachers who could understand the complexities of their lives, the situations they were frequently fleeing from, the responsibilities they had at home, the daily struggles of living in poverty and the street lives they had become accustomed to. This was also the era of HIV and AIDS, when little was known about the disease and many students had seen families members die in a short space of time, being called upon to nurse and comfort people who seemed to just wither away.

Moving from the West to the East Coast I began doing field research in New York public schools, based in institutions with some of the city's highest rates of reported violence. The contrast with San Francisco was striking, with relatively few gangs overtly present and little sign of gangs claiming these areas. The importance of contrasting contexts in which to study gangs was strongly apparent and a few years later this lesson becomes even clearer.

In 1996 I began working among the gang "nations" of New York City, mainly comprised of working-class native-born Latino/

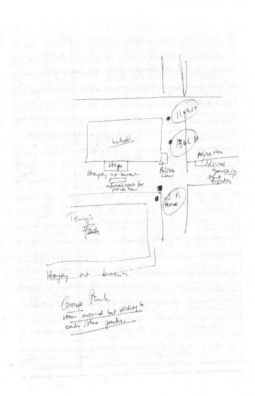

FIGURE 6.2 A sketch made of City High School amid three of the competing Latino youth gangs during field observations.
Source: Brotherton, April 23, 1992.

as (primarily with Puerto Rican and Dominican heritages) and African-Americans.[3] Like their San Francisco counterparts, members spoke of past struggles to escape poverty and the volatility of their family's economic fortunes, which veered between periods on welfare and in the segmented labor market, though, for the most part, these members were much closer to the working class than possessing any of the characteristics deemed to define the so-called "underclass." We did not come across many who were post-school age and unemployed for any length of time, and although the drug trade was still omnipresent it did not have the same violent impact on the community's health and safety as I had seen less than a decade before.

The major issue for these youth was the growing social divide they felt in education and the massive intervention of the criminal justice system in their lives, both of which compounded the structured racism that so impacted life in the city, despite the oft-repeated notion that New York was this rich mosaic/quilt of cultures, etc. (i.e. through its unofficially segregated housing and school system leading to what some social scientists referred to as "American apartheid" (Massey and Denton 1998)). This was, after all, during the tenure of Mayor Giuliani, a time of unabashed coercive social control rationalized by such reactionary models of crime prevention as "broken windows" and "zero tolerance" used both in the streets and in the public schools. It was also a time when police chiefs were being increasingly feted and treated as public celebrities for their supposed crime-fighting prowess, and the prison population mushroomed by 138 percent from 1980 to 1990, leading prison experts to call it the most punitive decade of any in US history, with African-Americans incarcerated at 6.6 times the rate of whites.

> By year end 1999, far more prisoners will have been added to America's prisons and jails than in any decade in recorded history. The 532,448 prisoners added to America's institutions during the 1990s is 25% higher than the number of prisoners added during the 1980s, and is nearly 16 times as many as the average number added during the five decades before 1970 in which the incarcerated population increased. Our incarceration rate plays such a distorting role in the labor market, one study found that the U.S. unemployment rate would be 2% higher if prisoners and jail inmates were counted.
>
> (Justice Policy Institute 2000)

For working-class and poor youth there was no doubt that this was an era of punishment, with notions of rehabilitation widely viewed by powerful conservative policy makers as naïve liberalism and wrong-headed humanism. The same logics of tough-on-crime social control measures found favor in public education, with the widespread use of metal detectors and security guards eventually linked formally to the police department, fueling the school-to-prison pipeline. There was some evidence that schools were pushing out the undesirables (Fine 1991) and a deeper look at the school demographics across the city revealed that the system was one of the most segregated in the United States (Orfield and Frankenburg 2013), especially as the white middle classes moved into previously poor or minority neighborhoods and set about ensuring that their local schools offered the education required of their families' cultural capital. Testing also became far more pronounced with schools increasingly ranked according to their performance measures, which were said to delineate successful from failing institutions. Naturally many of the "failed" schools were in the city's poorest areas servicing students with the least cultural capital.

Faced with these powerful stratifying and exclusionary social and ideological pressures youth tried from below to put some form of order and meaning back into their lives and into their communities.[4] The gangs therefore took on a different form. They were more politicized, reflexive and open to progressive ideas and various forms of social solidarity outside of the group (Brotherton and Barrios 2004) than anything I had witnessed on the West Coast. Members, both leaders and the rank-and-file, saw themselves as agents of social change and cultural innovators, not just one-dimensional "deviants" adapting to their local contexts or conforming to and reproducing the negative representations of the dominant society (Brotherton 2007).

For their pains the groups were treated by the Establishment not with an eye to increasing youth empowerment through recognizing their extraordinary capacities to self-organize and relate to the most alienated youth, but as dangerous threats to the existing social order. Members of the governing class could not conceive of such groups as vehicles to energize the community and build a more engaged citizenry – even when gang-related violence was sharply down during this entire period.

To many of the youth those with societal power repeatedly demonstrated their lack of interest in reversing the processes of marginalization and Othering. The criminalization of poor communities that went on apace led members to recall the histories of past radical self-determination in their communities as recounted to them by family members and old heads. Such youth were striving to express themselves through the social and cultural resources available to them, looking for new meanings much as happened in the original hip-hop culture of a generation or more before that took shape amid the burned-out tenements and rampant poverty captured in memorable documentaries and photo journalism shot in the South Bronx and Brooklyn (see Chang 2005, Cooper and Chalfant 2009 [1984], Chalfant and Prigoff 1987, Silver and Chalfant 1983). Now it was happening again in many of the same neighborhoods, at a different level. As one active supporter of the Latin Queens during this time put it:

> Why New York? Why not? This is where so many of these youth movements start. We mix it all up, that's our lives. We have all the ethnic and racial influences here, all mixed up in the city, coming together in different neighborhoods. We're just taking it to a different place. Like we build on each other. We see what our brothers and sisters did in the past and now we have to do our thing, facing our problems, doing it our way.
>
> (Ms. R., August 7, 1996)

In the two largest gang conferences organized in New York since the 1960s (in 1997 and 2001 at John Jay College), attended by hundreds of gang-related youth from New York and beyond, there was no attempt at a dialogue and no effort to understand the worldviews of these youth or their historical circumstances by any social control agencies related to the criminal justice system (i.e. NYPD, Corrections, Probation or Parole) or anyone from city government. Instead there was a predictable and almost stereotypical rush to condemn and judge, with tabloid-led moral panics (e.g. the *New York Post* and the *Daily News*, see below) and local commercial radio leading the way.[5]

We concluded that we had to look to different youth cultural explanations to understand the forms gangs were taking, their diverse contexts, the life histories of the members, the stages that the groups

3 suspects in Tortola slay are free

By DEREK ROSE
DAILY NEWS STAFF WRITER

Three of the four Americans accused of killing a Connecticut artist on the island paradise of Tortola walked from a courtroom as free men yesterday.

Financial adviser William Labrador, 37, of Southampton, L.I., was left to stand trial in the slaying of Lois McMillen.

British Virgin Islands Judge Kenneth Benjamin ruled there was insufficient evidence linking the three freed men to the Jan. 14, 2000, slaying for which they had been jailed for more than a year.

"Michael Spicer, Alexander Benedetto and Evan George, you are discharged," Benjamin said as he directed the jury to enter verdicts of not guilty.

Benedetto, a 35-year-old Manhattan book publisher who had a brief relationship with McMillen, hugged friends and family. "It's nice that justice is done," he said.

Spicer, a 37-year-old law student from Virginia, patted Labrador on the shoulder as he left the courtroom.

"I want to jump in the ocean," he said. "Jump in the beautiful Caribbean ocean and wash off the circumstances of the prison for us."

Labrador remains on trial because a prison informer said he admitted killing McMillen, 34, of Middlebury, Conn.

Her fully clothed, beaten body was found near a beachside road in Tortola. An autopsy showed she had drowned.

The men admitted spending time with McMillen, a former model, abstract painter and ardent feminist, but they denied seeing her the day she died. She had been staying in her parents' villa on the island.

Labrador's family applauded the acquittals.

"Three down, one to go," said his mother, Barbara Labrador, also of Southampton. "I feel very good, and I think the judge made an excellent legal ruling.

"The only reason this is going to the jury is because of [prison informer] Jeff Plante."

Russell McMillen, the victim's father, was in the courtroom with his wife, Josephine, when the ruling was announced. "They were just released on a technicality," he told the Daily News.

The evidence against the men included .003 gram of sand that the prosecution said put Spicer on the beach where McMillen died. Benjamin called that "less than fit" to support a murder charge.

STREET GANG IMAGES   Erica Class points out photo of Latin Kings yesterday at exhibit at John Jay College.   ANDREW SAVULICH DAILY NEWS

Reputed gang chief to speak at college

By RALPH R. ORTEGA and JOHN MARZULLI
DAILY NEWS STAFF WRITERS

The reputed head of the Latin Kings is giving a seminar at John Jay College of Criminal Justice today "to alert young people" about law enforcement efforts to dismantle street gangs, the Daily News has learned.

News of the seminar, part of a four-day conference at the City University of New York school on the culture of street gangs, drew a strong rebuke yesterday from City Hall.

"John Jay should be a college for criminal justice, not for criminal practices," said Matt Higgins, a spokesman for Mayor Giuliani.

Hector (King Hector) Torres — who allegedly has run the Almighty Latin King and Queen Nation in New York since Antonio (King Tone) Fernandez pleaded guilty to a drug charge in 1999 — is the moderator of a panel discussion titled "State Counter-intelligence."

DAILY ❂ NEWS
EXCLUSIVE

"We feel the biggest danger is the snitch culture, where our young people are tricked by the police and federal authorities to say hurtful things about the organizations they belong to," Torres told The News yesterday.

"We want to alert our young people to how this snitch culture operates and manipulates them," he said.

"We will start with a skit where kings and queens will act out scenarios where the police and feds attempt to set them up as snitches and informants," Torres said.

Torres will be joined on the panel by King Tone's wife, Myrna. A member of the Los Angeles-based Bloods gang is scheduled to speak in another seminar about the West Coast.

A source close to the college said the presence of gang members at the school — which has educated thousands of cops and law enforcement officials — was unsettling. "It's a disgrace . . . It makes the gang lifestyle look ap-

pealing," said the source, who spoke on the condition of anonymity.

Jerry Capeci, a John Jay spokesman, defended the conference and Torres' right to speak his mind even though his views may not be those of the college.

"John Jay College believes strongly in cooperating with the police and other law enforcement agencies to root out crime, whether it's committed by street gangs, organized crime or any criminal group," Capeci said. "If Hector Torres is interested in giving a primer on what he plans to do is stop people from cooperating, that's his prerogative.

"In no way, shape or form is John Jay trying to glorify gang membership," Capeci added. "The agenda here is the exact opposite."

Relations between John Jay College and the NYPD have cooled in recent years because of what police brass viewed as criticism of department policies by several professors.

Police Commissioner Bernard Kerik, who has beefed up law enforcement against gangs, declined yesterday to comment on the conference.

Mayor slams judge on cop sex case

By LISA L. COLANGELO and HELEN PETERSON
DAILY NEWS STAFF WRITERS

Mayor Giuliani yesterday blasted a judge's decision to reinstate a cop who was fired for having sex with a prostitute in a district attorney's office.

The officer, Troy Jackson, 34, of Staten Island was caught with the hooker in a bathroom on the third floor of the Manhattan district attorney's office at 1 Hogan Place in 1999.

Giuliani vowed to appeal the "wacky decision" of Manhattan Supreme Court Justice Marcy Friedman, calling it "irrational and illogical."

"I don't think there's any sensible person that would agree with this," he said.

Jackson pleaded guilty to NYPD administrative charges but argued in a lawsuit that the loss of his job was too severe a penalty.

Friedman agreed, noting that Jackson had an otherwise exemplary record in his seven years as a cop.

"Troy Jackson is a human being who made a mistake," said his lawyer, Mitch Garber, who said Jackson admitted "this was embarrassing not only to himself and his family, but also to the department."

The NYPD declined to comment except to say it would appeal. In legal papers filed in response to Jackson's suit, the department called the incident a "major blow to the integrity of the NYPD and to public confidence in police officers."

Lois McMillen

FIGURE 6.3 Report in the *New York Daily News* following the "Globalizing the Streets" conference in 2001. © Daily News, L.P. (New York). Used with permission.

were passing through, their societal reception and the foreground of gang life, i.e. how it is lived, experienced and constituted in everyday settings. Consequently social movements theory and analysis seemed to be a much better fit to our data, and resistance theory as interpreted in cultural, performance and post-colonial studies.

FIGURE 6.4 Poster of "Globalizing the Streets" conference – NB there is no mention of gangs.
Source: Street Organization archives.

By the time of the new millennium the experiment of creative street politics engaged in by a number of gang-related youths in the city was essentially crushed, split and silenced by the state. *The experiment was feared not because of the participants' penchant for interpersonal violence but rather for their skills at self-organization and their audacity to suggest that barrio and ghetto youth advance a collective cause, united against the systematic injustices they face on a daily basis.* With social control agencies using all the same techniques of COINTELPRO[6] from decades before and now armed with RICO[7] laws to charge gang members with conspiracy even with the flimsiest evidence, there was little the street organizations could do. The organic intellectuals that led them, the assortment of liberal and leftist community leaders and academics that supported them and the will of the legions of young people now being engaged in political struggle for the first time were no match without a much broader level of mass radicalization to come to their aid.

Such radicalization did eventually transpire, albeit about a decade later, with the Occupy movements that filled the streets with hope across the entire United States, feeding into a seemingly endless wave of spontaneous and organized discontent across much of Europe and the Middle East. Perhaps in many ways the politicization of the New York gangs presaged this later movement of the disaffected. Where was the American Dream now, they asked? We work hard like these other ethnic groups so why do we get prison (Reiman 1998) and they move up the ladder? These race/ethnic and class questions constantly emerged from their discourses as they battled for respect, for the right to be heard, to be taken seriously, and to be consulted.

In the more recent period, during which time I have spent extended leaves outside the United States, there is no doubt that a "world of gangs" has begun to emerge in response to many of the effects of global neo-liberal policies that Hagedorn (2008) cites as behind the growing ubiquity of the gang subculture. But while there are gangs of the nature that Hagedorn describes, linked in different ways to organized violence and crime, at the same time there are other kinds of street formations and organizations. There is, as Katz and Jackson-Jacobs (2003) concluded, a great deal of "ambiguity" in the gang world and the putative links to acts of violence cannot be assumed but rather have to be proven.[8] The remarkable finding for this researcher is that despite the extraordinary measures taken to end the experiment in New York City we can still see the power of these subcultures almost fifteen years later.

Conclusion

In this chapter I return to some of the sites and populations I have been studying over the past twenty years. When I first started working with gang youth it was via their school connection, which very few researchers at the time were considering. It was also in the middle of the crack epidemic and the levels of societal violence and crime were much higher than they are today. Nonetheless, I found these youth and their subcultures to be anything but pathological and it took little to observe that so many members of these street organizations were coming from highly traumatized environmental and social backgrounds both at the local level and, if they were first generation immigrants, in their homelands.

After all, these were the years of the Central American civil wars, and mounting economic problems in the developing world in part due to the massive debt crisis as the first world maintained much of the post-colonial world in a grimacing state of dependency. However, when I moved to the East Coast I saw a very different gang scene to that I had been accustomed to and for the first time I witnessed a level of consciousness among the subcultures that at least began to resemble the very real relationship they had with systems of oppression and repression.

But such a consciousness and its accompanying practices were too much for the local elites and their apparatuses of social control. The Latin Kings and Queens were doubtlessly the exemplar of this heightened social and self-awareness among "gangs" and I, along with my research partner Luis Barrios, were privileged to be allowed to observe this subaltern movement and historical moment at such close quarters and for so long. These are experiences that are difficult to duplicate in a lifetime.

Notes

1 Notwithstanding the criticism of Katz and Jackson-Jacobs (2003) that gangs should not be simply used as a "window" through which we see the larger social ills of society.

2 It was extremely difficult to assess the true drop-out rate of the school, for it depended on whether one took the base year in the analysis as the incoming cohort and then traced how many graduated four years later or the year-to-year drop out rate, i.e. if someone failed to register in the 12th grade and could not be found in the educational system. If the former is the case then around 50 percent was the number I was told by many of the teachers. If the latter is the accepted method, then the percentage was around 15 percent according to the school's records at the time, while the average attendance was 77 percent, one of the lowest in the city, as one teacher told me: "What they're doing is denying everything. Out of 500 in the freshman year there were 400 sophomores and 200 who graduate. But you know they can't say

that. That's not acceptable. No-one wants to hear it but until somebody does then nothing is going to happen" (November 25, 1991).

3 The main groups were the Almighty Latin King and Queen Nation, the Ñetas, Zulu Nation and La Familia.

4 The *New York Times* recently ran an editorial under the heading "In Search of Second Chances." It was prompted by a recent report highlighting the extent to which citizens are prevented from fully participating in civil life. The report stated that at least 65 million people in the United States have a criminal record (which was gained because they were in prison or arrested) and that "This can trigger severe penalties … Laws can restrict or ban voting, access to public housing, gun possession and professional and business licensing. They can affect a person's immigration status, parental rights, credit rating, ability to get a job, and eligibility for benefits."

5 Prior to the conference I had given a half-hour interview to radio station 1010 WINS News, a local subsidiary of CBS, about the aims of the event and who might be participating. During the interview I mentioned that members of street organizations/gangs would be attending from various parts of the United States, including Los Angeles. I explained that various social actors related to the gang issue would be presenting and participating, including public school teachers, social workers, community leaders, trade unionists, media workers, academics, gang members, film-makers, etc. The radio station took a single sentence from the interview in which I referred to the participation of LA gang and ex-gang members who will participate on panels with Latin Kings from New York and other such groups and repeatedly broadcast it for several days, billing the conference as a "gang summit." Needless to say on the day of the conference there was a heavy presence of the local gang task force who stationed their cars prominently around the institution. On the second day of the conference various journalists went in search of a "story" related to violence at the conference. No such violence happened and on the second day members and leaders of the local Bloods group and the Latin Kings/Queens signed a peace pact on the steps of John Jay College. Such news never made it into any corporate media outlet at the time.

6 COINTELPRO is the acronym for the Counter Intelligence Program started by the FBI in 1956 that continued in operation until the early 1970s. It was designed to infiltrate and subvert the actions of domestic political groups that the FBI deemed "subversive."

7 RICO stands for Racketeer Influenced and Corrupt Organizations Act, passed in 1970 under then President Richard Nixon. It was originally intended to combat the power of the US Mafia but has since been used against a range of subjects including leftists and, increasingly, street gangs.

8 The decline of violence and crime in the United States over the last two decades alongside the continuing appearance of gangs has to be explained and yet it rarely is addressed in the literature.

7

THE NEED FOR A CRITICAL GANG STUDIES

> Thinking is a struggle for order and at the same time comprehensiveness. You must not stop thinking too soon – or you will fail to know all that you should; you cannot leave it to go on forever or you will burst. It is this dilemma, I suppose, that makes reflection, on those rare occasions when it is more less successful, the most passionate endeavour or which the human being is capable.
>
> (Mills 1959:223)

In the following I have isolated five themes that are useful to consider if we are to approach the gang from a critical and increasingly global perspective to understand the structure, the drift and the meanings (see Mills above) of this phenomenon in a world that is made and remade. These themes have all emerged from observations and data from the field or via collaborations with an international array of gang researchers drawn from different disciplines. They might be seen as foci within a set of perspectives that depart from the usual orthodoxy in gang studies and in particular from the increasingly dominant criminal justice approach to the subject. There is a growing body of research studies, both within and outside the United States, that support and inform some of these areas and together could begin to constitute a critical study of the gang. I have listed them in no

Recuerdo de mi Visita al Palacio de Carondelet
Quito, 22 de agosto del 2007

FIGURE 7.1 Members of the Ecuadorian Latin Kings in the Presidential Palace of Ecuador's President Rafael Correa. Image courtesy of Fernando Zambrano.

particular order and the foci will to some degree depend on the access of the researcher to these groups and his/her sociological/criminological imagination, interests and training. The list is not supposed to be exhaustive but rather a summary of some of the most glaring omissions in gang research that has suffered from the general pathologization of the gang and, in particular, from the overwhelming emphasis on violence and drugs in relation to gang formation and membership.

Social citizenship and transnationalism

In many countries where gangs proliferate there is a direct link to the lack of social citizenship, or what T.H. Marshall (1950) famously defined as: "from the right to a modicum of economic welfare or security to the right to share to the full the social heritage and to live the life of a civilized being to the standards prevailing in society."[1] The lack of social citizenship is particularly apparent in neo-liberal times when the state is withdrawing from its obligation to its citizens (and residents). A critical approach to gangs would have to begin from this premise that societies with low rates of social citizenship and high rates of transnationalism will likely experience high rates of gang membership.

In the United States, with its large number of undocumented residents, hundreds of thousands of "deportable aliens" and residents/ citizens who live their lives between nation states, the gang can provide a group setting, a sense of belonging and an identity through which to resolve one's in-betweenness. Such youth may seek to reaffirm or anchor their cultural and ethnic identities via this medium, thereby creating their own imagined community. These populations, unloosed by both the porosity and reinforcement of borders in late modernity, are one reason for the multiplication of gangs at the global level in certain socio-political areas. Within such areas we also see intense geographies of exclusion (Sibley 1995), for example as stigmatized emigrants are repatriated with the mark of the felon and the failure, which of course compounds the lack of social citizenship.

Central America, as mentioned, is an excellent example of such a space where gang proliferation has been principally caused by the mass expulsion of undesirable/undeserving immigrants from the United States. This might be seen as the unintentional consequences of the US policy to export its social problems during an era of extreme security state punitiveness and/or the consequence of integrating its "impossible subjects" (Ngai 2004). But gang transnationalism is found in many settings. In Europe we also see the phenomenon as immigrant youth "sin papeles," i.e. the undocumented, join and form street groups/gangs to survive socially, economically and culturally. Some of these youth, after losing their lifelines in depression/recession-hit Southern Europe, have been cast adrift by the global labor market and the particular ways capital is being accumulated on the European stage. Others are the children of adults who migrated during better times from developing countries, particularly in Latin America. Both are seeking some form of stability, place and societal attachment and the gang provides a level of sociality and acceptance that is difficult to attain in Western Europe with its racialized policing practices, border controls and politics of containment, all of which have intensified under the pressures of an ascendant extreme-right. In New York we saw street organizations perform a similar transnationally supportive role when members from the Dominican Republic, for example, felt the pressures of "liminal legality" (Menjivar 2006),[2] or among Puerto Rican youth who felt both culturally alienated and socially subordinate and hence invented their own nation within a nation.

These groups are in similar though different circumstances to those imagined in classic Chicago renditions of urban social disorganization. The borders of Thrasher's day were different zones to those of today with little of the contemporary militarization, surveillance and punishment meted out at these points of transit (Miller 2014).[3] This analytical issue of borders is crucial for an understanding of the contemporary formation of gangs and as legal, political, social and cultural entities. It is, as Mendoza-Denton has argued, a way to see history collide and given meaning by these subcultures at the base of society.

But who or what is going to redraw these boundaries such that they make sense to these vulnerable communities? In late modernity it is precisely the liquidity of daily life that is a chief characteristic of the era, reinforced inevitably by the penchant for societies to adopt market fundamentalism (see Somers 2008) as some form of panacea for so many of our social and economic problems. What is the meaning of citizenship, therefore, in this environment where risk and deep levels of precariousness are the norm? This question is crucial and in many ways is the elephant in the room in so many gang studies regardless of the location.

The intersectionality of the gang

It is difficult to approach the gang today without thinking seriously about its race/ethnic, gender and class make-up and where these analytic and constructed categories intersect. However all these categories are unstable. Gender, for example, is constructed along a continuum, intersecting with race, ethnicity and class in multiple ways. The gang adapts to these categories, reinforcing some while undermining others, producing what appear to outsiders as certain overtly gendered norms and practices (captured stereotypically in the notion of hyper-masculinity) while other norms are closeted, concealed and not so easily revealed. In the generalized communities outside of the gang these norms are also in flux, with traditional familial roles, especially in cross-cultural settings, under a great deal of pressure.

For example, females might use the gang to assert their independence to break from traditional models and expectations within their ethnic culture. Males might similarly utilize gang membership to live up to their gendered expectations but beneath their assumed and often master status might live another life involved in quite different sexualized subcultures. Flores (2014) argues, drawing on ethnomethodological sociology, that gender is done in gangs and is created in negotiations both within the gang and outside of it. He concludes that gang masculinities are fluid and this is particularly the case as members seek ways out of the subculture.[4] Mendoza-Denton (2008) shows how gender and ethnicity are closely linked in gangs facing a demeaning colonizing society that produces different forms of cultural resistance rather than cultural conformity, while others (e.g. Miller 2001 and Campbell 1991) argue that the gang helps to reproduce gendered subordination. Beyond the United States, Steinberg's (2004) work on prison gangs in South Africa reveals highly organized same-sex relations within these subcultures in a generalized culture that is heavily homophobic.[5]

Empirically in my own work I have observed a range of gender-related sexualities within the gang scene that are never referred to in the literature. While researching the ALKQN during the 1990s members of the group approached my research partner Luis Barrios to ask if he could help negotiate a social and political space to allow them to come out openly as gay-identified. Luis raised the issue with the leader at the time, King Tone, who, while receptive to the idea, thought that the majority of the members were not ready for such a development. Another group, the Ñetas, we studied in New York and Puerto Rico around the same time allowed gay-identified inmates and transsexuals into its membership in prisons. It was the only prison "gang" that openly did so and was a result of the group's early days in Puerto Rico when it went to war against "Los Insectos" and gay-identified prisoners allied with the Ñetas against the abuse of the guards as well as the predatory practices of other inmates. In Brooklyn, one of the leaders of the Bloods gang in recent years was a gay-identified female who was very politicized and militant and a fervent advocate of gay rights. In short, we have observed a range of masculinities and feminities in gangs that contrast strongly with both hyper-masculine and submissive feminine stereotypes.

Class identities and locations are similarly going through multiple changes and belie many assumptions of outsiders as well as the tropes reproduced in much gang criminology. The notion of the underclass gang, for example, while still relevant in some quarters (see Hagedorn 1998), is not a characteristic of all such groups or its members despite the era of post-industrialism. We found the Latin Kings and Queens in New York and in Europe to be largely part of the working classes, with members engaged in both the formal and informal economies (but not necessarily the drugs economy). In other settings with high rates of unemployment and underemployment the gang may have a different class constitution and its character will depend on the opportunity structures available to its members.

The issue of class is complicated, however, by the different approaches to this category and whether we adopt an orthodox sociological analysis using socio-economic status (i.e. SES usually based on income, education and occupation) as a framework or a more Marxist approach that sees class membership in relationship to the ownership of the means of production and exchange. In such an approach we would be interested in the level of class-consciousness of the membership and how such a class awareness is manifested in the activities of the group and its ideological properties (see also White 2013 on conditions in Australia).

Finally, regarding race and ethnicity, we assume that race itself is a social construction and therefore changes markedly across society. The meaning of "Blackness" in the United States, where it is primarily applied to those with African-American heritage, is not the same as in Britain where it often includes subjects from the Caribbean and East Asia. In South Africa it is different again, especially due to the residual effects of apartheid, and in Brazil, with its myth of a racial democracy (Oliveira 1996), the construction and identification process is of great contrast. Moreover, subjects with mixed ancestry are often denied part of their identity; this is particularly true of Black Latino/as in the United States, partly because the United States has often operated on a dualism (i.e. black and white) in race-ethnic relations, and the extraordinary range of race-ethnic identities and heritages become lost in this dichotomizing discourse.

Further, we now live in what some call a hyper-pluralist world (Young 2011) with constant and rapid changes in population demographics and cultural hybridity increasingly the norm, all of which are particularly noticeable in urban and urbanizing areas. These processes are leading to the reconfiguration of traditional race and ethnic enclaves where lines of spatial separation were reinforced not just by culture but by institutional discrimination and overt white supremacy in different national contexts. Thus, racism and racial constructions are certainly alive and well and many gang-prone youth are still schooled in unofficially segregated schools and neighborhoods in the United States while they might attend highly racially marginalized public schools in Latin America where the white middle and upper classes would never send their children.

Nevertheless the racial-ethnic results for the gang are extremely diverse, as I have witnessed through my own research, and as is reinforced in on-the-ground studies by other critical researchers, which is not at all to deny the impact of racial structures on the dynamics of marginalization (see Vigil 2002). For example, in Chicago Conquergood (1992) referred to the range of ethnicities in his long-term ethnographic study of the Latin Kings (whose founder is actually Italian-Puerto Rican), whereas in Spain Palmas (2010) reveals the variety of ethnicities in the same group.[6] In Los Angeles Weide (2014) writes about the numbers of Latino/as in black–dominated gangs and vice versa, while in South Africa, Steinberg (2004:53)[7] recounts the extraordinary development of the "numbers" prison gangs under the strict racial coding system of apartheid, as he describes:

> And so the three camps were formed, each with their self-made philosophies of banditry and their collectively assigned roles. The 26s were to accumulate wealth, which was to be distributed among all three camps, and acquired through cunning and trickery, never through violence. The 28s, in turn, were to fight

on behalf of all three camps for better conditions for inmates. They would also be permitted to have sex, in their own ritualized manner, among themselves. They were never to touch a 26.

As for the 27s, they were the guarantors of gang law; they were to keep the peace between the three camps. They would learn and retain the laws of all three gangs, as well as the laws of the relationships between gangs. And they would right wrongs by wreaking revenge; when blood is spilled, they would spill blood in turn.

Gangs and the politics of space

I wrote earlier of the importance of situated space and place in understanding the formation and evolution of street gangs. Of course, this was originally comprehended by the Chicago School, with its emphasis on social ecology; however in the world of rapidly privatized public space, the emergence of global cities, the increasing urbanization of both developed and developing societies and the maze of legal codes aimed at controlling the dangerous classes,[8] the question of spatial politics is essential to a critical appreciation of the gang. An example of such an approach is that of my colleague Lucas Palmas (2014:93) who has analyzed the five different field sites in our collaborative research, creating a comparative grid (see Table 7.1).

For Palmas the struggle for space[9] is appreciated through looking at groups in their relationship to local governmental forces, the politics of such government entities and the memberships of the various groups. Based on their complex interaction within the larger politics of the society, Palmas argues that it is possible to discern an evolved spatial position of the group that reflects both subcultural and dominant cultural power dynamics working themselves out through discourses and social practices, from crime control to youth empowerment to immigration and settlement and post-colonial cross-national relations. Gangs, thus, represent a highly expressive form and segment of the urban subaltern and their spatial imprint on society, while it can be interpreted and measured in a discourse of danger and threat, can also be seen as both a spontaneous and a conscious effort at creating a counter-public.

TABLE 7.1 Street organizations, young Latinos and local political spaces

	New York	Genoa	Barcelona	Quito	Santo Domingo
Aims of local governmental politics	Contrast between the street economy and businesses linked to the world of gangs	Recognition of the social goals of the group and their visibility in public spaces	Legalization and issuance of democratic statutes enabling the establishment of a democratic association.	Recognition, issuance of democratic statutes enabling the establishment of a democratic association at the national level	Involvement in community actions in the poorest neighborhoods
Key actors	City council, police, correctional system, media, academia	City council, university, social centers, spaces occupied as community centers, absence of public management of process	Strong management by city council/local bodies; social research and non-profit involvement	City council, university, and government	Presidential Commission on AIDS; neighborhood associations and non-profits
Membership characteristics	Ethnic minorities in segregated neighborhoods	First and second generation immigrants, often undocumented	First and second generation immigrants, often undocumented	Citizens, youth from the most impoverished neighborhoods	Citizens, deportees from the United States, youth from the poorest neighborhoods
Results	Imprisonment; invisibility of the group; reproduction of street economy	End of inter-group violence and major increase in group's social capital plus more legitimacy in public spaces	End of inter-group violence and major increase in group's social capital plus more legitimacy in public spaces	Increase in social capital and legitimacy in public spaces	Legitimacy and recognition of social value in public spaces

Source: table courtesy of Lucas Palmas.

The role of the state is central to his analysis though it is understood not simply from above, through its structures, rules and *pronunciamentos*, but from below and within, through the eyes and articulations of state agents and their impacts on and interrelationships with gang-related youth. From a critical perspective, the politics of space is intrinsically linked to the politics of security and the emerging role of the state in late modernity. In the United States this is manifestly obvious with the various wars against the Other, but there are similar processes clearly present in the states of exception as decreed in Central America or the pacification programs aimed at privatizing and clearing the slums and favelas of Brazil in the interests of big capital. Virtually all such coercive social control policies implemented by the state under various auspices involve a spatial cleansing of gangs which unites the class interests of elites with state bureaucracies, systems of (in)justice and militarized apparatuses.

Such a complex, multi-layered spatial analysis is present to different degrees in the work of Zilberg and her notion of security space in the context of El Salvador, Hagedorn's (2008) and Venkatesh's (2000) gang research vis-à-vis the race-based and spatial demarcations of Chicago,[10] Davis' (1990) radical geography of Los Angeles, Mendoza-Denton's (2008) Latina socio-linguistic research tied to hemispheric gang localism in California, Gutierrez Rivera's (2013) political geography of the "maras" in Honduras and less directly Caldeira's excavation of the race and class-based redivision of Brazilian cities or Sassen's (2014a:222) recent treatment of global systems of expulsion and her concluding question: "what are the spaces of the expelled?" All of these studies point to the reconstituted role of space and can be interpreted as a politically infused socio-economic and cultural analytic, especially if the gang is conceived as occupying and developing alternative subterranean grids and counter-spaces to those of the dominant society.[11]

However, there is still an important ingredient that is frequently omitted in such discussions: gangs in prison. To date there is missing a rigorous analysis of the spatio-political relations between the street gang and the prison gang. How is prison space configured by the "gang" (see Steinberg 2004)? What lies between the prison and the street? How do gang members negotiate space after prison in the security state (see Goffman 2013)? Despite the decades-long mass incarceration industry in the United States and the expansion of prisons in many other societies these zones of inquiry receive relatively little attention. Perhaps this reflects the difficulties of doing such research, but it is also likely the result of the dearth of critical questioning of the current gang phenomenon.

The culture of gangs

One would think that the culture of gangs would be foremost in gang research, but this is far from the case. It is still largely the background narratives of gangs that are privileged over their foregrounds. Cultural criminology,[12] in particular, has insisted that research needs to approach the subject from the opposite direction and that without understanding the cultural and existential life of gangs[13] the meaning of gangs is lost and the crucial naturalistic warnings of Matza (Chapter 3) are ignored. Gangs and gang members become little more than the cardboard cut-outs of urban, "dark" stereotypes (Conquergood 1992).

Contemporary street gangs wherever they are found are engaged in intense cultural projects, especially as they tap into the network society (Castells 1997). There are few street gangs today whose members do not utilize social media to broadcast their reputations or claim their space in the virtual world. Papachristos (2005) talks about the virtual street corner, no doubt reflected in the fact that most police gang units devote considerable resources to tracking this development as part of their intelligence-gathering endeavors.

Aside from the Internet I have argued that we need to think more concretely about the cultural gang and its relationship to resistance as well as to social reproduction. As mentioned, gangs are producers of an extraordinary array of cultural meanings, some of which are gratefully exploited by capitalist enterprises as part of the global culture industry. Nonetheless, such subcultures are ongoing incubators of a staggeringly wide-ranging semiotic fare, with the rites, rituals and resistances that befit their location between the aporias of late modern capitalism, globalization and post-colonial relations. A critical gang studies would have to address the following:

Spiritualities and syncretism

In the United States many gangs express themselves through both religious symbolism and syncretic narratives. This has been the case for some time but seems particularly to have been enhanced in the post-1960s period when gangs started to reclaim or assert their identities as part of an oppressed people, with the language and rhetoric of organized and more popular religious belief systems becoming integrated into gang texts and ideologies. Below, for example, the authors recount the spiritual evolution of Chicago's Almighty Black P. Stone Nation in the 1970s:

> When he first joined the Stones, Harris was given a uniform along with a list of bylaws that explained the dos and don'ts of membership. Among them were: no drinking in public, no drugs, no fighting each other, respect the black woman. He also received background about the meaning of his uniform. The new teaching of the MSTA explained the older Blackstone uniforms. The red beret stood for the blood of the black people, who were supposed to be descended from the Berber tribe in West Africa that the white man later named Moors, who invaded Spain. Harris was told that the Romans threw one of the leaders – who donned a white fez that represented purity and godliness – from the Berber tribe into a lion's pit, they discovered that the white fez was now red with blood. The green represented the motherland of Africa, and the black jump boots symbolized the black man's foot upon the white man's neck.
>
> (Moore and Williams 2011:137)

Despite a range of gangs clearly adopting religious insignia such as beads (from rosaries), tattoos of the Virgen de Guadalupe, prayers (for example the many benedictions of the ALKQN and the Ñetas), the Islamic-influenced texts and norms of African-American groups such as the 5 Percent Nation and the group mentioned above, the natural disciplinary home of such research, the sociology of religion, has shown little inclination to explore this domain. Two recent studies by Flores (2014)[14] and Brenneman (2011)[15] provide some insights into these spiritual-gang relationships, both focusing on religion as a vehicle to exit gangs, but there is scarcely a study (apart from our own earlier work) on how gangs absorb and appropriate the symbols of and/or express a syncretic spiritual outlook. In the literature the relationship is frequently dismissed despite many gang-related youth coming from very religious backgrounds. Thus it should not be surprising that baptisms, weddings and deaths are often celebrated with overtones that are strongly religious, nor is it illogical that many of the primary outreach efforts come from priests, particularly progressive clergy who seek to connect to those deemed so marginal and soulless. From a critical perspective we need to explore these dimensions of the gang world and see how religio-spiritual narratives such as those in the quote above are used to create a metanarrative for the group. Of course the pathological interpretation of these tendencies is that the gang is building a cult-like following behind a charismatic leader, and perhaps there is some truth to this in certain cases, but it willfully ignores the inner dimensions of youth and adults who are often dealing with extreme levels of social and physical trauma and whose psycho-social as well as political needs are many.

Gang embodiment

Tattoos, physical gestures, and various forms of clothing are all the typical subjects of media and certain academic treatments when it comes to gangs and embodiment. We seek a critical sociology and criminology of the body to better understand why the gang is represented in this way, turning to the body as a space and site of signification to insert the group and the individual in to a specific landscape of signs. Within the gang these signs are languages unto themselves and, of course, tattooing has a long history, particularly in incarcerated communities, but the body for many gang members is their natural canvas. It is the one place that they can control and if it means dying for that then so be it. In a world that is so chaotic, stigmatizing and excluding it is quite natural for the subjected to declare themselves present, to rupture their silencing and invisibility on the only platform available to them. The gang body, then, has multiple uses, meanings, properties and possibilities that have still to be appreciated and, of course, it often changes from group to group. In many respects the history of the group is written on the body just as it is often written on the walls of its territory, if it claims one.

But more than this, the body is a site to be controlled by the state and where possible made "docile" (to borrow from Foucault). The presence of the gang in neighborhoods not only represents a threat to public security, as often surmised by law enforcement; it is a challenge to the presumed calm of the normalized social order. This is why groups of three are defined as a gang by many police and judicial authorities, which enables such authorities to proscribe such bodies from a certain area, hence the proliferation of injunctions. I would argue that this proscription of the gang body relates to the authoritarian urges in contemporary society just as we saw such proscriptions meted out to more overt political bodies such as communists, anarchists and socialists in the past.

Conquergood, gangs and communications/performance

Again it was Conquergood who was one of the first to shine a light on the complex communicative systems used by gangs to convey their innermost meanings to each other and to the outside society. What was often misread simply as primitive gang graffiti by outsiders (particularly the police) was interpreted by Conquergood as a deep expression of the subculture's place in society and its internal economy of signs used to convey threat, sorrow, hope, peace, disapproval and other displays of collective emotion and identity (Conquergood 1997). He called this a form of street literacy and contrasted it to the literacy of texts and codes produced by the dominant culture which frequently used them to marginalize, control and criminalize gang members in communities that often felt like occupied zones. Drawing on multiple disciplinary sources his gang research became an important part of the growing field of performance studies, with communication by means of texts, speech, gestures, graffiti, clothing and bodily adornments all incorporated into a plastic system of street vernacular that has emerged over time within a field of contested urban power relations.

Both the written and visual analysis of communications vis-à-vis gangs is critical in a world saturated by images and copies of the

Other and various struggles for authenticity (and against exoticism). A critical study would draw on these activities, practices and elements of the gang culture, radically listening to and observing the articulations of the creators, archiving their creations and documenting the impacts they have at both the micro and macro levels of society (e.g. the torrent of images that are created as societies go to war against the gang Other and the reaction of the gang to such images, or the rise of global hip-hop and the powerful influence of gangs as subjects, progenitors and settings).

Conquergood felt that it was difficult to capture adequately the "moral outrage and repression"[16] that such literacy spoke to and of. He assumed that such cultural products were an essential part of a gang's subjugated knowledge, which consisted of: "street sense, survival wisdom, underground history, cultural codes, and protocols of communication" (Personal Communication 1999). In an articulation of the felt exclusion/inclusion dialectic of gang members living under the constant gaze of the state he says the following:

> The insult of effacement is compounded by surveillance. In the ocular politics of the ruling classes, subordinate groups are expunged from spaces of respectability, and then rendered hyperinvisible in the surreal zone of the panoptic power.

It is in responding to such pressures and infiltrations that gangs produce communications that are extremely contradictory, i.e. both overt and secret, opaque and transparently clear, camouflaged and pointedly direct. Conquergood felt that these subjugated knowledges could be seen as constituting an alternative street curriculum, which for him meant "all the manifold genres of cultural performance" (Personal Communication 1999), including the global development of hip-hop influenced by various outlaw subcultures and, of course, the gang. I would argue that there is no better place to start a critical study of gang communications than with Conquergood's rich theoretical and empirical legacy.

Resistance or social reproduction?

This issue of resistance versus social reproduction in the actions and practices of gangs/street organizations is extremely important for

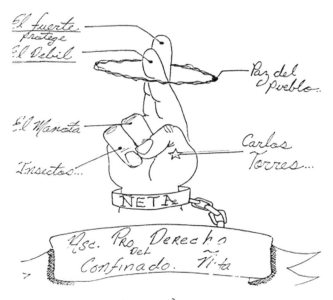

FIGURE 7.2 A hand sign from the Ñetas group in which each finger connotes a different meaning and relationship depicting the history of the group.
Source: Street Organization archives.

any critical research. To what extent do these subaltern groups break through their structured confines and transgress or subvert existing power relations such that a new imaginary is constructed? Do the ideological "penetrations" by these gang members of these often colonizing structures always succumb to the habitus and to their "limitations" (Willis 1977)? If gangs are creating counter-publics what are they a counter to?[17]

As I have already pointed out, I found quite different group formations on the West and East Coasts, which was especially highlighted by the level of street politics in New York City compared to San Francisco. This, in turn, was quite different to the research emerging from Chicago and Los Angeles and the more resistance-based street subcultural worlds outside of the United States, for example in Spain, Italy and Ecuador. Clearly, both resistance and social reproduction are going on simultaneously in many gang subcultures, which evolve and pass through different stages and processes of development. Levinson (2008) makes this point with regards to the street gangs in Guatemala, for example, and Rivera (2013) asks why the maras in Honduras are not more like street organizations. A critical project would subject the actions/practices, symbols, cultural products, ideologies and intentionalities of these groups to a test of these two analytical categories as opposed to the assumptions of most orthodox interpretations that they are generally socially reproductionist.

Gangs, violence and the political economy

Finally, we come to a brief discussion of the topic that most gang studies begin with. Throughout this book I have tried to place the gang in relationship to the changing pressures of the political economy and its mediations through social agents. It is impossible to see the gang without this context, but it is context and not simply a determining structure in the sociological and criminological causal sense. Structures can be made and unmade; nonetheless they frame what we do and crucially provide an array of resources, both containing and liberating, depending on the balance of class forces in any historical moment and the dominant ideas of the day.

In the current period, from a critical perspective, it would be folly to ignore the violence engaged in by gang-related youth and adults. I have attended my share of gang funerals and wakes and visited the homes of grieving family members and friends of gang youth whose lives have been ended so prematurely through the dramas of the street – ended not just by other gang members but by the police or other state-paid agents. Thus any research on the gang and violence relationship must deal with the following:

Direct and indirect violence and the gang

While it is important to engage all aspects of the foreground of gang behavior, so much attention is placed on interpersonal and intergroup violence that the relationships of such acts and group norms to the structured environment, or what Salmi (1993) calls "indirect violent" (see also Galtung 1969), is often occluded or not coherently expressed. Violence itself is often wedged into a dualism of either being expressive or instrumental, but the complexity of the violent act, its psycho-social, cultural, transactional and behavioral manifestation and its contingent social setting is what should set the critical perspective apart. There is no substitution for the direct observation of such acts over time. It must always be remembered that there are myriad ways to interpret such violence regardless of whether it is said to be tied to clear goals through a vocabulary of motives of the perpetrator or not.

Further, we need to understand much better the levels of state violence within these vulnerable communities and the cultures of exclusion and social humiliation that fuel the interlocking processes of the internally violent encounter. Sampson (2013), for example, argues that in cities as different as Chicago and Stockholm it is possible to see similar trends in neighborhoods with high rates of violence and relatively high rates of infant mortality and other negative health outcomes related to poverty. Of course, one cannot make a causal link here but there is always a host of correlations, both weak and strong, that need to be explored within a critical sensibility that can make the case for what I earlier described as a holistic approach to situated agency, within which violence could be one of a number of foci.[18]

Narcotics trade and the gang

While certain street gang members are involved in the drugs trade it is not the case that all gangs have this characteristic, nor do street gangs make particularly good entrepreneurial conduits for a trade that is normally based somewhere else, usually with strong ties to society's elites. Street gangs that become corporatized (Venkatesh 1997) as drug gangs represent particular forms of the gang and undergo quite specific changes in an historical context. However, the drugs trade should be seen as part of a broader informal economy that has grown immeasurably due to the restructuring and deregulation of the formal capitalist economy (Venkatesh 2006), forcing many poor communities to rely heavily on this sub-economy especially as provisions of the welfare state have been massively cut back and we enter an endless period of "austerity."

Nonetheless, it is important to seek historical parallels between this illegal trade and the penchant of the state to "legislate morality" (Duster 1970). A number of researchers have drawn parallels between the entrepreneurial transformation of such groups and the period of Prohibition in the United States, which created a massive black market for alcohol and saw the growth of organized crime with the involvement of various street groups in the profitable sale of this commodity (Hayden 2004). When crack was introduced into the inner cities during the 1980s, during the deindustrialization of the United States and the restructuring of the economy, a number of researchers saw two important developments: (1) gang members were less likely to mature out of the gang and into meaningful employment, and (2) the opportunity structures of poor neighborhoods changed, with drugs becoming an equal opportunity employer and inter-gang violence escalating, driven by turf wars and various other socio-economic tensions related to the now debilitated social fabric of an already vulnerable community (Fagan 1996, Hagedorn 1988, 1998).

But how should this development be viewed critically without engaging in more pathologizing of the gang and its social habitat? How do we study gangs, drugs and violence without accepting the tropes of the dominant culture or the orthodox, largely empiricist discourses that get endlessly repeated at criminology and criminal justice conferences without a shred of theory or sociological/criminological imagination? A critical inquiry must start with the historical emergence of the phenomenon and then a situated analysis of both the players and the structures within which the purported relationship has emerged, cognizant of the need to constantly question the analytical categories we are employing. Further, we need to look not just down but up and see the links between the phenomena and those more powerful interests that are intrinsically involved in all aspects of the political economy, both formal and informal.

For example, one of the most powerful and most violent gangs in Mexico at the moment is the Zetas, made up principally of ex-police officers from a so-called elite anti-drug squad. The drug cartels in Colombia have long been related to governing political parties with the vast sums of money that accrue from the global cocaine trade, routinely washed by mainstream banks with global reaches.[19] In the Dominican Republic, one of the centers of the Caribbean illicit drugs trade it is no secret that this informal economy would not exist or be so prevalent without the complicity of the military and the police or and the connections to leading politicians, including the presidency.

Consequently, any discussion of the drugs trade and the corresponding violence that is usually linked to street gangs must be placed and excavated in these contexts, within these sets of relationships and with these provisos. Further, it is impossible to talk about these aspects of the global political economy without citing the amplifying effects of US-dominated global drug policy which has given us the infamously failed "War on Drugs" (see Phillips (2012) for a particularly edifying case study set in Los Angeles) as well as the highly vindictive and socially corrosive "Mano Dura."

And finally, it is incumbent on any research into these relationships to consider the social harm caused by the drugs trade on gangs and the surrounding community through the use of highly addictive narcotics. Since many gang members with histories of drug use and abuse come from areas with the least health service availability it is likely that they are not receiving the kinds of treatment therapy their condition requires. Such an analysis will require deep inquiry into the politics of health in poor communities and the particular trajectories of drug-using gang members who often have to rely on internal resources to treat their habit or sustain their recovery.

Gangs and peacemaking

Finally, it is essential that we recognize that while gangs are organizations that emerge from marginalization and various forms of social conflict which they themselves often engage in, they are also profoundly social entities whose members seek resolutions to the various contradictions and problems they face on a day-to-day basis. Any gang researcher who has spent significant amounts of time in the field will be able to recount the countless efforts by gangs to resolve differences without resorting to violence. This, of course, sounds counter-intuitive, especially since most definitions of gangs

FIGURE 7.3 The leaders of the Latin Kings and the Ñetas in Genoa, Italy, after a bill was passed recognizing such groups as cultural organizations of immigrants. At the national press conference held after the vote Paolo Ferrero, the Italian Minister of Social Solidarity, said the following: "This national government of the left has a consciousness … this is why it must be in favor of this process in Genoa. Everybody has the right to hope, to dignified work, and to social services." Image courtesy of Luca Palmas.

ascribe to them the characteristic of seeking conflict to increase their cohesiveness or affirm their identity. On one hand this is true, since gangs are usually operating in a competitive arena in which groups vie to build their reputations and increase their status, however this is always done through a set of relationships which, in turn, are based on a range of individual and collective affiliations, e.g. group, familial, fictive kinship, friendship, ethno-racial, class, gender, neighborhood, etc. Consequently, it is hardly surprising that gangs are often involved in peacemaking activities as they seek to resolve differences through internal and external pressures.

Hayden (2004) takes up this point through his own involvement in gang truces in his former constituency in Los Angeles. He found working with both present and past gang members critical to the sustainability of any peace in areas with large numbers of competing gangs. But he makes a number of important observations that need to be taken into account in any research in this area. First, gang rivalries often have very long, complex histories, which must be considered before any lasting peace can be restored. Second, gangs are often rid-dled with informers working for the police, who make peace between groups not always easy to achieve. Third, there is often a strong rela-tionship between the street and prison in coming to terms with the dimensions of the conflict. Fourth, while conflicts can be regulated in the short term, perhaps through such interventions as "Operation Ceasefire" (which attempts to contain the contagion of violence as a social currency through the intervention of neighborhood peace-makers) or "Pulling Levers" (which asserts that most gang violence can be attributed to a few powerful figures in gangs, whose services and influence can be enlisted through threats of outstanding warrants and other "deterrents" while organizing open meetings for the gang in which job training and other incentives are proposed), Hayden argues that without long-term, guaranteed investment in these highly marginalized communities any reduction in violence will be short-lived. Hayden (2004:351) concluded that, while these interventions were more progressive than the "zero tolerance" or "broken win-dows" policing adopted elsewhere, they did not amount to a:

> structural reform or an institutional shift of power ... The police retained ultimate control of policy, operations, and, of course, budget. The ministers [involved as community go-betweens] represented a moral authority, a citizen base, and an ability to generate headlines. But the fundamental difference was that the police could deliver swift and certain punishment while the coalition [the organization of forces behind the intervention] couldn't deliver swift and certain jobs.

Consequently, while conflict often gets all the attention in gang research it is equally important from a critical perspective that we shift the gaze in understanding the gang and look more closely at what happens to the processes of peace that are started in gang communities.

We must take stock of the lessons that can be learned in furthering a more peaceful environment through considering both overt and covert power relations and the possibilities of reaching resolutions without recourse to coercive controls from above or the sowing of internal divisions through the classic strategies of social control (Durán 2013).

Conclusion

In this chapter I have discussed what I think could and should be some of the main foci for an alternative school of thought that I have termed critical gang studies. Naturally there is much more to say on this subject and there is beginning to develop a healthy amount of gang-related literature and research that bucks the highly uncritical positivist and empiricist trend in gang studies through the disciplinary lenses of criminology and criminal justice. I have emphasized the need for both a global and comparative approach to the topic and skepticism toward many of the organizing concepts we often inherit from a conformist social scientific discourse.

As in so many approaches to the study of social phenomena we only have to shift the gaze a small amount to see a very different picture of what we take to be the social problem. Gangs are particularly vulnerable to this partial and often prejudiced gaze as their construction is filled with the criminalizing and pathologizing tropes of the outside society. It is hoped that the student of gangs, armed with the tools of reflexivity and sensitive to the theater of absurdity that has often come to resemble this "upside down world," will get close enough to the gang world to ask the difficult questions and come away with the level of complex answers that the gang phenomenon intrinsically requires.

Notes

1 For an excellent contemporary study and application of the notion of social citizenship, particularly in relation to the victims of Hurricane Katrina, see Somers (2008).
2 Menjivar (2006) is simply referring to the legal ambiguity and "in-betweenness" of non-citizens, mainly undocumented immigrants. Their legal

status not only affects their relationship with the labor market but has profound socio-cultural implications, a focus which she argues is often missing from the literature.

3 "In *Border Patrol Nation*, I document a number of instances that could seem as if they were a part of an area under a state of exception. I describe people pulled out of cars and handcuffed, as gunmen crouch with their rifles pointed. I describe a Native American man pepper-sprayed by agents, pulled out of his truck and knocked briefly unconscious with a baton. I describe instances of home invasions and the Homeland Security tactic of the early morning raids, pounding on people's doors while they are still asleep, and handcuffing people who are still in bed and disoriented. In a way, you can describe the United States as a country in a constant low-intensity wartime posture, and if you fit a certain profile, if you have a certain skin complexion, an accent to your tone, are from a particular place in the globe, if you are associated with certain communities, or even carry certain political ideologies, you could be easily targeted by this enforcement regime.

In the conclusion, I also describe my hometown Niagara Falls, a city like many in the rust belt that has been left to disrepair, that has more than 5,000 derelict houses, buildings and churches, many collapsing before our eyes. There are potholes in some streets that look like craters, as if some bomb from above has already been dropped. A high poverty rate makes the streets, in places, look like they were filled with refugees. And likewise, there are some places in the city that look like it has already been blasted by the artillery, yet we still justify the billions and billions funneled into Homeland Security saying that the true, yet not-well-defined enemy, lurks on the other side of an international boundary line. In other words, it already looks like the war has come." (Interview with Todd Miller by Mark Karlin 2014)

4 Messerschmidt is a leading proponent of this approach to gender and masculinity, which he describes as follows: "men construct masculinities in specific social settings … the study of masculinities shows that men are involved in a self-regulating process whereby they monitor their own and others' gendered conduct. These practices, do not, however occur in a vacuum. Instead they are influenced by the gender ideals that we have come to accept as normal and proper and by the social structural constraints that we experience" (Messerschmidt 2001:67).

5 Formally, of course, South Africa has a set of progressive laws to protect the LGBT community, and was the first African country to recognize same-sex marriage, in 2006. However, there are many reports of violence against members of this community (see Human Rights Watch 2011).

6 Palmas (2008:120) reports "the research findings in Genova and Barcelona emphasize the presence of members from Russia, Peru, Rumania, Tamil, Pakistan, the Philippines, and other countries that have little to do with the rhetoric of the 'Latin race.'"

7 Steinberg goes on to describe how these gangs were formerly prison-only but how, with the opening up of South Africa to the rest of the world in 1990s, such gangs quickly transferred their subcultural norms to the street. How the gang is changing in post-apartheid society is the source of some debate in South Africa and its comparative development adds to the countless questions to be explored through a focus on gang intersectionality in a global theater.

8 For example in Los Angeles County alone there are over 100 gang injunctions, supposedly in efforts to control the movement and formation of these subcultures.

9 Hagedorn (2008) notes, for example, that the increase in "defensible space" in urban areas provides a strong impetus for new and continuing gangs that are committed to organized violence. His argument accords with many critiques of the neo-liberal city, particularly in developing nations, in which the city is seen as becoming increasingly stratified and fragmented, leading to cities within cities. Thus the gangs are left to maintain order and expand their control over the informal economy while the state concentrates its forces on a politics of containment rather than a commitment to provide universal public security. While this is certainly one trend it is by no means the only one, and it is important to be open to new sources of data and counter-intuitive developments in which the state does not necessarily remove itself from civil society and gangs do not automatically regress to the Hobbesian mean. As Katz and Jackson-Jacobs (2003:105) caustically note: "After Thrasher, criminologists have essentially been engaged in a graffiti war, competing to tag the gang and the gang member."

10 This work is in such contrast to that of Suttles (1968) who rarely mentions the police or the criminal justice system (it is literally never mentioned) at all in his classic highly Durkheimian and social ecological work on "ordered segmentation" and street-corner groups in a "slum" (the Adams area of Chicago).

11 Sampson's recent new Chicago School undertaking of explaining the enduring "neighborhood effects" on this great city is clearly an important contribution and, if read critically, supports this thesis on the politics of space. As Sampson concludes throughout, despite the impact of globalization in many areas of Chicago the slums are still the slums. "Durable spatial logic organizes or mediates much of social life, with neighborhoods and local communities a key component" (Sampson 2013:21). He argues, therefore, that while the structural is crucial to understanding change, e.g. capital accumulation (although he never engages a Marxist perspective), we cannot discount the extraordinary variety of social action and organization at the local level as residents struggle meaningfully with their range of stratified life chances. Gangs are obviously part of this living organism that is the community and place clearly matters. But the enduring political economy within which this struggle is embedded is never confronted either by the new or the old Chicago School.

12 An excellent, pithy description of cultural criminology is provided by Stephanie Kane (2004:315): "we fill the empty categories and shade the lines of significant difference with thick descriptions of everyday life in particular locales; we analyze the circulation of paradigms of institutional power, accounting for our positions on the insider-outsider axis and other determinants of information access; we have strategies for examining the centers from the edges; we take the time to establish ethical relationships of trust with the people with whom we seek dialogue; we speak in, record and transcribe discourse in languages other than our native (or otherwise familiar) tongues; we explore different ways of understanding and representing truth and authority."

13 Almost twenty years ago Decker and Van Winkle (1996) produced a study based on interviews with ninety-nine gang members in St. Louis that was informative but rarely delved into the layered cultural lives of the subjects or the complex interplay between background and foreground factors. Contreras (2012) does a better job more recently in his grounded interpretation of a gang of stick-up artists in the Bronx, aided by his own personal involvement in this subculture and his later training as a sociologist. This work is more in the vein of Bourgeois (1995), presenting the inner-city gang deviant as the violent outgrowth of racism, poverty and the intersecting cultures of the street at a time of a thriving crack economy.

14 Flores looked at Chicano gang members and their involvement in recovery as part of two ministries in Los Angeles.

15 Brenneman focused on the Evangelical church and the gangs in Central America, particularly looking at the movement out of gangs by their members and their adoption of the evangelical credo.

16 Who other than Conquergood would talk about the "moral outrage" of gang members? Most outsiders would see such subjects as either immoral or amoral but Conquergood again and again pointed out the deeply human personal and social properties of these groups and, if anything, saw the dominant society as largely immoral and amoral, which is one reason he was so committed to exposing the barbaric practice of the death penalty (see Conquergood 2013).

17 For example, Ferrell (2000) raises an important area of research which is rarely attempted in gang studies regarding the criminology of boredom. Drawing on both the Situationists and the Frankfurt School, Ferrell argues that a wide range of criminalized practices have developed in reaction to the collectivized boredom enforced by modernism. As he states (Ferrell 2000:293): "The deployment of carefully honed survival skills in dangerous situations, the on-the-spot integration of practiced artistry and illicit adventure, the embracing of emotional rituals that predate modernist rationality – all suggest experiences that are not boring, and not boring precisely because they recapture, if momentarily, the lost immediacy of self-made human experience."

18 Scholars from both left-liberal and neo-conservative perspectives have made a number of claims regarding gang violence that attempt to be

generalizable but tend to be highly apocalyptical. For example Downey (2004) and Hagedorn (2008) argue that gang violence has become so institutionalized due to the absolute (not relative) marginalization of so many youth across the globe that gangs have become quasi-armies of the poor based on a commitment to nihilism or the instrumentalist currency of the drugs trade rather than any socially conscious effort at planned resistance. Meanwhile Manwaring (2005) and Sullivan (1997) propose that street gangs have become not only universally pathologically violent but have their sights on national take overs and are actively working to bring about "failed states." Such divergent interpretations and views of the violent gang within popular and seductive narratives of global chaos and decay will likely gain a lot of adherents as we careen from crisis to crisis socially, politically and economically.

19 It is worth remembering the role of drugs money in the banking system during the 2008 financial "meltdown." Antonio Maria Costa, head of the UN Office on Drugs and Crime, said he has seen evidence that the proceeds of organized crime were "the only liquid investment capital" available to some banks on the brink of collapse last year. He said that a majority of the $350 billion of drugs profits was absorbed into the economic system as a result.

8
CONCLUSION

> What social science is properly about is the human variety,
> which consists of all the social worlds in which men [*sic*] have
> lived, are living and will live.

> (Mills 1959:132)

In this book I have attempted to offer an alternative way to think
about the street gang as just one of the extraordinary variety of social
worlds that Mills (above) encouraged us to study and ponder.[1] It is
an unabashed critical vision of the gang and I have mainly referred
to other critical voices in this endeavor. I do this unapologetically as
so many young students of gangs today rarely know that another way
of seeing and knowing the gang exists, such is the domination of an
orthodox, uncritical version of gang criminology and criminal justice,
especially in the United States. This is a pity since the original gang
research in the United States was so promising.

I began by arguing about the role of history in gang research and
the sad lack of attention it has received in most of it. This ahistor-
ical approach is rife in orthodox criminology and helps to remove
the street gang from its multivalent societal connections, formational

FIGURE 8.1 C. Wright Mills, leader of the radical sociology gang in the 1950s. Image courtesy of Nik Mills.

processes and community attachments. The gang has to be seen comparatively and across time and must be located in the materialist as well as symbolic conditions in and from which it is constructed. There is a rich body of critical social history with which students of gangs need to be acquainted before they can hope to conceive of the web of meanings that gangs produce as well as represent. Further, we need to see these groups with their own histories and their members as historical agents rather than as simply performers of social deviance or as pathological carriers of risk, which is the current preference in most criminal justice circles. It is crucially important for students to understand something about the history of capitalism, its uneven development and the class nature of society to fully appreciate the emergence and transformation of this social phenomenon.

I then discussed the different gazes and theoretical approaches to the gang and laid out both humanistic and Hobbesian perspectives as well as the more recent social reproductionist paradigms within which gangs have been studied. Each of these approaches I suggest has its problems, especially when it comes to a class analysis and the nature of the political economy, but I am especially critical of the

Hobbesian model which still dominates so much of the gang discourse particularly within any discussion of the gang's social control. I argue that few criminological students today know much about the sociology of knowledge within which the street gang has been crafted and explored, yet it is essential to understand how the gang has been constructed, reconstructed and deconstructed across the decades.

Thrasher's approach was open, based on a strong humanistic concern for youth and for a progressive, rational urban social development. Thus he resisted the temptation to pathologize and reify these groups in a dynamic Chicago buffeted by race and class pressures, the domination/dominion of capital and its accumulation and the major thrusts of both immigration and migration. Following the Chicago School came the humanist tradition, theoretically advanced by Merton and later developed by Cohen, Cloward, Matza and others; this work, so hopeful yet critical of the failings of the Good Society, has now firmly taken a back seat to an atheoretical positivism and empiricism reflective of neo-liberalism's dominance in the field. When theory is applied it is usually via a neo-conservative set of base assumptions under the aegis of control theory or, more recently, an amalgam of behaviorist root paradigms loosely termed theories of deterrence.

In contradistinction to these theories and in efforts to extend them, I am in favor of a situated resistance approach to the gang. A perspective that places the phenomenon in a dynamic historical location, viewed holistically in all its aspects of emergence and evolution and then working from the position of possibility. Unlike so many gang researchers I have followed the careers of street gangs and their members in multiple national and international settings and spent many hours in their company rather than waiting for my assistants to bring back the latest interview, survey or field note. I have long argued that there is an agency in the gang that can only be understood at the cusp of its dialectical relationship to society, at the point at which it reflects both its inclusion and exclusion. It is precisely out of this tenuous relationship that the gang exhibits a range of ambiguous meanings that we need to explore to better understand the transcendental qualities of the group for its members and its transformational, subversive potential.

I went on to discuss how a critical methodology might look in order to study the gang up close and in context. In this endeavor I support the approaches of critical ethnographers who struggle for a reflexive relationship with their subjects, continually questioning their epistemological assumptions and the politics and ethics of their roles. Such a methodology must not just focus on the gang per se but on the social controllers and those who are complicit in the extended work of the poor's pathologization. There is a rich tradition of rigorous qualitative work in this aream from the Chicago School on, but we need to carefully examine the strengths and weaknesses of these bodies of knowledge that reflect the domain assumptions and both research norms and possibilities of the time. In the contemporary period there is a dire need to hear other voices and to see our work as part of the ongoing struggle for a just society. This requires new types of data, new interpretations and a respect for the lived and felt experiences of those who are both everywhere and nowhere, be they in excluded neighborhoods saturated with consumerist ideology, prison confines whose populations are now almost a parallel state, or global no-go areas that function as cities within cities. The appeal of such research is starting to have more adherents as the gang becomes accepted as a global phenomenon.

And then there is the symbolic creation of the gang. The moral panics that are continuous and which have become intrinsic to society's inexorable processes of hyper-consumerism, commodification, stratification and social containment. We cannot underestimate the prevalence and utility of gang simulacra in the modern epoch for the industries that thrive off these images and narratives, particularly as the world increasingly views security in para-militaristic terms, replacing the pastoral imaginary of modernity with that which handily complements the power of financial elites.

Finally, I argue for a new school of thought, a critical gang studies that can measure up to the challenges of research in a world as complex and as global as ours. With post-industrial, precarious vistas staring most of us in the face the domination of the field by theoretically thin, politically empty and morally bereft perspectives leaves us with a growing vacuum of ideas, interpretations, methodologies, data and policies. As most gang research drifts along on automatic pilot the same tropes are repeated in journal article after journal article, usually based on "American" data, and doing so without a hint of

comparative contexts, social formations or processes. For those straying outside the canon the penalties are non-publication, denied funding and non-recognition of one's contributions through low impact
factor scores or some similar invidious metric conjured from schools
of business management. In a sardonic article the noted sociologist
Tom Scheff (1995:158) describes these specialized groups of academics as follows:

> The loyalty of academic gang members to each other and to
> the code of the gang is easily as fierce as that of street gangs.
> It is fortunate that academic gangs use words and not bullets,
> or the homicide rate would be at least as high as that of street
> fighters.

The heretical case of the esteemed pioneer of performance studies
Dwight Conquergood (Brotherton and Barrios 2004), as I have suggested, is a clear example for all to contemplate. A similar argument, of
course, was made by an array of critical scholars in the past. C. Wright
Mills called for a sociological imagination to combat the "habitual
distortions" (Mills 1959:24) of the discipline by grand theorists and
"specialists", particularly by "abstract empiricists"; Jock Young (2011)
invoked a criminological imagination to resist contemporary criminology's (particularly the US variety) awe of the methods of the dismal science and its practices of "voodoo criminology"; Stanley Cohen
powerfully argued "Against Criminology" (Cohen 1987), taking to
task the rising power of managerial and conservative criminology (as
well as critiquing other left and liberal traditions) although he had little idea then of the extent of this shift; and Foucault, of course, made
knowledge and power central to his critique of enlightenment forms
of punishment, cautioning us about what happens to those who stray
outside disciplinary boundaries (Foucault 1977).[2]

Despite these forebodings, I get the sense that the hermetically
sealed world of much gang criminology today is having a difficult
time maintaining its relevance if not its legitimacy for students who
have long wondered how the study of gang deviance could so assiduously avoid any mention of culture, politics or epistemology, or
deal with the inconvenient ambivalences of street action and social

reaction, or consider the possibility that states of exception might not just be for developing nations often said to have the characteristics of a failed state. For, despite the hubris of the United States constantly reminding the world of its democratic essentialism and superiority, it might itself be in just such a condition (Chomsky 2006). If gangs tend to find their reflections in each other as well as mirroring the contradictions of the enveloping society, it is important to bear this moment of historical demise in mind. This is true in particular when we compare the gangs in advanced capitalist society and those in developing and often neo-colonial nations.[3] So how then should we proceed?

While I have suggested a number of areas that are worth exploring to advance a more critical tradition there are surely others which students in different societal contexts and with other interests and training might prefer to undertake. One thing we can agree upon is that we need to move forward and away from these narrow discursive domains and pay more attention to what the participants of these subcultures are actually saying, doing and thinking.[4]

Perhaps recent insider accounts can help us do that (e.g. Durán 2013, Rios 2012, Weide 2014), plus working through long-established networks of informants embedded in local communities can bring us closer not only to the participants in the subcultures but the range of perspectives from neighborhood residents whose contextualization of the presence of gangs will also aid in this process (see for example Stoudt *et al.* 2012). Further, struggling for the development of theory, recognizing that so much more needs to be explained and explored far beyond extant Hobbesian imaginaries of crime can ever hope to address or even conceive, is an increasingly urgent undertaking. We are now theorizing in global cities whose youth experience, with greater intensity, unrelenting economic exclusion, cultural inclusion and extreme social liquidity. It is precisely in this world that, as Castells asserts, resistance identities prosper as power asymmetries inform and insinuate themselves into individual and collective identities which are in tension with the constraints, provisions and expectations of a global, networked capitalism evolving (or perhaps devolving) into different processual stages of development, overdevelopment and underdevelopment (Marable 2000). As Castells concludes:

we have also observed the emergence of powerful resistance identities, which retrench in communal heavens, and refuse to be flushed away by global flows and radical individualism. They build their communes around the traditional values of God, nation and the family, and they secure the enclosures of their encampments with ethnic emblems and territorial defenses.

(Castells 1997:356)

Continuing to situate (both discursively and socially) gang members within a colonizing discourse, one might ask: can they be viewed as a reaction to our disalienation, as Fanon (1965) would have it, as our souls become occupied by the state? Or, as Young might postulate, are they part of the contemporary and perhaps universal search for ontological security in late modernity? Is this, perhaps, one of the reasons such youth will never find those routes to attachment which are supposed to forestall that infamous condition known as "maladjustment"? Are they prototypically beyond the reach of the "legitimating identities" (Castells 1997) bequeathed by our socializing institutions, which very much belonged to those progressive epochs of modernity? Does the gang site represent a "third space," in the words of Soja (1996), an urban zone or frontier that is lived intensely through the roles, rituals and communicative systems of "bonded communitarians" (Conquergood 1993)?

It is not at all clear where we are headed. One thing is certain, however: many of the domain assumptions about these subcultures need to be seriously questioned and revisited in the light of changes to the political economy, the state, the production of culture, the politics of law enforcement and incarceration and the globalization processes we now take for granted. Meanwhile, of course, the same functionaries in the US criminal justice industry will continue to administer gang survey after gang survey (see Egley and Howell 2013) to the same law enforcement agencies over countless years, thereby creating all manner of graphs that supposedly tell us whether we are in a critical gang period, a lull, or something in between. All indicators, naturally, still point toward the gang as the problem sui generis and the usual empiricist reasoning abounds with unanswered questions, such as why is Los Angeles now the "epicenter" of gangs in the United States? Or, why is New York no longer the city with "critical" gang problems as it had been in the 1990s, the 1970s and as long ago as the 1880s?

It is not that the questions are themselves irrelevant but that the empiricist research used to answer them only exposes the thinness of the discourse and the lack of any social scientific imagination beyond the usual positivist banter that avoids systematic inquiry into the socio-historical processes behind intergenerational marginalization, white supremacy, mushrooming rates of relative deprivation and the vast interlocking systems of punishment and vindictiveness now enmeshing the poor and the most vulnerable from the cradle to the grave.

The lack of introspection compels one to question the levels of uncritical training provided in criminal justice colleges across the nation and beyond. But the policy recommendations, if there are any, are just as inadequate, prompting one to wonder whether we are caught in a time warp. Recently I was visited by a European police officer who also works among his country's gang-related youths and thought he would learn something comparatively by coming to the United States. I met him one afternoon after he had spent some time with one of New York Police Department's gang units. He sat shaking his head as I approached him. "I know you warned me but I thought they had evolved. No chance," he said. "After they showed me all their statistics and numbers of take-downs and which groups are poised to grow and which no longer posed a threat I asked them, 'don't you guys do anything on the prevention end?' They looked at me like I was crazy. 'That's for wusses' they said, 'we're not social workers.'"

He was not exaggerating the mindset, and it would seem to be getting worse, not better. In the United States our solutions still primarily lie within law enforcement and a range of half-baked programs aimed at belatedly changing the perspectives of individual youth by offering them some mediocre opportunities so they can change themselves, i.e. we are not the problem; they are. We do this rather than mobilizing them to change the world, convincing them that we are in this together, affirming with them that this brutally irrational societal condition cannot be tolerated for generation after generation but that they must become the subjects and not the objects of this history.

Thus, there continues to be little real thought given to prevention efforts or to any long-term solutions to the appalling prospects of inner-city youth whose life chances continue to dwindle as we wring our hands and wonder why non-elite college drop-out rates are so high, over 40 percent of inmates have never completed high school, social mobility has virtually ground to a halt, and the kids feel they are not alright.

Neither do we take seriously the legions of men and women graduating from prison, often traumatized after years in solitary, facing the world with no psychological counseling, no financial resources, often fragmented and non-existent family support and confronting extraordinary structural and societal constraints as well as prejudices that make reintegration difficult if not impossible. All this is occurring during what Harvey calls an investment strike by corporations, who prefer to transfer their massive accumulation of assets into forms of speculative capital rather than into jobs or socially useful plans to rebuild the nation's crumbling infrastructure. This question, of how is value accrued under current conditions of capitalism, is a critical part of the gang conundrum as I have argued, regardless of the national context, since without its consideration gang-prone youth are reacting not abstractly but concretely to the virtual certainty of "wasted lives" (Bauman 2004).

We live in a world where the elites have amply proven that they are not fit to lead the world into any next stage of history. Despite ongoing revolutionary transformations in technologies of production and communication the hackneyed mantras of "economic growth will conquer poverty" ring hollow on a planet in which three billion are living on a dollar a day or less. Such is the current status of the human condition, combined with incessant religio-ethnic conflicts that bear the stamp of imperialism's and colonialism's legacy and a devastating disequilibrium in the development of the relationship between humankind and nature. All of these processes will influence new and current gangs better conceived as cultural communes and survivalist subcultures responding to a dystopic environment. But, alas, the elites will never leave their taken-for-granted political and economic posts voluntarily and neither will their fear and hatred for the marginalized abate any time soon.

Consequently, gangs will always be both organized and spontaneous resolutions to these endless struggles waged by the subaltern to be seen, validated, respected and meaningfully included. I therefore contend that the key to understanding the gang, to grasping its contours, its social formations and its contexts, is always found in this dialectical relationship between inclusion and exclusion viewed historically and holistically. We have a choice. We can continue to use the lenses of the dominant culture with its various apparatuses of social control and its host of paid functionaries, informers and apologists or we can create a counter body of knowledge and alternative methodological inquiries to illuminate all those (over)shadowed spaces of criminalized social action where hope mixes with survivalism, creativity with accommodation and, yes, resistance with social reproduction.

Meanwhile, the reality in the United States is that there continues to be little disagreement among representatives of the elites when it comes to militarized preparations to defend its historically conceived borders and rights to raw materials and market spheres (see Robinson 2014), but suggest that a small fraction of this taxpayer bounty go toward the absolute eradication of want and we will likely be called unAmerican. Such is the sliver of space within which a public debate on such momentous societal questions as fairness and justice, dissent and accommodation is supposed to reside. In a different world the gang would be an intrinsically important part of that debate because it tells us something about ourselves, rather than being held at arm's length as the pathologized Other isolated in society's multiple forms of "special housing units" (both in captive and civil societies) or contained within the plethora of legal codes designed to quarantine the urban primitives. I argue that it is imperative to rescue the gang from its deviant seclusion so it cannot be used as convenient fodder for politicos when scapegoats are required, and neither can it be reduced to urban or suburban exotica for social scientists to dissect and analyze. Rather it must be humanized and politicized, made part of our hermeneutic quest to understand the human condition, and brought to the fore, in plain sight, as another form of what C. Wright Mills called the human variety.

Mills argued that we had to get out of our class-based, professional cages and sociologically engage these social phenomena, always seeking to link them to the great questions of the day, which in the current situation has to turn on the questions of power and powerlessness and the desperate need for societal change and transformation. My final plea is that we harness our critical sensibilities, channel our moral opprobrium and roll up our sleeves to work with men and women of the gang, bearing in mind the words of one of our late, great radical scholars of "deviance":

> Transformative research traces the concealed links between the observer and observed, makes visible the invisible, seeks to break down barriers between the social scientist and their objects of study, its success is to defamiliarize the investigator and to facilitate change in the investigated. It seeks what Sibley calls "dangerous knowledge." So should we.
>
> (Young 2011:173)

Notes

1 One of the best examples of the Mills approach to this social phenomenon is Tim Black's (2010) *When a Heart Turns Rock Solid*.
2 It is interesting to note that most students graduating from my own institution's Criminal Justice PhD program will never have read Foucault but will be able to cite chapter and verse from any number of works from a situational crime perspective!
3 I am thinking here of links and contrasts between the street gangs of the United States and those of Central America, principally El Salvador, Guatemala and Honduras. These are all collectivized youth (mostly) co-existing within a punishing politics of simultaneity that extends across borders. One kind is living with a system built on a surplus of ideological promises beset by a deficit of material opportunities and another in a system in which they are seen and treated as social dirt and which has a history of fascist intrigue and dictatorial rule over the poor, the oppressed and the indigenous. The social pathologies are intensely interwoven and see their reflections in the extraordinary crisis on the US Southern border, with children fleeing from the destabilization now often blamed on the gangs that originated in the class and ethnic cleansing of US deportation camps.
4 As opposed to what we want them to say or how we would like to observe them behave so that the categories we have constructed might be filled by these "types," thus continuing to make our preferred theoretical (and ideological) frames relevant.

Appendix
CULTURAL CRIMINOLOGY AND ITS PRACTICES

A dialogue between the theorist and the street researcher

Jock Young and David C. Brotherton

Jock Young

Let us start with considering what is this phenomenon called "cultural criminology." It is above all the placing of crime and its control in the context of culture. That is, of viewing both crime and the agencies of control as cultural products: as creative constructs. As such, they must be read in terms of the meanings which they carry. Furthermore, to highlight the interaction between the two, the relationship and the interaction between constructions upward and constructions downward – the continuous generation of meaning around inter-action and rules created, rules broken, a constant interplay of moral entrepreneurship, moral innovation and transgression.

But let's go further and place this interplay deep within the vast proliferation of media images of crime and deviance where every facet of offending is reflected in a vast hall of mirrors (see Ferrell 1999), where the street scripts the screen and the screen scripts the street, and where there is no linear sequence so the line between the real and the virtual is profoundly and irrevocably blurred.

All of these attributes, the cultural nature of crime and control, their interaction in an interplay of constructions, and the mediation through fact and fiction, news and literature, have occurred throughout history and are a necessary basis for any criminology which claims to be naturalistic. But what makes cultural criminology quintessentially late modern is twofold: the extraordinary emphasis on creativity, individualism, and generation of lifestyle in the present period coupled with a mass media which has expanded and proliferated so as to transform human subjectivity. The virtual community becomes as real as the community outside one's door – reference groups, vocabularies of motive, identities become global in their demesne. And it was at the beginning of the late modern period that the antecedents of cultural criminology emerged. For it was in the mid-1970s that the cultural turn occurred within the social sciences. Paramount here is the work of Clifford Geertz, whose symbolic anthropology has had influence across disciplines from history through literature and political science to labor history (see, for example, Berlanstein 1993).

Explicit in this endeavor is a stress on the interpretative rather than the mechanistic and the positivistic. It stands against the reduction in human action to a reflex of the material situation or a positivistic enactment of a pre-given culture. Rather, it stands for an interpretative analysis focusing on the way in which human actors generate meaning.

Parallel to this cultural shift in anthropology, we saw something similar happening in sociology, where a tendency developed that was both cultural in its focus and postmodernist in its sensibility. The radical phenomenological tradition of Becker, Kitsuse and Lemert, supplemented by the social constructionist work of writers such as Berger and Luckmann, was extraordinarily influential, involving the existential sense of freedom confronting the curtailed and constructed by the labels and essentialization of the powerful. This shift saw one of its earliest expressions in David Matza's book, *Becoming Deviant* (1969), with its concepts of naturalism, shift, pluralism, ambiguity and irony, on the one hand, and crime as transgression on the other. The synthesis of such an approach with subcultural theory commenced in the late 1960s with Downes' book *The Delinquent Solution* (1966) which, in its emphasis on subcultures as the site of problem solving and on the expressive rather than instrumental nature of much juvenile delinquency, began to neutralize the rather wooden American subcultural theory of the Mertonian tradition. In other words, culture was not a thing out there to be learnt and enacted; rather lifestyles were something which were constantly evolving. Such an orientation developed in the work of Brake (1985), S. Cohen (1972) and Young (1971), which focused on how deviant subcultures were both created by the actors and mediated and constructed by the impact of the mass media and the interventions of the powerful. It crystalized around the work of Cohen (1972) and Taylor (1999), with its evocation of a humanistic sociology of deviance and ethnographic method. Finally, it came of age at the Birmingham Centre for Contemporary Cultural Studies with the work of Stuart Hall, John Clarke, Dick Hebdige, Tony Jefferson and Paul Willis (see, for example, Hall *et al.* 1975, Hebdige 1979, Willis 1977). Here, youth culture is seen as a hive of creativity, as an arena of magical solutions where symbols are bricolaged into lifestyles, a place of identity and discovery and, above all, a site of resistance.

Thus, this reworking of American sociology replaced an all too mechanistic subcultural theorization with a notion of expressivity, style, and a relocation in leisure, evoking as it did so a rich narrative of bricolage and symbolism and an awareness of mediated reality. By the mid 1980s, such a humanistic sociology, buttressed by strong critiques of positivistic methods, was a major force within criminology. Since then, however, there has been a palpable return to positivism. It is in this context that cultural criminology seeks to retrace its roots and move on into the twenty-first century.

Let us now look briefly at five major tenets of cultural criminology, each of which will be exemplified by field work drawn from Brotherton's ethnographic studies on gangs and, in particular, on the Almighty Latin King and Queen Nation.

The lens of adrenaline

Rational choice theory and positivism are the two dominant approaches to crime that dominate contemporary sociological theory: the first stresses the mundane, the second the measurable. Both have very simple rational/instrumental narratives. In the first, crime occurs because of choice – depicted as an availability of opportunity and low levels of social control, particularly where individuals are impulsive and short-term oriented (see Felson 2002). Curiously (or perhaps not), every intellectual attempt is made to distance crime from structural inequalities and social injustice. Rather, we have pallid, calculative individuals committing crime where it is possible, coupled with putative victims who as likely targets are in turn attempting to calculate their optimum security strategies. In sociological positivism, inequality, lack of work, community breakdown, lack of social capital, etc. is recognized, but the jump from deprivation to crime, particularly violent crime, is scarcely attempted, rather it is assumed (see Katz 2002). It is a desperately thin narrative, like that of rational choice, where intensity of motivation, feelings of humiliation, anger and rage – as well as love and solidarity – are foresworn. If the first is the criminology of neo-liberalism, the second is that of social democracy – but in truth there is little to choose between them. Even in terms of determinism, rational choice theory might be better renamed market positivism, for between the determinants of poor character and opportunity for crime there is only a small space for the most pallid of market choices.

David C. Brotherton

This notion of emotional investment in the act of deviance is extremely important in the study of gangs. So often in gang studies, we read about one-dimensional cardboard cutouts which are rarely more than middle-class representations of the gang subject/object that concur with a particular search for examples of interpersonal violence, decision-making in the illicit economy or static notions of place built around the trope of territorialism. Lost also on much gang "mapping" of the inner city, particularly the security-state versions that now fill criminal justice textbooks, is any consideration of working-class space as an outgrowth of the dynamics of political economy, globalization and regimes of surveillance. Many of these master narratives are a result of research that takes its cue from moral entrepreneurs in the political classes and the ensuing panics aided and abetted by the interlocking criminal justice agencies. There are few gang studies, for example, that take seriously indirect violence in the shaping of inner-city communities and their identities; instead there are endless studies focusing on the "direct" interpersonal violence that is supposedly enabled by adolescent peer subcultures, mainly of the black or brown (and always of the lower-class) variety.

In the first excerpt below, we see an example of a not atypical street drama and the affective states of gang youth who often thrive on the "highs" and "lows" and unpredictability of their life-worlds, and on the challenges that come from the expected and unexpected. We can also glean how such youth (and adults) are culturally imbued with the importance of being "there," both physically and emotionally, for their "manitos" and "manitas." This is a "class act", not necessarily a "rational act", made possible by real and mythical histories of local barrio power plays. In this act, honor, loyalty, physical and emotional transcendence and social commitment are all in flux, with the means-end result often ambivalent, for it is always contingent on the personal and collective allegiances that are formed and reformed in the moment. Moreover, the memory of it all depends on who is telling the story. In King Tone's account below, the respondent (the Inca or leader of the Almighty Latin King and Queen Nation in New York) emerges victorious, relieved and sanguine, with his account becoming part of the group's oral history from below, an example of its historicity, and a key property of what constitutes his "Nation."

> King Tone: There is about 600–700 people. And one half has guns for King E. and the other half got it for King T. Now, I'm looking in there, I'm saying: "We all gonna die today!" You know, this is me and my mind. So they read the letter and they going to strip him. Me and C., in our minds, always planned this, we had to get rid of this coward. But what we didn't realize was now we gave over … instead of Brooklyn having the main manpower, the Bronx and Manhattan took it. So now we not only losing our main piece of power, we become the herbs of the Nation if we give them T. So me and C. stepped up in the circle and we went: "Nah. You strip but you can't violate him." They wanted to give him the five slap violation – it's something he created. Blood's frame of thinking was: "Give him what he gave out." So the five slaps were coming. So Z. and me

we started screaming: "Let's love." You know the love speech: "Please, let's end it here." They settled right. But then I seen a funny movement. Everyone left before Brooklyn left. And it was storming and a cold day, I remember it clearly as we came out. And when I'm next to T., all of the stuff from the roofs, like AKs start going off: "Cluck, cluck, cluck…" Now here's Z., here's her daughters – Z.'s got four daughters and I'm stuck with protecting them. So of course, I'm like: "They shooting at me. I can't shoot. I'm not going to reach them." But all the security guards ran away from Z. So at that minute I have to think quick. So, Z. and C. knew how really I loved her. I took out my guns – I'm shooting at the roof to try to hold fire, then I take my other gat out – 'cause I always carried two gats when I was out there, you know that was my frame of thinking from when I was young. And I start pointing at the rest of the Kings and I say: "If you don't come back and pick Z. up, I'm going to kill youse." There's me screaming in the middle of the night. They get Z., they throw her in the car, I back up and we get away.

(from Brotherton and Barrios 2004:138)

In the second example, we see another type of "high," this time speaking to the experience of constraint perpetrated by the state and its agents. It is remarkable how mainstream criminology neglects or rather avoids the vindictive qualities of the state in the ideological and bureaucratic achievement of social control. In a time of barbaric executions of inmates in their seventies, demented and barely able to function even in prison, or of torture normalized in our local, national and international gulags, we are obliged to excavate the state's subjectivity, its penchant for sadism, and its revelry in punishing, confining and purging the "Other."

Below is an excerpt from a letter to the author sent by King Tone dated 10/27/ 99. It was received four months after he was sentenced to a 13 to 15 year sentence for bagging three hundred dollars' worth of heroin. Tone's transgression occurred after being denied legitimate work opportunities due to his gang leadership stigma and during a period in which he faced homelessness with his two children and his wife. The evidence against him was recorded on a wire tap in a small-time drugs operation planned by the New York City Police Department using long-time "informers" and "snitches" within the Latin Kings and Queens. Although he was classified as a non-violent offender he was sent to the Federal Prison at Leavenworth, Kansas, the nation's oldest maximum security prison, and kept in a segregated unit under a single status category, virtually solitary confinement, for the next two years.

> "Dear Dave,
>
> I have been doing ok under the demoralizing way I'm living. Before I get into me, I hope that you and the family are doing fine in the hands of god. Myrna [Tone's girl-friend] has had the baby already, her name is Laylani Antonia Fernandez 9lbs 20.5 in Long Island, Oct 15, 99 5:05am. I really need to hold her as I do Javon and Shash [his other children] …
>
> Dave let me start from the beginning. When I left MCC (Manhattan Correctional Center) the Court told me I'm coming to Leavenworth so I can do my education. When I got here they had some problems with some brothers so they put me in the box and say I must stay for close supervision to await transfer. This was two months ago. Today I remain in single status with a question mark on my back. Picture me with one blue and one orange skimpy too tight boxers, one T-shirt, a too big orange jump shirt. oh yeah, one pair of socks, no mirror to shave, long hair, long nails etc. I'm starting to believe I'm not human no more, that is how I'm treated. Locked up 24 or 23 h a day. No Chaplin services. One call a month when the COs' [correctional officers] want, as long as its every 30 days for 15 min. No kids under 15 to visit due to plexiglass. 1 or 2 per visit only that means I can't see my girls. The cell contains a toilet, shower, dim light, bunk beds. One hour rec maybe 5 times a week, alone. Mail is censored, sometimes I get it a week later. Don't have a adequate law library or education supplies. No proper cleaning supplies. If they decide it, a hot tray can come frozen or warm, fresh or old. No adequate doctor. No check-ups, mental or physical … I have done nothing to be stripped of all my rights … Please tell Luis and R. Perez [the

late founder of the Puerto Rican National Congress] and Hec [the late King Hector Torres] what we must do to let them know that I am not on death row."

The soft city

Jock Young

Raban, in his book *Soft City* (1974), contrasts two city centers. On the one hand, the conventional depiction of the city as mass planning rationalized consumption and production, the urban grid of neighborhoods and zones, an iron cage where humanity is channeled and pummeled, and on the other, the soft city where all sorts of possibilities are on offer; a theater of dreams, an encyclopedia of subculture and style. Similarly, de Certeau (1984) depicts the city of planners, of rationalistic discourse, of quantitative data and demographies, with the "experiential" city, the street-level interaction that occurs beneath the interstices of plans and maps (see Hayward 2004a, 2004b). And there is a close parallel between this and Bakhtin's notion of the "second life of the people" (1984, see also Presdee 2001).

This dual city, not of spatial segregation and division within the city – although these, of course, occur – but of an "underlife" of the city, runs throughout cultural criminology and is a key concept. It is reminiscent of the sociology of deviance, where deviance is not marginal but the world bubbling up just under the surface of appearances (a place, incidentally, where ethnography can go, whereas social surveys merely reflect the surfaces) – or Goffman's "underlife" of institutions. It is not that the soft city is the only reality. Far from it; the bureaucratic rationalistic world impinges increasingly on every aspect of human existence. It is that this world by itself is imaginary of planners, politicians, official spokespersons. It does not grasp the existential fears, hopes, joys, resentments, terrors of everyday existence – and such a pronouncement is evident, of course, way outside the questions of crime or delinquency. This is the world where transgression occurs, where rigidity is fudged, where rules are bent, and lives are lived. It is the world upon which the imaginary of the powerful impacts upon the citizen.

FIGURE A.1 The Almighty Latin King and Queen Nation during a monthly meeting in a Brooklyn park (photograph Steve Hart).

Dave Brotherton

The soft city was everywhere in the organization and in its everyday practices. While the group's members were often raised in close-knit, somewhat parochial communities of poor, working-class neighbor-hoods, segregated by housing type, educational possibilities and job opportunities, served by infrequent mass transit systems, and policed by both public and private security forces, they saw the entire city as their rightful domain. They were, after all, Latinos whose imagined community was a diaspora that stretched transnationally across the local, national and international perimeters and parameters (super) imposed on them by a colonial and post-colonial political order. To counter their "felt" displacement both physically and historically, they had created a subculture that they called a "nation." In this world of the invisibles, they had decided quite logically that the borders extended to wherever their "gente" were situated. Unlike many other gang formations, they rejected the notion of territory, with its limited horizons and jealously guarded in-group ports of entry. Rather the entire city–its Spanish Harlems, East New Yorks, Lower East Sides, Jackson Heights, South Bronxes, Bushwicks and Williamsburgs–were all within its orbit of operations, as were other, lesser-known Latino and Puerto Rican enclaves such as Buffalo, Albany and Rochester in upstate New York, as well as Yonkers and Hempstead and Brentwood in Long Island. At large general meetings, delegations would be sent from Florida, Illinois, Pennsylvania, New Jersey, Connecticut and Massachusetts. I recently visited highly organized groups in Barcelona, Spain and Santo Domingo, Dominican Republic, and I am aware of members developing their own subcultural traditions in Genoa, Italy, San Juan, Puerto Rico and Quito, Ecuador. In Spain and the Dominican Republic, leading representatives told me they were inspired by the open-endedness and political effrontery of their New York comrades.

In other words, an important characteristic of the "soft city" property of the group is its glocalization, in which the migration and immigration flows of the group's members, instead of being seen as a sign of the larger community's social disorganization, were perceived as some of the community's strengths, an indication of its resilience and adaptability. Organized locally by tribes, which elected leaders who met regularly to plan city and state-wide activities, the group created its own spatial structures that were superimposed on bourgeois urban and suburban planning systems, thereby transgressing both private and public geographic spheres, and penetrating the deepest crevices of social exclusion (i.e. the global prison system).

In Figure A.1, we see the group rendezvousing in a public space. What we do not see are the helicopters circling above, the police on bikes and in their patrol cars avidly taking photographs to satisfy the limitless appetites of their intelligence apparatuses. In these meetings, organized on their time, in their spaces and with their agendas, they (the group's members) engaged the world, talked freely about their possibilities, made plans based on their hopes and expressed their vulnerabilities without fear of criminalization or of middle-class judgment. In Figure A.2, we see this other side of the group's assemblies.

FIGURE A.2 A monthly universal meeting of the ALKQN in Washington Heights, New York City (photograph by Steve Hart).

The transgressive subject

Jock Young

Crime is an act of rule breaking; it involves an attitude toward rules, assessment of their justness and appropriateness, and a motivation to break them whether by outright transgression or by neutralization. It is not, as in positivism, a situation where the actor is mechanistically propelled toward desiderata and on the way happens to cross the rules; it is not, as in rational choice theory, a scenario where the actor merely seeks the holes in the net of social control and ducks and dives his or her way through them. Rather, in cultural criminology, the act of transgression has itself attractions; it is through rule breaking that subcultural problems attempt solution.

Important here is the stress in cultural criminology on the foreground of experience, the existential psychodynamics of the actor, rather than on the background factors of traditional positivism (e.g. unemployment, poverty, poor neighborhoods). In this, the cultural criminologists follow Katz but are critical of his position, which tends to dismiss any focus on social background as a mistaken materialism and irretrievably positivistic.

Dave Brotherton

This relationship between background and foreground factors, which is a major social scientific contribution enabled by the cultural crim-inological approach, is brilliantly demonstrated by the very nature of the subculture. The notion of mediation as developed by the Birmingham School and its adherents is nowhere better understood than through the deliberate though contradictory transformation of the group from a "gang" to what we have termed a "street organiza-tion," i.e. a hybrid group formation somewhere between a street col-lective and a social movement. In our demographic data, collected from a portion of the group's members (sixty-seven out of about 1,000 active agents), we found that respondents came from a range of working-class family backgrounds; e.g. the majority (thirty-six) came from two-parent families, while the minority (twenty) came from one-parent families. Nonetheless, they all had origins in the working class; even if their parents had criminal records, there were few whose parents might be called "career criminals" (i.e. members of the supposed "underclass"). Consequently, their class, racial and gendered experiences, while certainly pushing them in the direc-tion of social exclusion, were not uniform, which explains to some extent why the subculture held so many overt and covert meanings for its members and could be interpreted (and frequently misinter-preted) by outsiders through both its instrumentalist and expressive representations.

Thus, those expecting to find a traditional gang were gener-ally confounded. Journalists, criminologists, law enforcement agents and judges could not easily classify what they were observing in the group's practices nor believe what they were hearing in the group's interviews and testimonies. What we, along with the group's members, observed was a great deal of cognitive dissonance among scouts sent by the mainstream as the group failed to conform to the contours of their discourse (which, of course, should be the point of departure for good social science – an "anomalous outcome" as Burawoy would have it). Alas, for social scientists of the statist variety, such a subculture is an "outlier" and should be dismissed for fear of polluting the sample of five or six "typical" gangs that have been studied for longer than it takes to secure twenty or thirty interviews. In this way, signs of performance creativity, magical solutions, evolving consciousnesses, ontological inquiries and complex spiritual and materialist identity constructions are considered beyond the research design. It is as if to say, "There will be no code switching here!" This hostility from the academic world, its colonizing gaze having barely been averted in criminal justice circles despite the trenchant critiques of post-structuralists, postmodernists and critical theorists over the last three decades, was well understood by the group, especially its organic intellectuals. As the "Santo" (spiritual adviser to the Inca or President) of the ALKQN put it early in our research:

> We are not gonna let ourselves be represented by academics. We ain't fish in a bowl to be looked and dissected – you better get that straight! We're not here in your laboratory, doing your bidding, helping your careers. We ain't nobody's fools and we're not gonna be used by no poverty pimps. If you wanna work with us that's fine but you ain't gonna take us for granted. We don't care what the rules of the game are ... We gonna change the game.
>
> (Brotherton and Barrios 2004:6)

As for our own transgressive acts as researchers, we adopted somewhat contradictory roles, both acceptable to the group and to ourselves, as insiders (who were close to the group's community and instrumental to some of its designs) and outsiders (who carried out interviews with preset questions, who took notes at activities and who generally kept outside of any decision-making processes within the group). This was how we interpreted the notion of a collaborative relationship in the service of a critical ethnography, which was especially borne out in the pivotal role of my academic colleague, Luis Barrios. For it was through Luis, a radical priest in the community and the first person in New York City to give the group a "home" (through opening his church to the group), that our research with the group began. However, quite in contrast to most orthodox approaches in which the "outsider" maintains at all times his/her distance from the researched in pursuance of the evasive goal of value neutrality, we concluded that a direct, open, reciprocal and engaged relationship with the group was necessary. How else could we come close to its lived meanings, gain insights into members' feelings of frustration, joy, anger and confusion, and learn to discern the points at which oppression is felt and resisted?

This was not entirely the same as "edge work" (Lyng 1998), that form of cultural criminology in which the act of deviance itself must be experienced in all its existential potential. Rather, our work was more akin to reflexive sociology (see Gouldner 1970, Bourdieu and Wacquant 1992), in which we sought to disabuse ourselves of our domain of assumptions and worked assiduously to learn from and with the respondents under similar conditions of constraint, possibility and ambiguity. This sociologist-as-partisan relationship can be seen in the following field notes from Barrios, who is reflecting on his role at a critical juncture in the group's developmental process:

> I remember the day when Father Castle told me that he had made a decision to end the ALKQN's sanctuary in St. Mary's Church. It was very difficult for me to understand his motivation and I reminded him of how dangerous this decision was for the Nation and for our community ministry. But I realized I was not going to change his mind. He was the senior priest, my supervisor, and at that moment he was intent on demonstrating that he was in charge. I prayed and meditated looking for answers and for the best way to approach the ALKQN leadership to share this bad news. I was angry because I was aware that this arbitrary and racist decision would give the police and other outside enemies an opportunity to dismantle what we had created in the last few years. Taking

away this physical space from the group was the most effective way to create chaos and destroy the collective identity of
those who were resisting oppression. I knew that it might
come to this from the beginning, but I didn't know what to
do. Father Castle was and is an incredibly progressive priest.
He was there for the Black Panthers and he is a person who
knows how to take risks and how to challenge the status quo.
Yet, he was making a unilateral decision for which the only
explanation he could give was: "These Latinos are growing
too large in numbers and one of these days they are going
to take over the church." Since that day our relationship was
deeply affected. In my pain and anger I thought about this
whole question and went back into my many years of experience in the struggle and began thinking of how often it is
that white progressive people, when it comes time to give the
power to those who are being oppressed, want to continue
with their paternalistic approaches.

(Field Notes 7/1/02)

The attentive gaze

Jock Young

Ferrell and Hamm talk of the methodology of attentiveness, of a
criminological verstehen where the researcher is immersed within
a culture. The phrase "attentiveness" is redolent of Matza's (1969)
"naturalism," the invocation to be true to the subject – without
either romanticism or the generation of pathology. It is reminiscent also of Agee and Evans who, in *Let Us Now Praise Famous
Men* (1960 [1941]), write and photograph with such a sensitivity,
respect and feeling for the lives of Southern sharecroppers during
the Depression.

This is an ethnography which is immersed in production, the
"thick description" of Geertz which is interested in lifestyle, the
symbolic, the aesthetic and the usual quotidian. But qualitative data
must be dislodged from their claims of scientific objectivity, precision
and certainty. They must be re-conceptualized as imperfect human

constructions and carefully situated in time, place (Ferrell and Sanders 1995) and history (Brotherton and Barrios 2004). In an inversion of orthodoxy, Ferrell and Hamm note that "they can perhaps sketch a faint outline of (deviance and criminality) but they can never fill that outline with essential dimensions of meaningful understanding" (1998:11). Finally, the cultural criminologists stress the mediated nature of reality in late modernity, so that subcultures cannot be studied apart from media representations and ethnography and analysis cannot be separated. Hence, the orthodox separation of media and its effects cannot be maintained.

Dave Brotherton

The role of the critical ethnographer is to take note of all things cultural, to look up and down the class, racial and gender hierarchies (ethnographically speaking), to be endlessly fascinated by the obvious and the opaque, and to search consistently for the official and unofficial transcripts (Scott 1985) of resistance and its attendant mentalities. To this end, we collected everything we could to shine a light on the becoming of the subculture, to capture its dynamism, its processes of articulation, its interpenetrations with the dominant culture, its anguish (as in Sartre's existentialist explanation of the progressive-regressive method of analyzing history). Prison letters, "insider" photographs (see below), "outsider" photographs (see above), field observations, oral diaries from King Tone (while under house arrest), interviews with a range of gang-related "insiders" and "outsiders," videos of meetings, rituals and social events, tapes of gang-produced music, fliers of group-originated events, and Internet Web pages by group members. This list of data types increased the longer we remained in the field, and our research horizons broadened with the group's development. Yet with all our research flexibility, we are under no illusion that we have captured but a slice of the lived reality. In other words, we are not here to proclaim "the truth" but we are here to make a claim that has to be tried and tested against other claims: otherwise there is no point to social science, which, in my view, is a major sociological problem with the relativism of some post-structuralist and postmodernist positions.

FIGURE A.3 A Latin Queen during a meeting in Luis Barrios' church.

Nonetheless, cognizant of this tentativeness and the privileged nature of our "findings", and in order to achieve more accuracy and more accountability, we of course submitted our accounts to the group's members for commentary and critique. But the distance between the cultural capitals, between our respective elaborated and restricted class vocabularies, made such an undertaking difficult though not worthless. However, the biggest problem of all was that the final draft of the project, i.e. the book of the case study itself (Brotherton and Barrios 2004), would never reach our most important critic, cultural broker and consultant, King Tone, the leader of the "Nation." This was due to our work being deemed an item of contraband within the federal prison system. Perhaps this in itself is an indirect gauge of the book's subversive nature, an ironic indication of its truly dangerous quality, which might be considered testimony to the degree to which we succeeded in critically and culturally engaging the subject matter (see next section).

Dangerous and subjugated knowledge

Jock Young

David Sibley, in his *Geographies of Exclusion*, talks not only of spatial and social exclusion – the exclusion of dangerous classes – but the exclusion of dangerous knowledge. It is either the traditional positivism of sociologists or psychologists, or the new "crime science" and the rational choice/routine activities theorists that have exceptional interest in maintaining rigid definitions and demarcations between science and non-science, between criminality and "normality," between the expert and the criminal, between criminology and the more humanistic academic disciplines – and even between the individuals studied themselves as isolated atoms incapable of collective activity. It is the nature of cultural criminology that it questions all these distinctions and is intrinsically opposed to the project of criminology as a natural science of crime. As such, cultural criminology's "intellectual lawlessness" (and sometimes its actual lawlessness) is an anathema to such an orthodoxy.

Dave Brotherton

As mentioned above, the end result of a quasi-cultural criminological approach to gangs can and should be intellectually unsettling to the dominant culture and its various apparatuses. But it is even more illuminating to see the extent to which gang criminology's gatekeepers of the canon have gone to declare any questioning of their basic suppositions "off limits." One striking example of this modern-day clericalism is the treatment meted out to the late, brilliant urban gang ethnographer Dwight Conquergood, formerly Professor and Chair of Performance Studies at Northwestern University.

Conquergood had been studying the Latin Kings of Chicago for more than fifteen years (1987–2002), living in the same inner-city housing tenements as many of its members and producing an award-winning documentary on this group in the early 1990s, followed by several theoretically rigorous and empirically rich articles later in the decade (see Conquergood and Siegel 1990, Conquergood 1992, 1993, 1997). Essentially, Conquergood's work profoundly changed our understanding of gang semiotics and of gang interactional rituals by drawing together disparate schools of thought in the deviance field into a radical culturalist analysis of class and ethnic warfare mediated through Chicago's street subcultures. Until today, with the exception of myself and Venkatesh (1997), Conquergood's name is erased from the bibliography of almost every gang study, achieving what is essentially a ruthless act of intellectual purgation. Nonetheless, without Conquergood's insights and risk-taking forays into and between different literatures, it would have been difficult–perhaps impossible–for us to make the analytical leaps that were necessary in our New York study.

This same notion of "danger" in the area of knowledge production was and continues to be at the center of our ongoing investigation with these subcultures. For example, we argued in our book that any discussion of politics as a form of consciousness or as an act of empowerment was always missing from the gang literature. Yet, through the multivalent data we had collected, this activity was a core ingredient of the group's transformation. Further, we argued that the alternative/subjugated knowledge being developed among the socially excluded through their self-organizations was having a radicalizing effect on other youth and other groups in the city. In fact, one of the primary reasons for the massive assault by the state on this group was to prevent its "dangerous knowledge" practices from spreading. Finally, we traced how this "dangerous knowledge" was carried across generations and how historically many radical groups had been involved in gang subcultures and vice versa (e.g. the Black Panthers, the Vice Lords and the Brown Berets), as street cultures meshed with radical orators and the high culture of the academy seeped into the discourses of the imprisoned, both physically and metaphorically. In the quote below, taken from a relatively recent field interview, we see this intellectual journey that "dangerous knowledge" can make:

Interview with Raymundo, 10/18/2002 – Santo Domingo.

> We're sitting in front of two huge portraits painted on the walls of the Fuerza de la Revolucion, Revolutionary Force, the old Communist Party of the Dominican Republic. One of the portraits is of Che, the other is of Commandante Camano – both

heroes of the 1965 Revolution (the latter is the army general who led the resistance to the Yanqui invasion). Raymundo is a thick-set young man of 22 years, a son of the barrio, born in Santiago, the second city of the Republic. He is the leader of the Communist Youth League and a 3rd year student of Law and Politics at the public university. Raymundo is also a leader of the Latin Kings, although he never fully divulges his tribe or his rank to me in the 12 months that I spend talking to him.

"I'm reading *Empire* by Hardt and Negri," Raymundo states, "Do you know it?"

"Yes," I answer, a little taken aback at the level of his theoretical ambition.

"I've been telling the brothers in the Kings that we need to start a study club. You know, to try to help us get into these theories. Try to see how they apply to us out here in the Caribbean. I like their notion of Imperialism. I don't know if I agree with it but we have to listen to it, work it through. It's not all about Che and Lenin."

"Yes, I agree Raymundo. Just tell me when you want to begin. You know, when you can get it organized and I'll be there to help in any way I can. It's a great idea."

"You know the party doesn't like me being in the Kings. They have a very traditional view of the working-class (he chuckles). They think the street youth are 'negativos' (he raises his eye brows). 'They don't learn discipline.' 'They're too opportunistic.' 'They won't join the struggle.' 'They're too involved with drugs.' I tell them, 'If you want to be relevant you have to start with them. These kids are the proletariat. How can they help it if 50% of us are unemployed!'"

Conclusion

In the above, we have argued for a very different approach to criminology and to deviance than is currently de rigueur in the United States and lamentably in many other countries, both English speaking and non-English speaking. We have presented our arguments in the form of a conversation, a dialogue between the active researcher and the active theorist which builds on the already impressive work of Ferrell, Hamm, Lyng, Presdee and others who have begun to show how a new criminology, a cultural criminology, can be achieved. In the field of street research, we essentially need an ethnography of ethnography, a double awareness of the process of research in contrast to conventional quantitative research which wantonly imposes survey categories and the Likert scale upon its subjects.

Further, we argue that cultural criminology points to the way poverty, marginalization and oppression, often perceived in an affluent society as an act of exclusion, the ultimate humiliation in a consumer society, is an *intense* experience. In other words, it is not enough to formally take into account a state of material deprivation, a condition of joblessness, etc., but rather we must understand, document, share and imagine the sense of injustice and of ontological insecurity that necessarily accompanies such a lived condition in all its contested and accommodated aspects. Thus, crime and transgression in this new context can be seen as a breaking through of restraints, a realization of immediacy and a reassertion of identity and ontology. In this fashion, identity becomes woven into the rules broken, into individual and collective acts of transgression that demand attention, and into movements from below that create alternative spheres of being. It is our conclusion that cultural criminology offers one of the most fruitful methodological approaches into such processes and a way to connect a drifting and quiescent criminology with its more critical, sociological roots.

REFERENCES

Adamson, Colin. 1998. Tribute, Turf, Honor and the American Street Gang: Patterns of Continuity and Change since 1820. *Theoretical Criminology*, 2: 57–84.

Agee, James and Walter Evans. 1960 [1941]. *Let Us Now Praise Famous Men*. Cambridge, MA: The Riverside Press.

Alexander, Michelle. 2010. *The New Jim Crow: Mass Incarceration in the Age of Colorblindness*. New York: The New Press.

Alvarez, Luis. 2008. *The Power of the Zoot: Youth Culture and Resistance during World War II*. Berkeley: University of California Press.

Anyon, Jean. 1980. Social Class and the Hidden Curriculum. *Journal of Education*, 162(1): 67–92.

Aronowitz, Stanley. 2000. *The Knowledge Factory: Dismantling the Corporate University and Creating True Higher Learning*. New York: Beacon.

Bakhtin, Mikhail. 1984. *Rabelais and this World*. Bloomington: Indiana University Press.

Bataille, Georges. 1986. *Eroticism, Death and Sensuality*. San Francisco: City Light Books.

Baudrillard, Jean. 1994. *Simulacra and Simulation: The Body in Theory: Histories of Cultural Materialism*. Ann Arbor: University of Michigan Press.

Bauman, Zygmunt. 2004. *Wasted Lives: Modernity and Its Outcasts*. Hoboken: Polity.

Becker, Howard. 1963. *Outsiders: Studies in the Sociology of Deviance*. New York: The Free Press.

Bell, Daniel. 1960. Crime as an American Way of Life: The Queer Ladder of Social Mobility. In *The End of Ideology*, pp. 127–150. New York: The Free Press.

Bennett, William, John Diliulio and John Waters. 1996. *Body Count: Moral Poverty and How to Win America's War Against Crime and Drugs*. New York: Simon & Schuster.

Berlanstein, L. (ed.). 1993. *Rethinking Labor History*. Urbana: University of Illinois Press.

Black, Tim. 2010. *When a Heart Turns Rock Solid*. New York: Vintage.

Bourdieu, Pierre. 1978. *Distinction: A Social Critique of the Judgment of Taste*. Cambridge, MA: Harvard University Press.

Bourdieu, Pierre and Loic Wacquant. 1992. *An Invitation to Reflexive Sociology*. Chicago: University of Chicago Press.

Bourgois, Philippe. 1995. *In Search of Respect: Selling Crack in El Barrio*. New York: Cambridge University Press.

Brake, Mike. 1985. *Comparative Youth Cultures: The Sociology of Youth Culture and Youth Subcultures in America, Britain and Canada*. London: Routledge and Kegan Paul.

Brenneman, Robert. 2011. *Homies and Hermanos: God and Gangs in Central America*. New York: Oxford University Press.

Brotherton, David C. 1992. *The Future is Up for Grabs: Success and Failure in an Inner-City High School*. Dissertation. University of California, Santa Barbara.

Brotherton, David C. 1994. Who Do You Claim? Gang Formations and Rivalry in an Inner City High School. *Perspectives on Social Problems*, 5: 147–171.

Brotherton, David C. 1996a. "Smartness," "Toughness," and "Autonomy": Drug Use in the Context of Gang Female Delinquency. *Journal of Drug Issues*, 26: 261–277.

Brotherton, David C. 1996b. The Contradictions of Suppression: Notes from a Study of Approaches to Gangs in Three Public High Schools. *Urban Review*, 28(2): 95–120.

Brotherton, David C. 1997. Socially Constructing The Nomads: Part One. *Humanity and Society*, 21(2): 1–21.

Brotherton, David C. 1999. The Old Heads Tell Their Stories. *Free Inquiry in Creative Sociology*, 2(1): 1–15.

Brotherton, David C. 2003. The Role of Education in the Reform of Street Organizations in New York City. In L. Kontos, D. Brotherton and L. Barrios (eds.), *Gangs and Society: Alternative Perspectives*, pp. 136–158. New York: Columbia University Press.

Brotherton, David C. 2007. Beyond Social Reproduction: Bringing Resistance Back Into the Theory of Gangs. *Theoretical Criminology*, 12(1): 55–77.

Brotherton, David C. 2013. Ethnographic Activism. Unpublished paper given to the Criminology Department at Erasmus University, Rotterdam.

Brotherton, David C. and Luis Barrios. 2004. *The Almighty Latin King and Queen Nation: Street Politics and the Transformation of a New York City Gang*. New York: Columbia University Press.

Brotherton, David C. and Luis Barrios. 2011. *Banished to the Homeland: Social Exclusion, Resistance and the Dominican Deportee*. New York: Columbia University Press.

Burawoy, Michael. 1998. Extended Case Method. *Sociological Theory*, 16(1): 4–33.

Burrows, Edward G. and Mike Wallace. 1999. *Gotham: A History of New York City to 1898*. New York: Oxford University Press.

Butler, Judith. 1993. *Bodies that Matter: On the Discursive Limits of Sex*. New York: Routledge.

Cacho, Leslie Marie. 2012. *Social Death: Racialized Rightlessness and the Criminalization of the Unprotected*. New York: New York University Press.

Campbell, Anne. 1991. *Girls in the Gang*, 2nd edn. London: Blackwell.

Castells, Manuel. 1997. *The Power of Identity*. New York: Blackwell.

Castells, Manuel. 2012. *Networks of Outrage and Hope: Social Movements in the Internet Age*. Cambridge: Polity.

Castoriadis, George. 1987 [1975]. *The Imaginary Insitution of Society*, translated by Kathleen Blarney. Cambridge, MA: MIT Press.

Cerbino, Mauro. 2010. *La Nación Imaginada de los Latin Kings, Mimetismo, Colonialidad y Transnacionalismo*. PhD dissertation. University of Taragona, Spain.

Chalfant, Henry and James Prigoff. 1987. *Spraycan Art (Street Graphics / Street Art)*. New York: Thames & Hudson.

Chang, Jeff. 2005. *Can't Stop Won't Stop: A History of the Hip-Hop Generation*. New York: Picador.

Chomsky, Noam. 2006. *Failed States: The Abuse of Power and the Assault on Democracy*. New York: Metropolitan Books.

Christie, Nils. 1993. *Crime Control as Industry*, 3rd edn. Florence, KY: Routledge.

Cloward, Richard A. and Lloyd Ohlin. 1960. *Delinquency and Opportunity*. New York: Free Press.

Cohen, Albert. 1955. *Delinquent Boys*. New York: Free Press.

Cohen, Phil. 1972. Subcultural Conflict and Working-Class Community. Working Papers in Cultural Studies, 1. Birmingham: University of Birmingham, Centre for Contemporary Cultural Studies.

Cohen, Stanley. 1972. *Folk Devils and Moral Panics: The Creation of Mods and Rockers*. London: McGibbon and Kee.

Cohen, Stanley. 1987. *Against Criminology*. New Brunswick: Transaction Books.

Cohen, Stanley. 1997. Intellectual Scepticism and Political Commitment. In P. Walton and J. Young (eds.), *The New Criminology Revisited*, pp. 98–129. London: Macmillan.

Coleman, James. 1961. *Adolescent Society: The Social Life of the Teenager and Its Impact on Education*. Glencoe, IL: The Free Press.

Comaroff, John and Jean Comaroff. 1992. *Ethnography and the Historical Imagination*. Boulder: Westview Press.

Conquergood, Dwight (Producer and Director) and T. Siegel (Producer and Director). 1990. *The Heart Broken in Half* [videotape]. New York: Filmmakers Library.

Conquergood, Dwight. 1992. *On Reppin' and Rhetoric: Gang Representations*. Paper presented at the Philosophy and Rhetoric of Inquiry Seminar, University of Iowa.

Conquergood, Dwight. 1993. Homeboys and Hoods: Gang Communication and Cultural Space. In Larry Frey (ed.), *Group Communication in Context: Studies of Natural Groups*, pp. 23–55. Hillsdale: Lawrence Erlbaum.

Conquergood, Dwight. 1997. Street Literacy. In James Floord, Shirley Brice Heath and Diane Lapp (eds.), *Handbook of Research on Teaching Literacy Through the Communicative and Visual Arts*, pp. 354–375. New York: Simon & Schuster and Macmillan.

Conquergood, Dwight. 1999. Personal Communication. December 12.

Conquergood, Dwight. 2013. Lethal Theater: Performance, Punishment and the Death Penalty. In Patrick E. Johnson (ed.), *Dwight Conquergood: Performance, Ethnography, Praxis*. Ann Arbor: University of Michigan Press.

Contreras, Randol. 2012. *The Stickup Kids: Race, Drugs, Violence and the American Dream*. Berkeley: University of California Press.

Cooper, Martha and Henry Chalfant. 2009 [1984]. *Subway Art*. New York: Chronicle Books.

Curtis, Richard. 1998. The Improbable Transformation of Inner-City Neighborhoods: Crime, Violence, Drugs and Youth in the 1990s. *Journal of Criminal Law and Criminology*, 88(4): 1233–1276.

Davis, Mike. 1990. *City of Quartz: Evaluating the Future of Los Angeles*. New York: Verso.

Dawley, David. 1992. *A Nation of Lords: The Autobiography of the Vice Lords*, 2nd edn. Prospect Heights: Waveland Press.

Debord, Guy. 1994 [1967]. *The Society of the Spectacle*. New York: Zone Books.

de Certeau, Michael. 1984. *The Practice of Everyday Life*. Berkeley: University of California Press.

De Genova, Nicholas and Nathalie Preutz. 2010. *The Deportation Regime: Sovereignty, Space and the Freedom of Movement*. Durham, NC: Duke University Press.

DeCesare, Donna. 2013. *Unsettled/Desasosiego*. Austin: University of Texas Press.

Decker, Scott H. and G. David Curry (eds.). 2003. *Confronting the Gang*. Roxbury: Roxbury Press.

Decker, Scott H. and Barrik Van Winkle. 1996. *Life in the Gang*. Cambridge: Cambridge University Press.

Decker, Scott H. and Frank H. Weerman. 2005. In the Grip of the Group. In Frank Van Gemert, Mark S. Fleischer and Scott H. Decker (eds.), *European Street Gangs and Troublesome Youth Groups*. New York: Alta Mira.

Di Leonardo, Micaela. 1998. *Exotics at Home: Anthropologies, Others, American Modernity*. Chicago: University of Chicago Press.

Douglas, Mary. 1966. *Purity and Danger: An Analysis of the Concepts of Pollution and Taboo*. London: Routledge.

Douglas, Mary. 1982. *In the Active Voice*. London: Routledge.

Downes, David. 1966. *The Delinquent Solution*. London: Routledge & Kegan Paul

Durán, Robert. 2013. *Gang Life in Two Cities: An Insider's Journey*. New York: Columbia University Press.

Duster, Troy. 1970. *The Legislation of Morality: Law, Drugs and Moral Judgment*. New York: Free Press.

Egley, Arlen Jr. and James C. Howell. 2013. *Highlights of the 2011 National Youth Gang Survey*. Washington, DC: Office of Juvenile Justice and Delinquency Prevention.

Erikson, Kai T. 1966. *Wayward Puritans: A Study in the Sociology of Deviance*. New York: Wiley.

Esteva, Juan. 2003. Urban Street Activists: Gang and Community Efforts to Bring Justice to Los Angeles' Neighborhoods. In Louis Kontos, David Brotherton and Luis Barrios (eds.), *Gangs and Society: Alternative Perspectives*, pp. 95–116. New York: Columbia University Press.

Ewen, Stuart and Elizabeth Ewen. 2008. *Typecasting: On the Arts and Sciences of Human Inequality*. New York: Seven Stories Press.

Fagan, Jeffrey. 1996. Gangs, Drugs and Neighborhood Change. In C. Ron Huff (ed.), *Gangs in America*, pp. 39–73. Thousand Oaks: Sage.

Fagan, Jeffrey. 2010. Expert report in Floyd vs. City of New York, Southern District Court of New York. Available at: www.ccrjustice.org.

Fanon, Franz. 1965. *Wretched of the Earth*. New York: Grove Press.

Fecher, Rita and Henry Chalfant. 1993. *Flying Cut Sleeves*.

Feixa, Carles, Laura Porzio and C. Recio. 2006. *Jóvenes latinos en Barcelona. Espacio público y cultura urbana*. Barcelona: Anthropos-Ajuntament Barcelona.

Felson, Marcus. 2002. *Crime and Everyday Life*, 3rd edn. Thousand Oaks: Sage.

Ferrell, Jeff. 1993. *Crimes of Style: Urban Graffiti and the Politics of Criminality*. New York: New York University Press.

Ferrell, Jeff. 1997. Criminological Verstehen: Inside the Immediacy of Crime. *Justice Quarterly*, 14(1): 3–23.

Ferrell, Jeff. 1999. Cultural Criminology. *Annual Review of Sociology*, 25: 395–418.

Ferrell, Jeff. 2000. Making Sense of Crime: Review Essay on Jack Katz's Seductions of Crime. *Social Justice*, 19(3): 111–123.

Ferrell, Jeff and Mark Hamm. 1998. True Confessions: Crime, Deviance and Field Research. in J. Ferrell and M. Hamm (eds.), *Ethnography at the Edge: Crime, Deviance and Field Research*, pp. 2–19. Boston: Northeastern University Press.

Ferrell, Jeff and Clint Sanders. 1995. Culture, Crime and Criminology. In J. Ferrell and C. Sanders (eds.), *Cultural Criminology*, pp. 304–308. Boston: Northeastern University Press.

Fine, Michelle. 1991. *Framing Dropouts*. New York: SUNY Press.

Fleischer, Mark. 1998. *Dead End Kids: Gang Girls and the Boys They Know*. Madison: University of Wisconsin Press.

Flores, Edward O. 2014. *God's Gangs: Barrio Ministry, Masculinity, and Gang Recovery*. New York: New York University Press.

Flores, Juan. 2000. *From Bomba to Hip-Hop: Puerto Rican Culture and Latino Identity*. New York: Columbia University Press.

Fordham, Cynthia. 1996. *Blacked Out: Dilemmas of Race, Identity, and Success at Capital High*. Chicago: University of Chicago Press.

Foucault, Michael. 1977. *Discipline and Punish: The Birth of the Prison*. New York: Vintage Books.

Freire, Paulo. 1970. *Pedagogy of the Oppressed*. New York: Herder and Herder.

Galeano, Eduardo. 1991 [1989]. *Book of Embraces*, translated by Cecil Belfrage. London: Norton.

Galeano, Eduardo. 1998. *Upside Down World: A Primer for the Looking-Glass World*. New York: Metropolitan Books.

Galtung, Johan. 1969. Violence, Peace and Peace Research. *Journal of Peace Research*, 6(3): 167–191.

Garland, David. 2001. *The Culture of Control: Crime and Social Order in Contemporary Society*. Chicago: University of Chicago Press.

Geertz, Clifford. 1973. *The Interpretation of Cultures*. New York: Basic Books.

Geertz, Clifford. 1983. *Local Knowledge: Further Essays in Interpretative Anthropology*. New York: Basic Books.

Gilbert, James. 1986. *A Cycle of Outrage: America's Reaction to the Juvenile Delinquent in the 1950s*. New York: Oxford University Press.

Gilmore, Ruth. 2007. *Golden Gulag: Prisons, Surplus, Crisis, and Opposition in Globalizing California*. Berkeley: University of California Press.

Gilroy, Paul. 1993. *Black Atlantic: Modernity and Double Consciousness*. Cambridge, MA: Harvard University Press.

Giroux, Henry. 1983. *Theory and Resistance in Education*. South Hadley: Bergin and Garvey.

Giroux, Henry. 2012. *Disposable Youth: Racialized Memories and the Culture of Cruelty*. New York: Routledge.

Gitlin, Todd. 1980. *The Whole World is Watching*. Berkeley: University of California Press.

Glasgow, Douglas G. 1981. *The Black Underclass: Poverty, Unemployment and Entrapment of Ghetto Youth*. New York: Vintage Books.

Goffman, Alice. 2013. *On the Run: Fugitive Life in an American City (Fieldwork Encounters and Discoveries)*. Chicago: University of Chicago Press.

Goffman, Erving. 1961. *Asylums: Essays on the Social Systems of Mental Patients and Other Inmates*. New York: Anchor.

Goffman, Erving. 1963. *Stigma: Notes on the Management of Spoiled Identity*. Englewood Cliffs: Prentice-Hall.

Gonzales, Alfonso. 2013. *Reform Without Justice: Latino Migrant Politics and the Homeland Security State*. New York: Oxford University Press.

Gouldner, Alvin W. 1970. *The Coming Crisis of Western Sociology*. New York: Basic Books.

Greene, Judith and Kevin Pranis. 2007. *Gang Wars: The Failure of Enforcement Tactics and the Need for Effective Public Safety Practices*. Washington, DC: Justice Policy Institute.

Hagedorn, John. 1988. *People and Folks: Gangs, Crime and the Underclass in a Rustbelt City*. Minnesota and Chicago: Lake View Press.

Hagedorn, John. 1998. *People and Folks: Gangs, Crime and the Underclass in a Rustbelt City*, 2nd edn. Minnesota: University of Minnesota Press.

Hagedorn, John. 2006. Race not Space: A Revisionist History of Gangs in Chicago. *Journal of African American History*, 91(2): 194–208.

Hagedorn, John. 2008. *A World of Gangs*. Minneapolis: University of Minneapolis Press.

Hagedorn, John. 2015. *The In$ane Chicago Way: The Daring Plan by Chicago Gangs to Create a Spanish Mafia*. Unpublished manuscript.

Hall, Stuart, Tony Jefferson, Chas Crichter, John Clarke and Brian Roberts (eds.). 1975. *Resistance Through Rituals*. London: Routledge.

Hall, Stuart, Tony Jefferson, Chas Crichter, John Clarke and Brian Roberts. 1978. *Policing the Crisis: Mugging, the State and Law and Order*. New York: Holmes and Meier.

Hallsworth, Simon. 2013. *The Gang and Beyond: Interpreting Violent Street Worlds*. London: Palgrave.

Hallsworth, Simon and David C. Brotherton. 2012. *Urban Disorder*. London: Runnymede Trust.

Hallsworth, Simon and John Lea. 2011. Reconstructing Leviathan: Emerging Contours of the Security State. *Theoretical Criminology*, 15: 141–157.

Hallsworth, Simon and Tara Young. 2008. Gang Talk and Gang Talkers. *Crime, Media, Culture*, 4(2): 175–195.

Hamm, Mark, S. 1993. *American Skinheads: The Criminology and Control of Hate Crime*. New York: Praeger.

Hardt, Michael and Antonio Negri. 2005. *Multitude: War and Democracy in the Age of Empire*. London: Penguin.

Harvey, David. 2000. *Spaces of Hope*. Berkeley: University of California Press.

Harvey, David. 2007. *A Brief History of Neoliberalism*. New York: Oxford University Press.

Harvey, David. 2014. Afterthoughts on Piketty's Capital. Reading Marx's Capital with David Harvey. David Harvey's website.

Hayden, Tom. 2004. *Street Wars: Gangs and the Future of Violence*. New York: New Press.

Hayward, Keith. 2004a. *City Limits: Crime, Consumerism and the Urban Experience*. London: Glasshouse Press.

Hayward, Keith. 2004b. Consumer Culture and Crime. In C. Sumner (ed.), *The Blackwell Companion to Criminology*, pp. 143–161. Oxford: Blackwell.

Hayward, Keith, Jeff Ferrell and Jock Young. 2010. *Cultural Criminology: An Invitation*. Los Angeles: Sage.

Hebdige, Dick. 1979. *Subcultures: The Meaning of Style*. London: Methuen.

Hebdige, Dick. 1988. *Hiding in the Light*. London: Routledge.

Hirschi, Travis. 1969. *Causes of Delinquency*. Berkeley: University of California Press.

Hobsbawm, Eric. 1969. *Primitive Rebels: Studies in Archaic Forms of Social Movement in the 19th and 20th Centuries*. New York: W.W. Norton.

Hoggart, Richard. 1957. *The Uses of Literacy*. London: Penguin.

Human Rights Watch. 2011. We'll Show You You're a Woman: Violence and Discrimination Against Black Lesbians and Transgender Men. Available at: www.hrw.org/reports/2011/12/05/we-ll-show-you-you-re-woman.

Jankowski, Martín S. 1991. *Islands in the Street: Gangs in American Urban Society*. Berkeley: University of California Press.

Jankowski, Martín S. 2003. *Cracks in the Pavement: Social Change and Resilience in Poor Neighborhoods*. Berkeley: University of California Press.

Jenks, Chris. 2003. *Transgression*. New York: Routledge.

Justice Policy Institute. 2000. *The Punishing Decade: Prison and Jail Estimates at the Millennium*. Washington, DC: Justice Policy Institute.

Kane, Stephanie. 2004. The Unconventional Methods of Cultural Criminology. *Theoretical Criminology*, 8(3): 303–321.

Karlin, Mark. 2014. Interview with Todd Miller. Truth Out. Available at: www.truth-out.org/progressivepicks/item/24167-border-patrol-nation-us-creates-war-zones-at-boundaries-with-mexico-canada.

Katz, Jack. 1988. *Seductions of Crime: Moral and Sensual Attractions in Doing Evil*. New York: Basic Books.

Katz, Jack. 2002. Start Here: Social Ontology and Research Strategy. *Theoretical Criminology*, 6(3): 255–278.

Katz, Jack and Curtis Jackson-Jacobs. 2003. The Criminologists' Gang. In Colin Sumner (ed.), *The Blackwell Compendium of Criminology*, pp. 91–124. New York: Blackwell.

Kelley, Robin. 1994. Kickin' Reality, Kickin' Ballistics, Gangsta Rap and Post-industrial Los Angeles. In *Race Rebels*, pp. 183–228. New York: Free Press.

Klein, Malcolm. 1971. *Street Gangs and Street Workers*. Englewood Cliffs: Prentice Hall.

Klein, Malcolm. 1995. *The American Street Gang: Its Nature, Prevalence and Control*. New York: Oxford University Press.

Klein, Malcolm and Cheryl Maxson. 1996. *Gang Structures, Crime Patterns and Police Responses*. Washington, DC. Report to National Institute of Justice on Grant 93-JJ-CX-0044.

Klein, Naomi. 1999. *No Logo*. New York: Picador.

Larkin, Ralph W. 1979. *Suburban Youth in Cultural Crisis*. New York: Oxford University Press.

Law, Victoria. 2013. California Prison Hunger Strike Ends After 60 Days. *Truthout*.

Lea, John and Jock Young. 1984. *What is to be Done about Law and Order?* Harmondsworth: Penguin.

Lefebvre, Henri. 1971. *The Production of Space*. Oxford: Blackwell.

Levinson, Deborah T. 2008. *Adios Ninos: The Gangs of Guatemala City and the Politics of Death*. Durham, NC: Duke University Press.

Lewis, Oscar. 1965. *La Vida: A Puerto Rican Family in the Culture of Poverty – San Juan and New York*. New York: Random House.

Loewen, James W. 1995. *Lies My Teacher Told Me: Everything Your American History Book Got Wrong*. New York: New Press.

London, Jack. 2011 [1903]. *People of the Abyss*. New York: Createspace Independent Publishing.

Lyng, Stephen. 1990. Edgework: A Social Psychological Analysis of Voluntary Risk-Taking. *American Journal of Sociology*, 95(4): 876–921.

Lyng, Stephen. 1998. Dangerous Methods: Risk Taking and the Research Process. In J. Ferrell and M. Hamm (eds.), *Ethnography at the Edge*, pp. 221–251. Boston: Northeastern University Press.

Macleod, Jay. 1995. *Ain't No Makin' It*, 2nd edn. Boulder: Westview Press.

Maher, Lisa. 1997. *Sexed Work: Gender, Race and Resistance in a Brooklyn Drug Market*. Oxford: Oxford University Press.

Manwaring, Max G. 2005. *The New Urban Insurgency*. Michigan: University of Michigan Library.

Marable, Manning. 2000. *How Capitalism Underdeveloped Black America: Problems in Race, Political Economy and Society*, 2nd edn. Cambridge, MA: South End Press.

Marcus, George and Michael Fischer. 1986. *Anthropology as Cultural Critique: An Experimental Moment in the Human Sciences*. Chicago: University of Chicago Press.

Marshall, Thomas H. 1950. *Citizenship and Social Class and Other Essays*. Cambridge: Cambridge University Press.

Massey, Douglas E. and Nancy Denton. 1993. *American Apartheid: Segregation and the Making of the Underclass*. Cambridge, MA: Harvard University Press.

Matza, David. 1964. *Delinquency and Drift*. New York: John Wiley and Sons.

Matza, David. 1969. *Becoming Deviant*. Englewood Cliffs: Prentice Hall.

McCorkle, Richard C. and Terance D. Miethe. 2002. *The Social Construction of the Street Gang Problem*. New York: Prentice Hall.

McDonald, Kevin. 1999. *Struggles for Subjectivity*. Cambridge: Cambridge University Press.

McRobbie, Angela and Sarah L. Thornton. 1995. Rethinking "Moral Panic" for Multi-Mediated Social Worlds. *The British Journal of Sociology*, 46(4): 559–574.

Melossi, Dario and Massimo Pavarini. 1981. *The Prison and the Factory: Origins of the Penitentiary System*. New York: Rowman & Littlefield.

Mendoza-Denton, Norma. 2008. *Homegirls: Language and Cultural Practice Among Latin Youth Gangs*. Oxford: Blackwell.

Menjívar, Cecilia. 2006. Liminal Legality: Salvadoran and Guatemalan Immigrants' Lives in the United States. *American Sociological Review*, 111(4): 999–1037.

Merton, Robert. 1938. Social Structure and Anomie. *American Sociological Review*, 3: 672–682.

Messerschmidt, James. 2001. Masculinities, Crime and Prison. In D. Sabo, T.A. Kupers and W. London (eds.), *Prison Masculinities*, pp. 67–72. Philadelphia: Temple University Press.

Miller, Jody. 2001. *One of the Guys: Girls, Gangs, and Gender*. New York: Oxford University Press.

Miller, Todd. 2014. *Border Patrol Nation: Dispatches from the Front Line of Homeland Security*. San Francisco: City Lights Publishers.

Miller, Walter B. 1958. Lower Class Culture as a Generating Milieu of Gang Delinquency. *Journal of Social Issues*, 14: 5–19.

Miller, Walter B. 1973. The Molls. *Society*, 2: 32–35.

Miller, Walter B. 1975. *Violence by Youth Gangs and Youth Groups as a Crime Problem in Major American Cities*. Washington, DC: U.S. Department of Justice, Law Enforcement Assistant Administration.

Mills, C. Wright. 1959. *The Sociological Imagination*. London: Oxford University Press.

Moore, Joan. 1991. *Going Down to the Barrio: Homeboys and Homegirls in Change*. Philadelphia: Temple University Press.

Moore, Joan and Robert García. 1978. *Homeboys: Gangs, Drugs and Prison in the Barrios of Los Angeles*. Philadelphia: Temple University Press.

Moore, Natalie and Lance Williams. 2011. *The Almighty Black P Stone Nation: The Rise, Fall and Resurgence of an American Gang*. Chicago: Lawrence Hill Books.

Morrison, Wayne. 1995. *Theoretical Criminology*. London: Cavendish.

Morrison, Wayne. 2006. *Criminology, Civilisation and the New World Order*. Abingdon: Routledge.

Myrdal, Gunnar. 1944. *An American Dilemma: The Negro Problem and Modern Democracy*. New York: Harper.

New York Civil Liberties Union. 2012. A Look at School Safety: School to Prison Pipeline. Accessed at nyclu.org, June 3, 2014.

New York Times Editorial Board. 2013. When ICE Ran Amok. A22, April 8.

New York Times Editorial Board. 2014. When Children Become Criminals. A16, January 20.

Ngai, Mae M. 2004. *Impossible Subjects: Illegal Aliens and the Making of Modern America*. Princeton: Princeton University Press.

Notes from Nowhere. 2003. *We Are Everywhere: The Irresistible Rise of Global Anti-Capitalism*. New York: Verso.

Oakes, Jennie. 1985. *Keeping Track: How Schools Structure Inequality*. New Haven: Yale University Press.

Ogbu, John. 1978. *Minority Education and Caste: The American System in Cross-Cultural Perspective*. San Diego: Academic Press.

Oliveira, Ney dos Santos. 1996. Favelas and Ghettos: Race and Class in Rio de Janeiro and New York City. *Latin American Perspectives*, 23(4): 71–89.

Orfield, Gary and Erica Frankenburg. 2013. *Education Delusions? Why Choice Can Deepen Inequality and How to Make Schools Fair*. Berkeley: University of California Press.

Pager, Devah. 2003. The Mark of a Criminal Record. *American Journal of Sociology*, 108: 937–975.

Palmas, Luca (ed.). 2010. *Atlantico Latino: Gang Giovanili e Culture Transnazionali*. Rome: Carocci Editore.

Palmas, Luca. 2014. *Enemigos públicos. La fabricación de las bandas en la España contemporánea*. Madrid: Traficantes del Sueño.

Palmas, Luca and Andrea T. Torre. 2005. *Il Fantasma delle Bande: Genova e i Latinos*. Genova: Fratelli Frilli Editori.

Papachristos, Andrew. 2005. Gang World. *Foreign Policy*. Available at: www.foreignpolicy.com/articles/2005/03/01/gang_world?page=full.

Parenti, Christian. 1999. *Lockdown America*. New York: Verso.

Pearson, Geoffrey. 1987. *Hooligan: A History of Respectable Fears*. London: Schocken.

Pfohl, Stephen. 1989. *Death at the Paradise Café: Social Science (Fictions) and the Postmodern (Cultural Texts)*. London: Palgrave.

Phillips, Susan. 1999. *Wallbangin': Graffiti and Gangs*. Chicago: University of Chicago Press.

Phillips, Susan. 2012. *Operation Fly Trap: L.A. Gangs, Drugs, and the Law*. Chicago: University of Chicago Press.

Piketty, Thomas. 2014. *Capital in the Twenty First Century*. Cambridge, MA: Harvard University Press.

Pleyers, Geoffrey. 2012. *Alter-Globalization: Becoming Actors in the Global Age*. Cambridge: Polity.

Portes, Alejandro and Min Zhou. 1993. The New Second Generation: Segmented Assimilation and Its Variants. *Annals of the American Academy of Political and Social Science*, 530: 74–93.

Presdee, Mike. 2001. *Cultural Criminology and the Carnival of Crime*. New York: Routledge.

Raban, J. 1974. *Soft City*. London: Hamilton.

Reckless, Walter. 1961. *The Crime Problem*. New York: Appleton-Century-Crofts.

Reed, Adolph. 1992. The Underclass as Myth and Symbol. *Radical America*, 24(1): 21–40.

Reiman, Jeffrey. 1998 [1979]. *The Rich get Richer and the Poor get Prison: Ideology, Class, and Criminal Justice*. Boston: Allyn and Bacon.

Reiss, Albert. 1951. Delinquency as the Failure of Personal and Social Controls. *American Sociological Review*, 16(2): 196–207.

Rios, Victor. 2012. *Punished: Policing the Lives of Black and Latino Boys*. New York: New York University Press.

Rivera, Gutierrez Lirio. 2013. *Territories of Violence: State, Marginal Youth and Public Security in Honduras*. London: Palgrave.

Robinson, I. William. 2014. *Global Capitalism and the Crisis of Humanity*. New York: Cambridge University Press.

Robinson, M. 2001. Whither Criminal Justice? *Critical Criminology*, 10(2): 97–106.

Robles, Frances. 2014. Fleeing Gangs, Children Head to U.S. Border. *New York Times*, July 11: A1.

Rusche, George and Otto Kirchheimer. 1968 [1939]. *Punishment and Social Structure*. New York: Columbia University Press.

Said, Edward. 1979. *Orientalism*. New York: Vintage Books.

Salmi, Jamil. 1993. *Violence & Democratic Society: The Need for New Approaches to Human Rights*. London: Zed Books.

Sampson, Robert. 2013. *The Great American City*. Chicago: University of Chicago Press.

Sassen, Saskia. 1998. *Globalization and its Discontents*. New York: New Press.

Sassen, Saskia. 2001. *The Global City: New York, London, Tokyo*. Princeton: Princeton University Press.

Sassen, Saskia. 2014a. *Expulsions: Brutality and Complexity in the Global Economy*. Cambridge, MA: Harvard University Press.

Sassen, Saskia. 2014b. Preface: Making Histories. In Luca Palmas, *Enemigos públicos. La fabricación de las bandas en la España contemporánea*, pp. 1–8. Madrid: Traficantes del Sueño.

Scheff, Thomas J. 1995. Academic Gangs. *Crime, Law and Social Change*, 23: 153–162.

Schneider, Eric. 1999. *Vampires, Dragons, and Egyptian Kings*. Princeton: Princeton University Press.

Schutz, Alfred. 1967. *On Phenomenology of the Social World*. Evanston: Northwestern University Press.

Scott, James. 1985. *Weapons of the Weak: Everyday Forms of Peasant Resistance*. New Haven: Yale University Press.

Sibley, David. 1995. *Geographies of Exclusion*. London: Routledge.

Silver, Tony and Henry Chalfant. 1983. *Style Wars* documentary first shown on PBS. Distributed by Public Art Films.

Simon, Jonathan. 2007. *Governing Through Crime: How the War on Crime Transformed American Democracy and Created a Culture of Fear*. New York: Oxford University Press.

Snodgrass, John. 1976. Clifford R. Shaw and Henry D. McKay: Chicago Criminologists. *British Journal of Criminology*, 16: 1–19.

Snow, David A., Colin Morrill and Lori Anderson. 2003. Elaborating Analytic Ethnography: Linking Ethnography and Theoretical Development. *Ethnography*, 4: 271–290.

Soja, Edward. 1996. *Third Space: Journeys to Los Angeles and Other Real-and-Imagined Places*. Oxford: Blackwell.

Solnit, Rebecca. 2010. *A Paradise Built in Hell: The Extraordinary Communities That Arise in Disaster*. New York: Penguin.

Somers, Margaret. 2008. *Genealogies of Citizenship: Markets, Statelessness, and the Right to Have Rights*. Cambridge: Cambridge University Press.

Spitzer, Steven. 1975. Toward a Marxian Theory of Deviance. *Social Problems*, 22: 641–651.

Standing, G. 2012. *The Precariat: The New Dangerous Class*. London: Bloomsbury.

Steinberg, Jonny. 2004. *The Number: One Man's Search for Identity in the Cape Underworld and Prison Gangs*. Johannesburg: Jonathan Ball.

Stoudt, Brett, Michelle Fine and M. Fox. 2012. Growing up Policed in the Age of Aggressive Policing Policies. *New York Law School Law Review*, 56(4): 1331–1370.

Stumpf, Juliet P. 2006. The Crimmigration Crisis: Immigrants, Crime, and Sovereign Power. *American University Law Review*, 56: 368.

Sullivan, Mercer. 1989. *Getting Paid: Youth Crime and Work in the Inner City*. Ithaca: Cornell University Press.

Sullivan, P. John. 1997. Third Generation Street Gangs: Turf, Cartels, and Net Warriors. *Transnational Organized Crime*, 3(3): 95–108.

Suttles, Gerald. 1968. *The Social Order of the Slum*. Chicago: University of Chicago Press.

Taylor, Ian. 1999. *Crime in Context*. Oxford: Polity.

Thomas, Jim. 1993. *Doing Critical Ethnography*. Newbury Park: Sage Publications.

Thomas, William I. and Frederick Znaniecki. 1920. *The Polish Peasant in Europe and America: Vol 4*. Boston: Gorham Press.

Thrasher, Frederick. 1927. *The Gang: A Study of 1,313 Gangs in Chicago*. Chicago: University of Chicago Press.

Toby, Jackson. 1957. Social Disorganization and Stake in Conformity: Complementary Factors in the Predatory Behavior of Hoodlums. *Journal of Criminal Law, Criminology and Police Science*, 48(12): 12–17.

Touraine, Alain. 1988. *Return of the Actor*. Minnesota: University of Minnesota Press.

Trinh, T. Minh-ha. 1991. *When the Moon Waxes Red: Representation, Gender and Cultural Politics*. New York: Routledge.

US Commission on Safety and Abuse in Prisons. 2006. *Confronting Confinement*. New York: Vera Institute.

Van Gemert, Frank and Mark S. Fleischer. 2005. In the Grip of the Group. In Scott H. Decker and Frank H. Weerman (eds.), *European Street Gangs and Troublesome Youth Groups*, pp. 11–34. New York: Alta Mira.

Venkatesh, Sudhir A. 1997. The Social Organization of Street Gang Activity in an Urban Ghetto. *American Journal of Sociology*, 103(1): 82–111.

Venkatesh, Sudhir A. 2000. *American Project: The Rise and Fall of an American Ghetto*. Cambridge, MA: Harvard University Press.

Venkatesh, Sudhir A. 2006. *Off the Books*. Cambridge, MA: Harvard University Press.

Vigil, James Diego. 1988. *Barrio Gangs: Street Life and Identity in Southern California*. Austin: University of Texas Press.

Vigil, James Diego. 2002. *A Rainbow of Gangs: Street Cultures in the Mega-City*. Austin: University of Texas Press.

Vigil, James Diego. 2007. *The Projects: Gang and Non-Gang Families in East Los Angeles*. Austin: University of Texas Press.

Wacquant, Loic. 1997. Three Pernicious Premises in the Study of the American Ghetto. *International Journal of Urban and Regional Research*, July: 341–353.

Wacquant, Loic. 1998. From Welfare State to Prison State. *Le Monde Diplomatique*, July 4: 1–14.

Wacquant, Loic. 2002. Deadly Symbiosis. *Boston Review*, May 1: 1–25.

Wacquant, Loic. 2007. *Urban Outcasts: A Comparative Sociology of Advanced Marginality*. London: Polity.

Weide, Robert. 2014. *Race War? Inter-Racial Gang Conflict in Los Angeles*. PhD dissertation. Sociology Department, New York University.

Weiss, Lois and Michelle Fine. 2004. *Working Method: Research and Social Justice*. New York: Routledge.

Welch, Michael. 2002. *Detained: Immigration Laws and the Expanding I.N.S. Jail Complex*. Philadelphia: Temple University Press.

Welch, Michael. 2004. *Ironies of Imprisonment*. Newbury: Sage.

Werthman, Carl. 1969. Delinquency and Moral Character. In D.R. Cressey and D.A. Ward (eds.), *Delinquency, Crime and Social Process*, pp. 613–632. New York: Harper & Row.

White, Rob. 2013. *Youth Gangs, Violence and Social Respect*. London: Palgrave.

Whyte, William F. 1943. *Street Corner Society*. Chicago: University of Chicago Press.

Whyte, William F. 1991. *Participatory Action Research*. London: Sage.

Will, Susan, Stephen Handelman and David C. Brotherton. 2013. *How They Got Away With It: White Collar Criminals and the Financial Meltdown*. New York: Columbia University Press.

Williams, Raymond. 1965. *The Long Revolution*. London: Penguin.

Willis, Paul. 1977. *Learning to Labor: How Working Class Kids Get Working Class Jobs*. Westmead: Saxon House.

Willis, Paul. 2000. *The Ethnographic Imagination*. Massachusetts: Polity.

Wilson, James Q. and George Kelling. 1982. Broken Windows: The Police and Neighborhood Safety. *Atlantic Monthly*, 249(3): 29–38.

Wilson, William J. 1987. *The Truly Disadvantaged*. Chicago: University of Chicago Press.

Yablonsky, Lewis. 1963. *The Violent Gang*. New York: Macmillan.

Young, Jock. 1969. The Zoo Keepers of Deviance. In Colin Ward (ed.), *A Decade of Anarchy: Selections from Anarchy, 1961–70*. London: Freedom Press Centenary Series.

Young, Jock. 1971. *The Drugtakers: The Social Meaning of Drug Use*. London: MacGibbon and Kee.

Young, Jock. 1999. *The Exclusive Society: Social Exclusion, Crime and Difference in Late Modernity*. London: Sage.

Young, Jock. 2003. Merton with Energy, Katz with Structure. *Theoretical Criminology*, 7(3): 389–414.

Young, Jock. 2004. Voodoo Criminology and the Numbers Game. In J. Ferrell, K. Hayward, W. Morrison and M. Presdee (eds.), *Cultural Criminology Unleashed*. London: Cavendish.

Young, Jock. 2009. Moral Panic: Its Origins in Resistance, Ressentiment and the Translation of Fantasy into Reality. *British Journal of Criminology*, 49: 4–16.

Young, Jock. 2011. *The Criminological Imagination*. London: Polity.

Zatz, Marjorie. 1987. Chicano Youth Gangs and Crime: The Creation of a Moral Panic. *Contemporary Crises*, 11: 129–158.

Zilberg, Elana. 2011. *Space of Detention: The Making of a Transnational Gang Crisis Between Los Angeles and San Salvador.* Durham, NC: Duke University Press.

Zinn, Howard. 2005 [1980]. *A People's History of the United States: 1492-Present.* New York: Harper.

INDEX